Growth and Development
SOCIAL WORK SERVICES FOR THE 21ST CENTURY

The Report of the Chief Inspector of Social Work Services for Scotland

Laid before the Scottish Parliament by the
Scottish Ministers, November 2002.

SE/2002/304

The Local Reports

Growth and Development – Social Work Services for the 21st Century, is the second annual report prepared by the Chief Social Work Inspector. Completed in 2002, it includes a national overview of social work services and short reviews of services in each of the 32 councils. This report contains the reviews of social work services in each of the 32 local authorities with the national overview contained in a separate document. The individual reports are based on an analysis of demographic information, statistical returns to the Scottish Executive and Accounts Commission (Audit Scotland), information provided on visits to the local authorities and other written information provided by them.

The introductory section of each report covers the demographic and social features of the area. The description of each authority is followed by subsequent sections on:

- Community Care
- Children and Families
- Criminal Justice
- Finance
- Staffing
- Modernising services
- The Future

The 32 local authorities in Scotland range from large cities such as Glasgow through to small island authorities such as Eilean Siar. Differences between authorities in terms of geography and demographic, social and economic characteristics and their effects on service provision are highlighted throughout the report.

This year, we have included more statistical information, including figures from previous years and Scottish figures. As part of this process, some figures have been presented as quartiles. Appendix 1 details the source of the statistics and includes an explanatory note on our use of quartiles.

The individual local authorities were given an opportunity to comment on their particular section of the report. In many instances, the local authorities commented on the statistics included in the reports, and offered us more up to date figures than the ones we have used or provided data that they use locally. For the sake of comparison, the latest available figures from local authority returns to the Scottish Executive or Accounts Commission have been used in the reports but it is acknowledged these statistics do not necessarily present the most up-to-date or accurate account of social work activity and that more informative figures may be available. This exercise has again reinforced the need to improve the social work information systems and the robustness of the statistical information.

Further appendices on national statistical information and population figures are also included.

Contents

	Page
The Local Reports	3
Map of Scotland showing the 32 local authorities	6
Aberdeen City	7
Aberdeenshire	17
Angus	25
Argyll and Bute	33
Clackmannanshire	41
Dumfries and Galloway	47
Dundee City	55
East Ayrshire	63
East Dunbartonshire	71
East Lothian	79
East Renfrewshire	87
Edinburgh, City of	95
Eilean Siar (in English)	103
Eilean Siar (in Gaelic)	111
Falkirk	121
Fife	127
Glasgow City	135
Highland	143
Inverclyde	153
Midlothian	161
Moray	169
North Ayrshire	177

	Page
North Lanarkshire	**185**
Orkney Isles	**193**
Perth and Kinross	**201**
Renfrewshire	**209**
Scottish Borders	**217**
Shetland	**225**
South Ayrshire	**233**
South Lanarkshire	**241**
Stirling	**251**
West Dunbartonshire	**259**
West Lothian	**267**
Appendix 1 — Notes on statistics used in the local reports	273
Appendix 2 — National statistical information	276
Appendix 3 — 2000 based population projections for 2000 and 2016, by local authority	281
Glossary	283

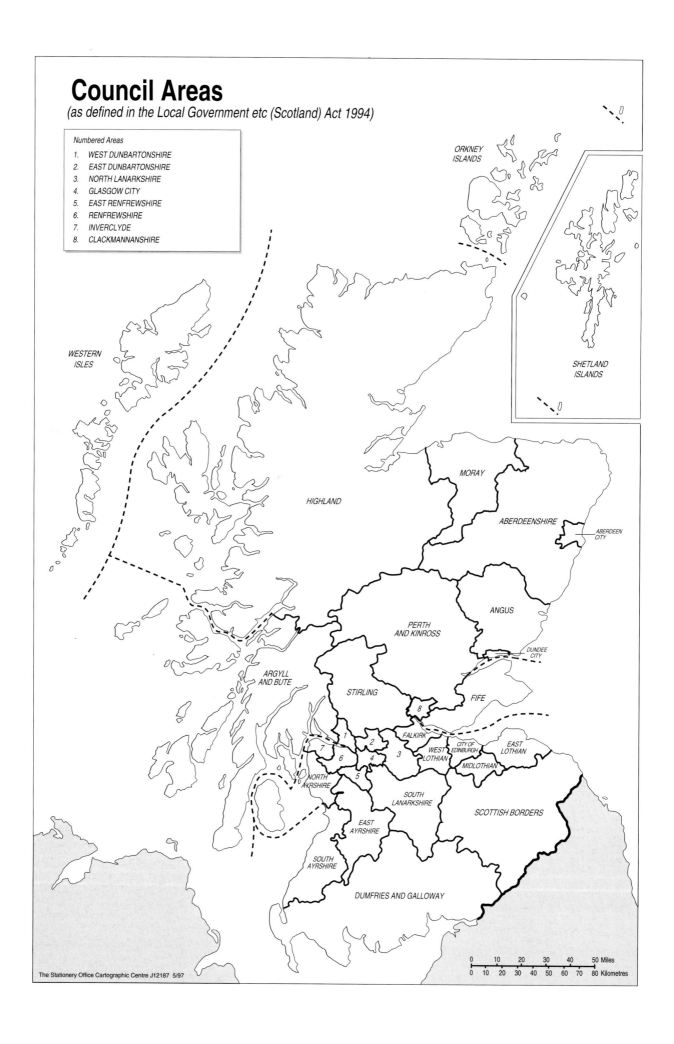

1. Profile at 2002

With an estimated population of 211,300 Aberdeen is the third largest city in Scotland. By 2016, the population is expected to fall by 11%. The older population is to rise but by less than the national average. The number of pre-school children is to fall by over a quarter. The number of 45 to 60 year olds will rise by over a quarter.

Whilst unemployment in the area is low (2% at January 2002), there are a number of areas within Aberdeen City where there are particular issues regarding poverty and deprivation.

Aberdeen has the third highest rate of drug misuse in Scotland (3% of 15-54 year olds).

1,329 crimes were recorded per 10,000 population in 2001. Although the rate has fallen since 2000, it is the second highest recorded rate in Scotland.

The Council is implementing a major programme of change, under the banner heading of aberdeen*futures,* which includes the Community Plan, the introduction of the Accord Card, the introduction of one stop customer service centres, work which is about to commence with a strategic partner to look at improvements to systems and processes within the Council and an internal service restructuring. To date, the major impact on social work services has been through the Departmental restructuring.

Strategic social work services have joined with strategic housing services to become Community Services. Operational Social Work services are now managed through three Neighbourhood directorates, with services currently being managed on an interim basis by their existing managers. In the longer term, it is proposed that services will be delivered on a multi-disciplinary team basis.

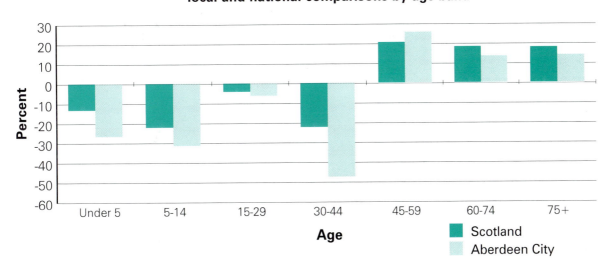

2. Performance: Community Care

Balance of care (aged 65+)	1999 actual	1999 per 1,000	Quartile	2000 actual	2000 per 1,000	Quartile
Older people in residential care homes	604	19	2	551	17	2
Older people in private nursing homes	841	26	2	737	23	3
Older people receiving home care	4,389	138	1	3,383	106	1
Older people in special needs housing	4,269	134.2	2	4,261	134	1
People receiving a community care service	1999-2000 actual	1999-2000 per 1,000	Quartile	2000-2001 actual	2000-2001 per 1,000	Quartile
Older people (aged 65+)	5,088	160	4	6,221	195.6	3
For mental health problems/dementia (aged 18-64)	118	0.8	4	920	6.8	1
For physical disabilities (aged 18-64)	1,494	11.0	3	1,546	11.3	3
For learning disabilities (aged 18-64)	299	2.2	4	321	2.4	4
For drug/alcohol abuse problems (aged 18-64)	41	0.3	3	105	0.8	3

In 2000, more older people received a home care service than in many other authorities but they were less likely to receive more than 10 hours of home care than in many other authorities. Aberdeen has a relatively high number of special needs housing places.

In May 2002, 172 people were awaiting discharge from hospital: 53 people were awaiting funding for homes and 30 were awaiting nursing home places.

Under an "Ageing with Confidence" joint strategy for older people launched by Aberdeen City Council and NHS Grampian, community care teams are aligned with GP practices. Features of joint care services are:

- an out-of-hours home care service, co-located with the Night Nursing Service;
- a Rapid Response Team operating 7 days a week and providing support for up to 4 weeks;
- a joint hospital admissions and discharge planning team; and
- a Rehabilitation and Assessment Pilot Scheme (RAPS) at Croft House, a residential home, where a multi-disciplinary team carries out assessments and arranges and co-ordinates activities and resources; most older people return to the community after their spell in Croft House.

Expansions are proposed for sheltered housing, the Crossroads attendant scheme and Care and Repair.

At the centre of Aberdeen, Aberdeenshire, Moray Council and the Health Board's plans to improve learning disability and mental health services is the closure of Woodlands and Ladysbridge, but immediate practical problems are transitional services and housing. A housing procurement group is looking at support models. The Change Fund has provided resources to improve local area co-ordination, develop autism services, introduce direct payments and restructure day services.

The three councils and health partners have a joint executive group to manage change and a joint project group for implementation. Specific changes introduced are:

- joint training, with a Grampian-wide training co-ordinator;
- creation of a community learning disability team; and
- involvement of users and carers in the commissioning process.

Between 1999-2000 and 2000-2001 there was a massive increase in the number of people who were receiving a community care service for mental illness. A Mental Health Framework Group is working on improvements in accommodation, employment, carers, service users, dementia/old age psychiatry, and monitoring and evaluation. Resources for change are derived from health development allocations, mental health and well-being funding, resource transfers and mental illness specific grant. Resources are being moved from hospital to the community. An outreach team for severe and enduring mental illness is being established.

Multi-disciplinary mental health and old age psychiatry teams have been linked to GP practices. Social workers purchase and provide the care, and home support workers are being introduced into teams. A resettlement co-ordinator is to bring forward joint projects.

On single shared assessment, the partners were progressing towards the Bottom Line. They have adopted the Moray tool, and will mainstream existing effective systems. Information sharing will be rolled out on the back of effective practice in, for example, the rapid response team.

The Joint Future agenda sits well with the Council's commitment to *aberdeenfutures*. Though partner agencies were still working towards the Bottom Line, real progress was made on agreeing the partnership arrangements, to align budgets, a new joint post of change manager and having an effective Staff Forum. The resourcing pot has been discussed but not yet finalised, for example to include housing and acute services. Integrated service management is in place for local teams and though agreed in principle has yet to be implemented above that.

Planning for sensory impairment services in Aberdeen is carried out by a sensory disability multi-agency task group, which secures the involvement of service users and carers and maintains links with Aberdeenshire and Moray Councils. Voluntary organisations carry out most assessments, provide a range of services commissioned and monitored by social work and supply awareness training to social work staff.

3. Performance: Children and Families

Balance of care – Looked after children (aged 0-17)	1999-2000 actual	1999-2000 per 1,000	Quartile	2000-2001 actual	2000-2001 per 1,000	Quartile
At home	288	6.7	1	227	5.2	1
With friends/relatives/other community	51	1.2	2	36	0.8	2
With foster carers/prospective adopters	174	4.0	1	144	3.3	2
In residential accommodation	80	1.9	1	56	1.3	2
Total	**593**	**13.7**	**1**	**462**	**10.7**	**2**

Key performance indicators	1998-1999 actual	1998-1999 per 1,000	Quartile	1999-2000 actual	1999-2000 per 1,000	Quartile
Child protection (CP) referrals (aged 0-15)	169	4.4	4	352	9.1	2
Children subject to a CP case conference (aged 0-15)	136	3.5	2	106	2.8	2
Children placed on CP register (aged 0-15)	136	3.5	1	100	2.6	1
Adoption applications in year (aged 0-17)	24	0.6	1	25	0.6	1
Stranger adopter applications (aged 0-17)	11	0.2	1	8	0.2	2

The number of child protection referrals almost doubled between 1998-1999 and 1999-2000. The rates of child protection referrals and of children subject to a child protection case conference are relatively high. The rate of children placed on child protection registers is high.

Despite a significant drop in the number of looked after children between 1999 and 2001, there are still relatively high rates of looked after children living at home, living with friends or relatives and foster carers, and living in residential care.

Family centre provision in Aberdeen has been refocused to:
- provide a high standard of childcare, education and support to young children who are in need;
- ensure that young children, whatever their social or economic backgrounds or circumstances have the best possible start in life; and
- provide opportunities and support to parents both in their parenting role and as adult learners.

In recognition of the increasing number of children adversely affected by parental substance misuse, family centres are providing more inclusive support, including outreach services designed to help with parenting skills, literacy or homelessness. Social Work, Education, Housing and Health are working jointly to promote the welfare of very young children whose parents are misusing drugs, with family support workers linked to the local maternity hospital assisting families with young children, who have drug dependency, mental health problems, learning difficulties and homelessness.

Behavioural support teachers underpin a strategy to reduce exclusions. A Barnardo's residential and outreach project includes specialist teachers who work with troubled young people to re-engage them within the mainstream education system. Joint social work/education projects are run from Craigielea Children's Centre:

- Acorn, for young people aged 14 and over, who fail to attend school, and in particular those looked after away from home; and

- Unicorn, aimed at helping the most needy young people make the transition from primary to secondary school.

A detailed action plan has been prepared to implement the recommendations of *Learning with Care*. In summer 2002 local guidance is being issued on multi-disciplinary assessments and arrangements are in train to monitor care plans. All schools have a nominated teacher for looked after children.

An audit of the educational environments in residential units is complete, and the recommendations flowing from the audit are being implemented, with imaginative spending plans.

A multi-disciplinary Moving On committee is at the centre of planning provision and purchase of a range of support and accommodation for care leavers. An external review has recommended further commissioning and purchasing focused on needs identified by young people themselves, particularly mental health needs.

4. Performance: Criminal Justice

Key Activities	1999-2000	2000-2001	2000-2001 per 10,000	Quartile
Number of social enquiry reports submitted to the courts during the year	1,830	1,573	103.5	1
Number of community service orders made during the year	261	258	17.0	2

The proportion of social enquiry reports reported to court within target time	2000-2001	Quartile		
Proportion of social enquiry reports submitted to the courts by due date	97.5	3		
The time taken to complete community service orders				
Average length of community service (hours) for orders completed during the year	143	3		
Average hours completed per week	2.8	4		

Fewer social enquiry reports were submitted to the courts during 2000-2001 than in 1999-2000, but the rate was higher than in most other authorities, reflecting the high crime rate in Aberdeen. Less than half social enquiry reports were allocated to social work staff within 2 days, but 97.5% were submitted to courts by the due date.

A relatively high rate of community service orders was made in 2000-2001. The average length of orders completed was relatively low, and the time taken to complete them was long – with just 2.8 hours completed on average per week.

Aberdeen is part of the Northern partnership which includes Aberdeenshire, Moray and Highland and is one of the three Pathfinder projects for the Getting Best Results initiative. The Council uses a range of quality assurance mechanisms and an external quality assurance manager in much of its assessment work. A new "QUASER" tool has been introduced to assess the quality of social enquiry reports and feed back to individual workers and their seniors. There is a 10% monthly audit of risk assessment. Risk assessment of sex offenders is subject to six monthly inspections and is to be extended.

The Council has introduced the CareJust management information package. It has undertaken client profiling, and expects to make full use of the system to identify needs and targets which can be fed into strategic planning and the Pathfinder initiative.

5. Finance

Service Area (£000)	GAE 1999-2000	Final net Out turn 1999-2000	GAE 2000-2001	Final net Out turn 2000-2001
Children's Services	£7,384	£13,480	£7,418	£13,849
Community Care	£32,959	£39,688	£34,233	£39,747
Adult Offenders		£72		£161
Other SW Services	£4,106	£4,060	£4,084	£3,976
Total	**£44,450**	**£57,300**	**£45,735**	**£57,733**

Spend per head	1999-2000	2000-2001
Spend per head	£271.24	£273.29
Quartile	1	1

Criminal Justice services receive funding from the Scottish Executive, £2,185,174 was provided in 2000-2001.

Community Care expenditure is one of the highest in Scotland. Spending on children's services is significantly above the GAE, attributed in part to the impact of drug misuse. The Aberdeen Child Care Audit highlighted the increasing number of children who are being adversely affected as a result of parental substance abuse.

Overall spend per head on social work services is high.

6. Staffing

Staff	WTE 1999 actual	WTE 1999 per 1,000	Quartile 1999	WTE 2000 actual	WTE 2000 per 1,000	Quartile 2000
Managers & central staff	162	0.8	1	150	0.7	2
Frontline staff	1,287	6.1	1	1,198	5.7	2
Other	269	1.3	2	248	1.2	2
Total	**1,717**	**8.1**	**1**	**1,596**	**7.6**	**1**

Vacancies	Vacancies 2000	% Vacancies 2000	% Vacancies 2000 Scotland	Vacancies 2001	% Vacancies 2001	% Vacancies 2001 Scotland
SWs with adults	0	0	7.8	8	8.3	10.9
SWs with children	6	5.3	7.4	6	5.2	10.7
SWs with offenders	3	7.3	7.5	6	16.9	7.2
Generic workers	0	0	8.0	0	0.0	12.7
Total	**9**	**3.6**	**7.7**	**19**	**8.0**	**10.5**

Rates of managers and frontline staff are relatively high although both reduced between 1999 and 2000. The overall vacancy level is below average but is high for criminal justice posts.

Local recruitment and retention are affected by the level of mobility in a labour market dominated by the oil industry. Staff turnover is very variable: for fieldwork staff it dropped from 45% in 1999-2000 to 23% the following year. Staff vacancies in May 2002 showed a reduction, but there were relatively high levels of sickness in some units. There is now a noticeable drop in applicants, and problems are being encountered in recruiting to specialist posts (such as drugs workers for children and families) which demand a combination of skills, experience and the capacity to develop services.

The Council has tackled the particular problems within children's services by:

- revising recruitment systems and publicity material;
- raising the profile of children's services at recruitment events;
- encouraging more placements in childcare settings;
- offering new staff a two year deal – an induction programme, weekly supervision for the first six months, mentoring for the first three months, attendance at a monthly support group and a protected caseload in the first year; and
- providing the opportunity of following the PQ Part 1 and locum relief for training.

In addition, demands placed on children's services workers are being examined to identify what support is needed for qualified staff.

7. Modernising services

An estimated 3% of the population of Aberdeen come from a minority ethnic background and the proportion of the Chinese population is relatively high. The Council has adopted race equality as part of its corporate approach to equal opportunities. The Council, Grampian Police and other partners have formed a racist incidents partnership, committed to systematic recording and response to racist incidents. Social work services in its race equality plan focuses on staff training, access to information, ethnic monitoring, and involving ethnic minority staff and community groups in planning services.

Accord Link is Aberdeen's Modernising Government funded programme to improve access to services, focusing on electronic delivery, smart card technology and web-based information. Social work services has a limited locus in these developments in 2002.

Material from the well-developed council Intranet is being migrated to the new Internet facility.

CareFirst information systems are being developed and updated by introduction of new software. New finance modules have facilitated more accurate budgeting in community care. A new criminal justice module has been brought on stream. The Council has hosted the development of a drugs information system, soon to be rolled out to other social work services.

8. The Future

To complement the substantial developments which have been introduced in joint arrangements for community care, the Council and its health service partners face a range of supporting priorities to:

- identify specific action to improve disability and mental health services in the areas already identified, for example, different ways to provide old age psychiatric services, joint needs assessments and means of involving users and carers;
- plan how that action can be implemented making use of various streams of funding which are becoming available and which reflect a shift of resources from hospitals to the community;
- drawing on progress to date, develop a firm implementation plan for delivering the Joint Future agenda by next April.

While tangible changes have been made in disability and mental health services, the three councils and health partners still have a major task in managing progressive change to community services, particularly as vulnerable people are moved out of Ladysbridge. Every impetus should be given to an outreach team for severe and enduring mental illness.

Real strides have been made in providing support for troubled young people at school and also for improving the education of looked after children. New measures for joint professional development for staff who deal with such young people would consolidate the progress which has been achieved. As the basis for reliably assessing the educational progress of looked after children, it is necessary to introduce a revised and improved information set as soon as possible.

The Council is still some way from delivering comprehensive services for care leavers. The major tasks arise over:

- identifying the numbers of care leavers for whom the Council has responsibility;
- establishing their main needs in setting out their futures lives;
- planning appropriate accommodation for young people who have chaotic lifestyles and who abuse substances; and
- assessing the budget required to make inroads into the support required.

A significant number of children are affected by disability and the provision of services to these children can require the deployment of significant resources.

In criminal justice services, the various aspects of risk assessment at present in use – including those for sex offender cases – fall short of a systematic and continuous mechanism for quality assurance of risk assessment and the Council and its partners in the grouping should explore the options for such a mechanism, which would improve service quality.

The problems which are emerging in social work staffing could impact on the City's capacity to meet its strategic plan, although in the past it has been able to use underspend in staffing budgets to offset other expenditure. The Council needs to urgently devise means of improving staff recruitment and retention, making use of the ADSW action plan for supporting front-line staff.

1. Profile at 2002

As one of Scotland's larger authorities, Aberdeenshire has a population of 227,200 which is predicted to increase slightly by 2016. The number of children under 14 is to fall significantly. The older population faces a larger than average increase.

Local unemployment is comparatively low (1.6 % at January 2002). 82% of people of working age are in work, against a Scottish average of 73%.

The drug misuse rate is well below average at 1.1% of 15-54 year olds.

The recorded crime rate has fallen slightly from 2000 and is well below average (446 crimes per 10,000 population in 2001).

Social services are provided by a Department of Social Work and Housing and headed by a director who discharges the functions of Chief Social Work Officer.

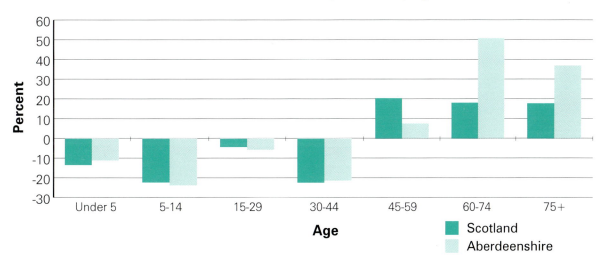

2. Performance: Community Care

Balance of care (aged 65+)	1999 actual	1999 per 1,000	Quartile	2000 actual	2000 per 1,000	Quartile
Older people in residential care homes	638	21	2	597	19	2
Older people in private nursing homes	1,047	34	1	1,033	34	1
Older people receiving home care	1,635	53	4	1,612	52	4
Older people in special needs housing	5,255	171	1	4,855	156	1
People receiving a community care service	1999-2000 actual	1999-2000 per 1,000	Quartile	2000-2001 actual	2000-2001 per 1,000	Quartile
Older people (aged 65+)	4,465	143.5	4	4,128	132.7	4
For mental health problems/dementia (aged 18-64)	179	1.3	4	184	1.3	4
For physical disabilities (aged 18-64)	1,040	7.3	4	1,111	7.8	3
For learning disabilities (aged 18-64)	174	1.2	4	262	1.8	4
For drug/alcohol abuse problems (aged 18-64)	74	0.5	3	108	0.8	3

Older people are more likely to be in residential or nursing home care than those in most other authorities. Around 50 people are waiting for placements in nursing homes, most for a placement in the locality of their choice. By contrast, the proportion of older people receiving home care is low, though many of them are in special needs housing, a significant feature of local community-based care. Enhanced care sheltered housing complexes have proved to be a cost-effective means of providing community-based care. With finance from the modernising community care incentive fund a mid-day meal service has been introduced in 5 project areas, to provide older tenants with good quality nutritious meals and social companionship.

Plans are at an early stage to establish up to 25 health and community care locality teams to provide integrated services, initially to older people. They are to be based on GP practices or groups of practices, and to comprise care managers, community nurses, health visitors, home care supervisors and occupational therapists.

Learning disability and mental health services are provided by teams which have shared social work and health management. Learning disability teams have been strengthened by additional care management posts financed from the Change Fund. A joint training co-ordinator covers the three North East authorities. Supported living options are being developed with partner agencies for people with varying levels of disability.

By developing individual care programmes the mental health team has helped to achieve a significant reduction in compulsory admissions, although there has been an increase in non-compulsory admissions. Stronger primary care support would consolidate improvements.

Considerable progress has been made towards developing single shared assessment, linking well with the effective development of the health and community care teams. A single assessment tool should be in place by the end of May 2002, with appropriate training programmes.

An implementation and review group of health, education, social work, voluntary and user representatives is driving change in sensory impairment services. Measures are being taken to improve co-ordination between social work, health and education on needs assessment.

Aberdeenshire and its health partners have made good progress by establishing joint management arrangements, to be called the Aberdeenshire Partnership for Health and Social Care. These arrangements will consist of a high level committee, a senior management group, local management groups and locality teams.

Resources will be aligned at the outset, rather than pooled. The services and functions to be included in the joint resourcing pot have been identified.

3. Performance: Children and Families

Balance of care – Looked after children (aged 0-17)	1999-2000 actual	1999-2000 per 1,000	Quartile	2000-2001 actual	2000-2001 per 1,000	Quartile
At home	191	3.6	3	176	3.3	3
With friends/relatives/other community	21	0.4	4	20	0.4	4
With foster carers/prospective adopters	118	2.2	3	112	2.1	3
In residential accommodation	39	0.7	4	35	0.7	4
Total	**369**	**6.9**	**3**	**343**	**6.4**	**3**

Key performance indicators	1998-1999 actual	1998-1999 per 1,000	Quartile	1999-2000 actual	1999-2000 per 1,000	Quartile
Child protection (CP) referrals (aged 0-15)	569	11.8	1	736	15.5	1
Children subject to a CP case conference (aged 0-15)	124	2.6	3	91	1.9	3
Children placed on CP register (aged 0-15)	105	2.2	2	78	1.6	3
Adoption applications in year (aged 0-17)	30	0.6	1	33	0.6	1
Stranger adopter applications (aged 0-17)	13	0.2	1	11	0.2	2

Although Aberdeenshire has a comparatively high rate of child protection referrals, the rates of children subject to a child protection case conference and placed on the CP register are lower than in many other authorities.

There are low proportions of looked after children in residential accommodation, living at home, living with friends or relatives or living with foster carers. The number of children in residential units has been significantly reduced but a number continue to be accommodated in residential schools. The children in the residential units present increasingly complex and challenging behaviour. In 2001-2002, residential units provided default placements for a number of children for whom no other care placement could be found.

Aberdeenshire's manual "Guidance for Foster Carers and Social Workers" covers the legal and professional context of fostering, the needs of children and a wide range of issues for Carers. Easily updated, it has contributions from a wide range of sources. Now in its 3rd edition, the Manual has been well received by carers in Aberdeenshire and other authorities.

In an Equal Chances project the Council audited the educational experiences and achievements of looked after children in 2000. In contrast to national research, it found that the attainment of looked after children in Aberdeenshire was not significantly below that of their peers. Following the audit and the publication of *Learning with Care*, the Council established a joint education and social work management group, which has an implementation plan and oversees the disbursement of specific funding.

As a rule, children looked after away from home receive full-time education. Joint assessments are undertaken with education and increasingly with the health service. The authority is piloting schemes of education for inclusion in the care plans of looked after children. By August 2002, each school is to identify a staff member to co-ordinate the needs of looked after children. An audit is to be conducted of educational experiences and additional support requirements.

Throughcare and aftercare support for looked after children varies according to where children live in the area. In the Northern Division, aftercare is provided by a Barnardos 16+ team; in the South and Central divisions generic staff are supported by a specialist team member.

4. Performance: Criminal Justice

Key Activities	1999-2000	2000-2001	2000-2001 per 10,000	Quartile
Number of social enquiry reports submitted to the courts during the year	830	621	38.9	4
Number of community service orders made during the year	131	143	9.0	4
The proportion of social enquiry reports reported to court within target time	2000-2001	Quartile		
Proportion of social enquiry reports submitted to the courts by due date	95.8	3		
The time taken to complete community service orders				
Average length of community service (hours) for orders completed during the year	151	3		
Average hours completed per week	3.4	3		

The rate of social enquiry reports submitted to courts was lower than in many other authorities in 2000-2001, having reduced since 1999-2000. The rate reflects the low crime rate. Aberdeenshire were only able to submit 95.8% of orders to courts by the due date.

The rate of community service orders made during the year was lower than in many other authorities. The average length of community service orders completed in 2000-2001 was relatively low and the time taken to complete the orders was similar to that in many other authorities.

The Council is part of the Northern Partnership for criminal justice social work services. The partnership, which includes Aberdeen City, Moray and Highland is working towards consistency of service, with practice development groups on transfer of cases, community service, social enquiry reports, and supervised attendance orders. There are plans for future work on probation, throughcare, prison induction, and structured programmes, and to co-ordinate their various arrangements for work with young offenders. There will also be an information strategy, taking account of the authorities' different information systems, and there is a quality assurance group.

The Council is currently developing a range of quality assurance mechanisms and plans to introduce the CareJust module of the information software package CareFirst. Currently the majority of the information is about process and there is a need to develop a range of outcome measures.

The Joint Young Sex Offenders Project is an extension of the partnership's adult sex offender project. Funding from the Youth Crime Review provides services for adolescents and children who are exhibiting sexually abusive behaviour. The focus is on preventing young people's inappropriate behaviour escalating into offending behaviour. The project uses a multi-disciplinary approach, involving Grampian Police, schools and educational psychologists. Preliminary indications from carers suggest positive results.

5. Finance

Service Area (£000)	GAE 1999-2000	Final net Out turn 1999-2000	GAE 2000-2001	Final net Out turn 2000-2001
Children's Services	£3,124	£9,164	£3,303	£9,715
Community Care	£29,921	£31,566	£31,414	£31,346
Adult Offenders		£773		-£75
Other SW Services	£3,945	£2,079	£3,979	£2,784
Total	**£36,990**	**£43,583**	**£38,695**	**£43,770**

Spend per head		1999-2000		2000-2001
Spend per head		£191.82		£192.64
Quartile		4		4

Criminal Justice services receive funding from the Scottish Executive, £947,300 was provided in 2000-2001.

Aberdeenshire spent two and a half times the GAE calculated by the Scottish Executive for children's services in 2000-2001. The principal reasons cited for this high spend are expensive residential care and the prevalence of misuse of drugs and alcohol, though Aberdeenshire as a whole has a far lower than average rate of drug misuse. Additional resources have been allocated, particularly in North Aberdeenshire, to provide specialist and intensive support to a small number of drug misusing parents of young children. This is particularly taxing work for staff and has necessitated additional training costs.

The overall social work spend per head is less than in many other authorities.

6. Staffing

Staff	WTE 1999 actual	WTE 1999 per 1,000	Quartile 1999	WTE 2000 actual	WTE 2000 per 1,000	Quartile 2000
Managers & central staff	137	0.6	2	149	0.7	2
Frontline staff	864	3.8	4	939	4.1	3
Other	274	1.2	3	237	1.0	3
Total	**1,274**	**5.6**	**3**	**1,326**	**5.8**	**3**

Vacancies	Vacancies 2000	% Vacancies 2000	% Vacancies 2000 Scotland	Vacancies 2001	% Vacancies 2001	% Vacancies 2001 Scotland
SWs with adults	0	0	7.8	0	0	10.9
SWs with children	0	0	7.4	3	2.9	10.7
SWs with offenders	0	0	7.5	0	0	7.2
Generic workers	0	0	8.0	0	0	12.7
Total	**0**	**0**	**7.7**	**3**	**1.5**	**10.5**

Numbers of managers and frontline staff per thousand population are below many other authorities. Vacancies are far lower in all areas of social work than in Scotland as a whole. Recruitment and retention have, however, deteriorated in 2001-2002. Increasing problems have emerged over recruiting experienced staff in children and family services; maintaining home care in remote areas; retaining mental health officers once qualified; and recruiting experienced drugs workers, where drug problems are most concentrated.

The Council is seeking support from voluntary organisations, which can provide more flexible working arrangements and, therefore, attract the return of qualified workers who might prefer sessional working. In children's services, family support staff now have a professional development scheme and are encouraged to develop specialisms.

The home care service has recently been reorganised to improve staff recruitment and retention and to promote continuity of personal care. Home carers are at three levels:

- practical support workers, employed by the independent sector in urban areas;
- personal carers (addressing personal and health care needs); and
- team support workers to co-ordinate packages and undertake low-level reviews.

Flexibility will be increased by shift working; a training package will enhance skill levels; a new uniform is being provided to signal different status, focus and image.

7. Modernising services

The Council has adopted a corporate approach to preparing a Race Equality Plan and has committed itself to level one of the Commission for Racial Equality's standards for local government. Having established close links with Grampian Race Equality Council, it is a partner in the racist incidents sub-group of the community safety steering group. A detailed action plan for involving social work services has been formulated by senior managers.

Modernising Government funding has been secured for a pilot project to help older people in rural areas to access services with the help of clear, uncomplicated and comprehensive information conveyed through a new Internet portal. Once piloted, a training package on use of the portal is to be rolled out across Aberdeenshire and made available throughout Scotland.

A bid is planned for second round funding for a common information system with NHS partners, which will enable the introduction of electronic single shared assessment.

8. The Future

The prospect of a steep increase in the older population continues to dominate the planning and development of community care across Aberdeenshire as a whole. The Council and the health service have laid the strategic ground but important development priorities are:

- to increase the number of older people receiving home care;
- to implement successfully the recent reorganisation of the home care service to achieve objectives of improved staff recruitment and retention and greater continuity of care;
- to extend from the present 5 project areas the meals service for older people who need support;
- to reverse the small increase in numbers of older people awaiting placement in nursing homes; and
- to carry forward plans to use smart technology in domestic settings.

To build on the achievements of the mental health team, it is necessary to plan for stronger support for the primary care of the mentally ill.

Sensory impairment services have been gradually improved, but there is an outstanding requirement to harmonise and improve the assessment process for these services.

The problems created by drug and alcohol misuse continue to put pressure on local resources and treatment and support will continue to be a priority calling for flexible responses.

To reduce the pressures on resources from expensive residential care for children and young people, it will be necessary to develop and extend further community disposals.

To ensure consistency of aftercare for young people, plans should be made to extend throughout the area the service approach used by Barnardo's in their local project.

For criminal justice services, collaboration with the two neighbouring councils is now far advanced and there is an opportunity to extend it further through such aspects of service as probation. Work already done to harmonise and improve information systems is ready to be taken to completion.

1. Profile at 2002

Angus is a medium-sized predominantly rural authority with a population of 109,200.

It has a higher than average percentage of households with pensioners and the number of people aged between 60 and 74 is projected to increase by a higher rate than the Scottish average in the next 14 years. The total population is projected to fall by 2016 and the number of under 5s is to decrease by more than the national average.

At 3.7% (January 2002) the rate of unemployment is lower than for Scotland as a whole. 83% of working age people are working – significantly higher than the Scottish average of 73%.

Angus has lower than average rate of drug misuse (1.2% of 15-54 year olds).

At 563 per 10,000 population the local crime rate has risen slightly from 2000, but is below the Scottish average.

Services are provided by a social work department under a director who carries the responsibilities of chief social work officer. Planning for integration of services in Angus involves a team of staff from social work, education, health and housing.

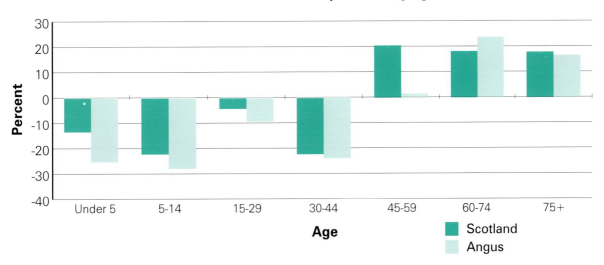

Expected % change in population, 2000-2016, local and national comparisons by age band

2. Performance: Community Care

Balance of care (aged 65+)	1999 actual	1999 per 1,000	Quartile	2000 actual	2000 per 1,000	Quartile
Older people in residential care homes	493	27	1	470	25	1
Older people in private nursing homes	495	27	2	477	26	2
Older people receiving home care	1,629	88	2	1,560	84	2
Older people in special needs housing	2,303	124.9	2	2,391	129.5	2
People receiving a community care service	1999-2000 actual	1999-2000 per 1,000	Quartile	2000-2001 actual	2000-2001 per 1,000	Quartile
Older people (aged 65+)	4,784	259	1	5,058	274.4	1
For mental health problems/dementia (aged 18-64)	263	3.9	2	225	3.4	3
For physical disabilities (aged 18-64)	667	10	3	717	10.7	3
For learning disabilities (aged 18-64)	258	3.8	2	255	3.8	3
For drug/alcohol abuse problems (aged 18-64)	30	0.4	3	28	0.4	3

The rate of older people receiving a community care service is relatively high, reflecting a higher than average percentage of households with pensioners. The Council has more residential home beds for older people than most mainland authorities in Scotland. The rates of older people in nursing home care and in special needs housing are relatively high. While the rate of older people receiving home care is also relatively high, indications are that relatively few have received more than ten hours of home care each week.

The home help service is being restructured into a home care service, which embraces the "Supporting People Agenda" and a new service for meals on wheels. The meals service will make use of vans which heat frozen meals on a staggered basis during the delivery process, so that the service can be provided to remote areas of Angus.

A joint planning group has developed the Partnership in Practice agreement (PiP) for learning disability services and is responsible for implementation and for allocating Change Fund resources. The PiP is being widely circulated, including to GPs and local health care co-operatives. Stakeholder events have been held to involve people with learning disabilities and their families.

Day care opportunities for people with learning disabilities are being modernised, and two resource managers have been appointed to help develop, as alternatives to traditional centre-based services, employment, educational and leisure and recreation opportunities. Co-ordinators help young people with learning disabilities and their families to experience a seamless transition between children's services and adult services.

The mental health strategy in Angus (now in its fourth year), has had an external evaluation by the Scottish Development Centre for Mental Health. The evaluation identified:

- positive progress in establishing the identity and role of the joint teams and in developing formal systems to support their operation; and
- integrated working within and between the teams.

The evaluation identified that further work was required to involve service users and carers, and to develop targeting, priority setting and gate keeping.

Across Angus, there are multi-disciplinary community mental health teams with service managers, team leaders, care managers, community psychiatric nurses, occupational therapists and support workers. They have very strong links to GPs and local health care co-operatives. Social Work leads for older people and health on adult services. An external reference group enables people with mental health problems and their carers to make their views known. The Council and NHS partners run joint training and have developed a joint protocol for the protection of vulnerable adults.

A single shared assessment tool covering all care groups has been developed. This is currently being piloted within older peoples services and will be implemented across all care groups by April 2003. It covers referral/screening, initial assessment, comprehensive assessment and access to specialist assessments.

A strategy group reviews sensory impairment services, with representation from social work and voluntary sector organisations. The Council purchases assessment, rehabilitation, mobility, and communication services from local voluntary sector providers. Arrangements for future needs assessment have been reviewed but the views have still to be taken of children and their parents about new arrangements.

The Council and its health partners have agreed to adopt joint management and aligned budgets incrementally. A member/officer partnership will sign off joint action plans. There are already single managers in learning disability and mental health, but there will be no overall single manager for older people's services.

The joint resourcing pot begins with mental health and learning disability services, and is to be extended to residential and home care budgets in time. Progress has been made on an agreed statement of intent, a joint development and training plan, and a joint staff forum.

3. Performance: Children and families

Balance of care – Looked after children (aged 0-17)	1999-2000 actual	1999-2000 per 1,000	Quartile	2000-2001 actual	2000-2001 per 1,000	Quartile
At home	48	2.0	4	59	2.5	4
With friends/relatives/other community	8	0.3	4	6	0.3	4
With foster carers/prospective adopters	90	3.7	1	75	3.1	2
In residential accommodation	18	0.8	4	16	0.7	4
Total	164	6.8	3	156	6.5	3

Key performance indicators	1998-1999 actual	1998-1999 per 1,000	Quartile	1999-2000 actual	1999-2000 per 1,000	Quartile
Child protection (CP) referrals (aged 0-15)	237	10.9	2	177	8.3	2
Children subject to a CP case conference (aged 0-15)	125	5.8	1	78	3.6	1
Children placed on CP register (aged 0-15)	77	3.5	1	53	2.5	1
Adoption applications in year (aged 0-17)	6	0.2	4	3	0.1	4
Stranger adopter applications (aged 0-17)	1	0.04	4	1	0.04	4

While the rate of child protection referrals is relatively high, the rates of children subject to a case conference and placed on the child protection register are particularly high. The number of adoption applications is very low.

The early years' service concentrates on preventive work. Family support teams working with 0-3 year olds and their parents have developed a targeted, non-stigmatising service. Outcomes are agreed with individual families and are measured against attainable targets. The strategy has achieved effective outcomes, which have prevented statutory involvement in the lives of the families involved.

Angus has a low number of looked after children. Comparatively few are in residential care, living at home and living with friends or relatives. A higher proportion live with foster carers.

The Council has a clear system for identifying the educational needs of looked after children and monitoring progress. The main features are:

- a small multi-disciplinary team, which includes a link teacher with expertise in special educational needs, who prepares initial care plans on children within three working days of them becoming "accommodated";
- the team identify the resources needed;
- care plans are monitored by this team using the LAC system;
- for the few children who reject all forms of mainstream education, individually tailored packages are arranged; and
- the single residential unit has been equipped with computers and other educational aids.

Progress on establishing a local budget for aftercare for young people is slow and no training has yet been organised. The Council intends to consult care leavers shortly.

A local youth crime strategy involves joint assessments and case conferences for young people in transition between children's hearings and adult criminal justice systems. Barnardo's Bridge Project provides services to young sex offenders.

4. Performance: Criminal Justice

Key Activities	1999-2000	2000-2001	2000-2001 per 10,000	Quartile
Number of social enquiry reports submitted to the courts during the year	794	1,022	135.2	1
Number of community service orders made during the year	130	163	21.6	1
The proportion of social enquiry reports reported to court within target time	2000-2001	Quartile		
Proportion of social enquiry reports submitted to the courts by due date	99.2	2		
The time taken to complete community service orders				
Average length of community service (hours) for orders completed during the year	139	4		
Average hours completed per week	2.8	4		

Although the crime rate is below average, the rate of social enquiry reports submitted to courts was high in 2000-2001, having increased significantly from the previous year. A relatively high proportion of social enquiry reports are submitted to courts by the due date.

A high rate of community service orders was made during 2000-2001, the number having increased from the previous year. The average length of community service orders completed during the year was lower than in most other authorities but the time taken to complete them was long, and on average just 2.8 hours were completed per week.

The Council is a member of the Tayside criminal justice grouping with Dundee and Perth and Kinross. It plans to form a single planning and performance team. The grouping already delivers the Tay Project for adult sex offenders jointly: quality assurance of criminal justice services in Angus has included use of balanced scorecards, which are in place for probation, community service, courts and social enquiry reports.

A monthly joint assessment group involving police, children's and criminal justice services provides a forum for sharing information about sex offenders, and other potentially dangerous offenders, of all ages.

The Fergus Programme is for men convicted of violent offences against their partner or ex-partner. Evaluation of the programme includes reports from the partner. 70% of orders have been successfully completed.

5. Finance

Service Area (£000)	GAE 1999-2000	Final net Out turn 1999-2000	GAE 2000-2001	Final net Out turn 2000-2001
Children's Services	£2,779	£5,201	£2,813	£5,592
Community Care	£18,502	£16,667	£19,303	£17,272
Adult Offenders		£5		-£22
Other SW Services	£2,124	£1,972	£2,133	£2,112
Total	**£23,405**	**£23,846**	**£24,248**	**£24,953**
Spend per head		**1999-2000**		**2000-2001**
Spend per head		£218.40		£228.54
Quartile		2		3

Criminal Justice services receive funding from the Scottish Executive, £815,218 was provided in 2000-2001.

The Council spends significantly above the GAE on children's services.

Social work expenditure per head of population is at a similar level to many other authorities.

6. Staffing

Staff	WTE 1999 actual	WTE 1999 per 1,000	Quartile 1999	WTE 2000 actual	WTE 2000 per 1,000	Quartile 2000
Managers & central staff	95	0.9	1	80	0.7	2
Frontline staff	539	4.9	2	536	4.9	2
Other	135	1.2	3	150	1.4	1
Total	**769**	**7.0**	**2**	**767**	**7.0**	**2**

Vacancies	Vacancies 2000	% Vacancies 2000	% Vacancies 2000 Scotland	Vacancies 2001	% Vacancies 2001	% Vacancies 2001 Scotland
SWs with adults	5	12.9	7.8	3	8.9	10.9
SWs with children	2	5.3	7.4	3	6.5	10.7
SWs with offenders	0	0	7.5	3	15.6	7.2
Generic workers	0	0	8.0	0	0	12.7
Total	**7**	**7.6**	**7.7**	**8**	**9.0**	**10.5**

The Council has relatively high rates of managerial and front-line staff, although the number of managers has fallen between 1999 and 2000. Vacancy levels in 2001 were lower than the national average, but high in the area of criminal justice. Vacancy rates have increased in children's services since 2001. Early in 2002 the vacancy rate among qualified childcare staff was 9%. New services in community schools and youth justice had the effect of attracting staff from core services. A working group is reviewing proposals for ensuring all qualified staff spend time in children's services, developing traineeships, and improving partnerships with education and training colleges.

Neither community care nor criminal justice teams currently have significant social worker vacancy rates. Community care staff can be recruited from a mix of professions wider than social work. While there is a growing number of home care vacancies, the restructuring of the home care service, with a greater emphasis on personal care, is expected to address the problem.

7. Modernising services

At the 1991 census, the largest ethnic minority population in Angus was Chinese. Angus Council engages with the local community in a variety of initiatives. Angus has been the subject of research into racism in rural areas. In preparation for the Race Equality Scheme, the social work department has been particularly involved in staff training and an audit of the needs of ethnic minority service users.

Angus Council is part of the Modernising Government funded Citizen Focus initiative developed by a number of councils. The initiative focuses on the development of one-stop shops and broadband links between local communities. Social work staff expect limited benefits for social work service users from this initiative.

8. The Future

A sound foundation of collaboration has been laid with the health service in developing important aspects of community care, but early action is required on two fronts to capitalise on progress:

- the reformed home care service needs to improve the range of home support, particularly for older people; investment in home support services needs to be increased if the increasing numbers of older people are to be provided with alternatives to residential care in future years; and

- sensory impairment services call for a higher priority; joint working between those providing services for people with a sensory impairment can be improved – that is between social, health and education workers and voluntary sector providers.

In order to consolidate and reinforce the progress already achieved to improve education for looked after children, the social work department should join with the education service to provide joint professional development for staff dealing with those children.

The new Tayside criminal justice grouping needs to come into operation as soon as possible, in order to maintain a consistent level of service throughout the whole area and realise the benefits envisaged from the larger group. Deciding and implementing standard procedures and systems for the new Grouping are now a matter of some urgency.

The vacancy rate early in 2002 for qualified staff put at risk the standards of service planned for children and families. The opportunity should be followed up to assess and implement recommendations from the expert working group to improve recruitment and retention of social work staff.

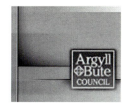

1. Profile at 2002

The third most sparsely populated authority in Scotland, Argyll & Bute has a population of 88,800 over a large geographical area, with an extensive coastline and a number of islands.

The area has one of the highest concentrations of older people in Scotland. 36% of households have a pensioner living in them and almost 9% of the population is over 75. All the islands have large concentrations of older people and there are now fewer younger people available to care for them. It is predicted that there will be reductions in all sectors of the population under 45 and that the number of people between 60 and 74 will increase by more than a fifth.

Unemployment is 4.2% (January 2002).

Argyll and Bute has a drug misuse rate of half the national average (1.0% of 15-54 year olds).

The crime rate is very low (480 recorded crimes per 10,000 of the population).

Argyll & Bute Council Community Planning Partnership embraces the principal statutory, voluntary and private organisations working in the area. The plan includes improvement of "care of the elderly and other vulnerable groups" under the umbrella of the aim to promote health and well being throughout the area.

Social services are managed within a joint housing and social work department, headed by a Director. There is a separate chief social work officer.

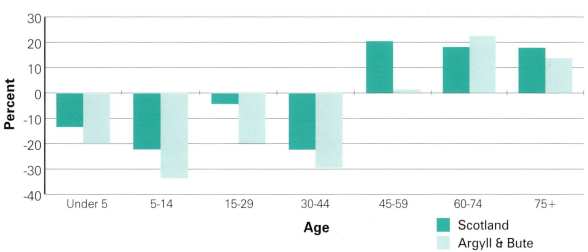

Expected % change in population, 2000-2016, local and national comparisons by age band

2. Performance: Community Care

Balance of care (aged 65+)	1999 actual	1999 per 1,000	Quartile	2000 actual	2000 per 1,000	Quartile
Older people in residential care homes	498	30	1	465	28	1
Older people in private nursing homes	193	12	4	178	11	4
Older people receiving home care	812	50	4	830	50	4
Older people in special needs housing	1,022	62.4	4	866	52.6	4
People receiving a community care service	**1999-2000 actual**	**1999-2000 per 1,000**	**Quartile**	**2000-2001 actual**	**2000-2001 per 1,000**	**Quartile**
Older people (aged 65+)	1,881	114.2	4	2,507	152.2	4
For mental health problems/dementia (aged 18-64)	127	2.3	3	142	2.6	3
For physical disabilities (aged 18-64)	268	4.9	4	256	4.7	4
For learning disabilities (aged 18-64)	227	4.1	2	273	5.0	1
For drug/alcohol abuse problems (aged 18-64)	9	0.2	4	12	0.2	4

Despite having one of the highest concentrations of older people in Scotland, Argyll and Bute provides a comparatively low number of older people with a social work service. A high rate of older people (though reducing recently), still live in residential care compared to many other authorities. The rate of older people living in special needs housing is low and decreased between 1998 and 2000. Older people are less likely to receive a home care service than they are in many other authorities, but if they do it is more likely to be an intensive service (more than 10 hours per week). The numbers of older people receiving home care are increasing as numbers living in residential care are falling.

Following a best value review of home care services the Council is implementing significant changes:

- introduction of 3 different services (domestic, personal and intensive) for children and adult service users;
- a more flexible service appropriate to the sparsely populated area in which staff work;
- enhanced remuneration for staff undertaking personal and intensive care; and
- separate management in the 4 principal divisions of the authority.

To enable more older people to live longer in their own homes with support the Council has:

- made significant increases in the number of houses with community alarms;
- enhanced budgets for Care and Repair; and
- increased the number of aids and adaptations completed.

The Council has established a framework for joint working with its health partners in a Partnership in Practice agreement (PiP) which still needs to be finalised. Features of joint working are:

- high priority for learning disability services, following best value reviews;
- replacement of residential provision where possible by independent living, in conjunction with local housing providers;

- provision for short respite breaks and improved care management; and
- increased diversity and community-based provision for users of traditional day centres.

The specialist NHS team and generic social work teams work jointly on learning disability services. However, access to treatment is limited; a half psychiatrist post and one psychologist do not stretch far over the dispersed communities. Involving groups of service users and carers has proved slow and time-consuming, given the geography of the area.

Mental health services are in a similar state of development but have been assisted by the extension of joint working, notably in the refurbishment of Argyll and Bute Hospital. The practicalities of redistributing resources throughout dispersed communities are still being worked out. Imaginative use of community psychiatric nurses and mental illness specific grant funding have developed community-based mental health services in Bute, Cowal, mid-Argyll, Kintyre and Lorne.

The Thomson Court Dementia Resource won the 2001 Community Care award in the mental health category. It provides residential, day and outreach care for people with dementia and includes a reminiscence room with a 1940s parlour, a sensory garden, a community laundry service, a bathing service and a 24-hour carers help-line. Users and carers were involved in the planning and are now participating in the operation.

Carenap E has been adopted as the single shared assessment tool. To prepare for its introduction:
- joint protocols and procedures are being developed;
- training is planned;
- assessors identified;
- simple, complex and specialist assessments agreed; and
- budgets devolved to area level, to be the responsibility of locality managers.

Work is however needed on information sharing and IT systems and equipment.

Some 3000 people with a sensory impairment are scattered throughout Argyll and Bute. Specialist social work staff are involved in future needs assessments. They also deliver an extensive programme of sensory awareness training. Specialist interpreting services are purchased from Deaf Communications. Joint working takes place at an operational level.

The Council and its health partners now have a joint management structure with a high-level joint strategy manager to drive the Joint Future agenda in 2002-2003.

There are already a number of joint posts, such as an island co-ordinator in Mull and islands' development worker. The partners are taking an evolutionary approach to joint management and joint resourcing of services.

3. Performance: Children and families

Balance of care – Looked after children (aged 0-17)	1999-2000 actual	1999-2000 per 1,000	Quartile	2000-2001 actual	2000-2001 per 1,000	Quartile
At home	71	4.0	2	103	5.7	1
With friends/relatives/other community	14	0.8	3	10	0.6	3
With foster carers/prospective adopters	34	1.9	3	29	1.6	4
In residential accommodation	44	2.5	1	32	1.8	1
Total	**163**	**9.1**	**2**	**174**	**9.7**	**2**

Key performance indicators	1998-1999 actual	1998-1999 per 1,000	Quartile	1999-2000 actual	1999-2000 per 1,000	Quartile
Child protection (CP) referrals (aged 0-15)	98	6.1	3	117	7.4	2
Children subject to a CP case conference (aged 0-15)	43	2.7	2	52	3.3	1
Children placed on CP register (aged 0-15)	24	1.5	3	42	2.7	1
Adoption applications in year (aged 0-17)	5	0.3	4	3	0.2	4
Stranger adopter applications (aged 0-17)	0	0	4	0.0	0.0	4

The rates of children subject to a case conference and of those placed on the child protection register are high in Argyll and Bute. The number of children on the child protection register increased significantly between 1998 and 2000. It has now stabilised around the low to mid 20s. There are very few adoption applications and there were no applications from strangers in 1999-2001.

The number of looked after children increased slightly between 1999 and 2001. The rate of looked after children living in residential care is falling but remains high in comparison to many other authorities. The rate of looked after children living with foster carers is low and fell between 1999 and 2001, but recently the numbers in foster care shifted and 48% of accommodated children now live in foster care.

The Council has boosted its foster care service. In 5 years the number of permanent carers has trebled to 30, and the number of temporary carers also increased to 30. The key to developments has been the work of 4 family placement social workers each located in a Service Centre, and an Early Years social worker. The introduction of training, carer support groups and a newsletter all contributed to the 96 placements achieved in 2001.

Prompted by *Learning with Care*, a joint social work and education working group has been set up to enhance the education of looked after children. It is addressing:

- a comprehensive assessment for looked after children; all those children currently have care plans and receive full-time education but few have individual educational plans and few teachers are involved in reviews;
- training for both social work and education staff who work with those children.

The Council has established standards for an audit of the educational environments in residential homes and foster homes, but it has not yet been carried out.

There is a detailed strategy for addressing the duties and responsibilities under the Children (Leaving Care) Act 2000. However, the Council has no dedicated throughcare or aftercare workers, relying on childcare staff and foster parents to provide support. Although a range of quality housing and support services is available throughout the area, there are fewer local employment and training opportunities, and young people often choose to live outwith Argyll and Bute. This makes it necessary to have extensive consultation with young people leaving care.

The Council intends to employ integration managers to oversee implementation of children's services plans in the four principal divisions covered by the authority. Using the Children's Change Fund, it plans to improve the joint working of education, health and social work staff.

4. Performance: Criminal Justice

Key Activities	1999-2000	2000-2001	2000-2001 per 10,000	Quartile
Number of social enquiry reports submitted to the courts during the year	370	470	75.6	2
Number of community service orders made during the year	71	95	15.3	3
The proportion of social enquiry reports reported to court within target time	2000-2001	Quartile		
Proportion of social enquiry reports submitted to the courts by due date	100.0	1		
The time taken to complete community service orders				
Average length of community service (hours) for orders completed during the year	137	4		
Average hours completed per week	5.1	1		

The rate of social enquiry reports submitted to courts during 2000-2001 was relatively high, the number having increased since 1999-2000. All social enquiry reports are submitted to courts by the due date.

A relatively low rate of community service orders was made during 2000-2001. The average length of order completed was low compared to many other authorities. The orders were completed more quickly than in other authorities with an average 5.1 hours completed per week.

The Council forms part of a criminal justice service grouping with East and West Dunbartonshire. It has developed a comprehensive system for quality assurance with elements from:

- 20% annual sampling, using a range of key performance indicators derived from national standards and departmental procedures;
- client and customer feedback for completion of orders; and
- use of need and risk assessment tools.

Information is fed back on a monthly basis to the teams as well as to external stakeholders.

Current management information systems are a mix of paper-based and stand-alone computer systems. However the department has recently introduced the OLM CareJust software module, which will be networked across the authority to allow electronic monitoring of all KPIs plus risk assessment procedures. The single system is being implemented as the standard across the grouping.

5. Finance

Service Area (£000)	GAE 1999-2000	Final net Out turn 1999-2000	GAE 2000-2001	Final net Out turn 2000-2001
Children's Services	£2,407	£3,385	£2,478	£3,321
Community Care	£16,340	£11,772	£16,878	£13,407
Adult Offenders		£32		-£4
Other SW Services	£1,794	£4,644	£1,792	£4,653
Total	**£20,542**	**£19,832**	**£21,149**	**£21,378**

Spend per head		1999-2000		2000-2001
Spend per head		£223.35		£240.77
Quartile		2		2

Criminal Justice services receive funding from the Scottish Executive, £483,577 was provided in 2000-2001.

Like many other authorities Argyll and Bute spends significantly above the GAE on children's services and less on community care. It spends more than two and a half times the GAE level on other social work services. Spend per head on social work services is relatively high.

6. Staffing

Staff	WTE 1999 actual	WTE 1999 per 1,000	Quartile 1999	WTE 2000 actual	WTE 2000 per 1,000	Quartile 2000
Managers & central staff	73	0.8	1	89	1.0	1
Frontline staff	475	5.3	2	522	5.9	1
Other	89	1.0	3	90	1.0	3
Total	**637**	**7.1**	**2**	**700**	**7.9**	**1**

Vacancies	Vacancies 2000	% Vacancies 2000	% Vacancies 2000 Scotland	Vacancies 2001	% Vacancies 2001	% Vacancies 2001 Scotland
SWs with adults	0	0	7.8	0	0	10.9
SWs with children	0	0	7.4	1	20.0	10.7
SWs with offenders	0	0	7.5	0	0	7.2
Generic workers	4	11.0	8.0	6	11.3	12.7
Total	**4**	**8.9**	**7.7**	**7**	**10.8**	**10.5**

The Council has a high rate of managers and frontline staff in comparison with many other authorities. There are no vacancies in adult services or criminal justice, but there is one vacant post in children's services and six generic posts are vacant.

Recruitment of qualified social workers and home carers is difficult, especially in isolated parts of Argyll. There are particular problems on some of the islands where singleton social workers might be widely known in the communities in which they live.

The Council has changed advertising procedures so that vacancies are available for longer, and has instigated use of its website. Training and development continues as a high priority: the Council is seeking to grow its own staff to fill shortages and the number of staff undertaking training continues to grow steadily. All new managers are speedily trained in recruitment and selection procedures.

7. Modernising services

The intention is to develop a Race Equality Scheme by November 2002, within the Council's framework for equal opportunities. A seasonal influx of travellers has focused council services on providing practical and educational support. There is limited local experience for developing a scheme without external assistance, the Council may benefit from seeking support from neighbouring and similar authorities.

The Council was recently the rural winner in the Scottish Executive's Digital Communities Competition, with its bid for a suite of e-initiatives which will provide every household on the North Argyll Islands with a computer, web camera, printer, software, and one year's free web access. Video conferencing is soon to be extended to three of the smaller islands.

The Council has expanded the number of community and passive alarm systems in the last year, making good use of new technology in a substantial rural area for many older people. Looked after children have also benefited from new technology, with grants for computer assisted learning, in both foster and residential care.

Client information systems inherited from Strathclyde are being replaced in a staged implementation: several modules remain to be rolled out. Arrangements are in hand to integrate education information systems, so that information about the educational attainment of looked after children can be accessed. Progress has still to be made in linking with local health information systems. Full use of Internet and Intranet facilities will not be possible until there is further upgrading of the telecommunications infrastructure.

8. The Future

The reorganisation of the home care service is a major task calling for a strong management lead and resources to ensure that it delivers better local services (and value).

In order to build on the considerable changes it has made to implement community care across its extensive area, the Council needs to address as succeeding priorities:

- improvement of access to treatment for learning disabilities;
- redistribution of resources to support mental health services, to consolidate the advances already made in community-based services;
- greater involvement of users and voluntary organisations, to boost further the standards of community-based mental health services;
- improvement of the supply and training of qualified mental health workers; and
- higher quality of sensory impairment services through increased joint working of social work, education and health staff, closer involvement of voluntary organisations, clear identification of priorities for service development and wider adoption of imaginative patterns of service delivery in particular localities.

The local working group should complete its work on plans to implement the recommendations from *Learning with Care* on the education of looked after children, and the Council should complete its audit of the educational environments of those children, as a basis for devising and implementing progressive improvements.

The practical difficulties of providing aftercare for young people are compounded by their tendency to move out of the area for work and educational opportunities; in order to develop a service which is responsive to the often complicated needs of those young people, the Council need to consider importing or commissioning expertise to help identify needs and shape effective services.

To take forward its commitments to race equality and to providing a responsive service to ethnic minorities, the Council might benefit from commissioning expert support from other authorities or organisations.

1. Profile at 2002

Clackmannanshire is a very compact area, with an estimated population of 48,500 it is the smallest of the mainland authorities.

It is predicted that there will be reductions in all sections of the population aged under 45. Large increases in population are expected in the over 65 age group over the next 14 years.

Unemployment has fallen but, at 4.6% (January 2002), is still above the national average.

The area has lower than average drug misuse (1.4% of people aged 15-54).

There has been a slight increase in crime, with 646 crimes recorded per 10,000 population in 2001.

Social work services are part of a Services to People Department which includes education, leisure and housing functions and which account for nearly 80% of the Council's staff. The new department, led by a Director, has 5 heads of service. The Director is responsible for education, housing and social work services. The Head of Adult Care Services is also the Chief Social Work Officer.

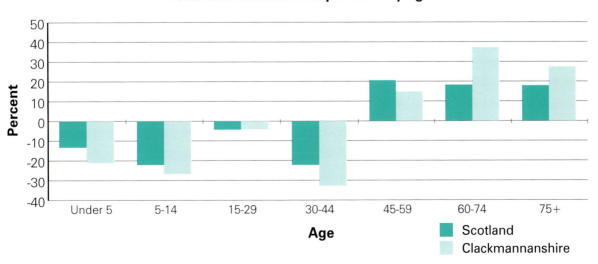

Expected % change in population, 2000-2016, local and national comparisons by age band

2. Performance: Community Care

Balance of care (aged 65+)	1999 actual	1999 per 1,000	Quartile	2000 actual	2000 per 1,000	Quartile
Older people in residential care homes	79	11	4	71	10	4
Older people in private nursing homes	59	8	4	102	14	4
Older people receiving home care	501	71	3	497	70	3
Older people in special needs housing	1,277	180.2	1	1,288	180.8	1
People receiving a community care service	**1999-2000 actual**	**1999-2000 per 1,000**	**Quartile**	**2000-2001 actual**	**2000-2001 per 1,000**	**Quartile**
Older people (aged 65+)	1,579	221.7	2	1,630	228.9	2
For mental health problems/dementia (aged 18-64)	346	11.5	1	138	4.6	2
For physical disabilities (aged 18-64)	391	13.0	3	398	13.3	2
For learning disabilities (aged 18-64)	93	3.1	3	78	2.6	3
For drug/alcohol abuse problems (aged 18-64)	20	0.7	2	17	0.6	3

Compared with most other authorities, rates of older people in residential and nursing home care are lower and rates of older people in special needs housing are higher. The number of older people living in nursing homes has increased significantly between 1999 and 2000. The rate of those receiving home care is less than in many other authorities, but indications are that the Council provides more intensive support. There are few delays in receiving equipment and aids to daily living. Recent joint investment has led to:

- expanded home care;
- better rapid response to individual needs; and
- improved access to services 24 hours a day.

The Council works with partner agencies in Forth Valley to plan and develop services for people with a learning disability. Users and carers have a prominent role in the local implementation group, which has advised on advocacy, respite care, modernising day care and the needs of people with autism.

Services for mental health have been developed in partnership with other Forth Valley councils and the Health Board. Day care and work skills have been priorities of the local implementation group which operates within the overall joint mental health strategy. However, between 1998 and 2000 the number of people receiving a community care service for mental health problems decreased sharply, due to a number of staffing vacancies which have now been filled.

The single shared assessment process will be implemented during 2002. Joint information and training sessions have been delivered to nursing and community care staff. Health and social work staff are to have access to the same services, with budgets held by team leaders.

A Forth Valley group plans services for people with sensory impairment. The group has started to work through the recommendations of Sensing Progress but cannot commit resources.

The Council, with European Social Fund resources, has established an integrated training, work experience and employment project. It undertakes vocational profiling, job matching, on-site job coaching and support for both employer and service users.

The Council and the Health Board have made a positive start in relation to joint resourcing. All community care services, both assessment and provision and specialist health services for the elderly, are to be jointly resourced, but district nursing or health visitors will not be covered in the first phase of change. Steps have been taken towards joint resourcing for mental health and learning disability services.

Joint management arrangements are still being developed. Clackmannanshire Health Alliance has established, as a sub group, a high level joint committee and it is planned for a senior health and social work manager to jointly manage the Joint Future implementation. A joint partnership group is in place and the Local Partnership Agreement is the subject of wide consultation.

3. Performance: Children and families

Balance of care – Looked after children (aged 0-17)	1999-2000 actual	1999-2000 per 1,000	Quartile	2000-2001 actual	2000-2001 per 1,000	Quartile
At home	31	2.7	4	35	3.1	3
With friends/relatives/other community	12	1.1	2	14	1.2	2
With foster carers/prospective adopters	33	2.9	2	35	3.1	2
In residential accommodation	13	1.2	2	11	1.0	3
Total	**89**	**7.8**	**3**	**95**	**8.4**	**2**

Key performance indicators	1998-1999 actual	1998-1999 per 1,000	Quartile	1999-2000 actual	1999-2000 per 1,000	Quartile
Child protection (CP) referrals (aged 0-15)	165	16.3	1	149	14.8	1
Children subject to a CP case conference (aged 0-15)	40	4.0	1	25	2.5	2
Children placed on CP register (aged 0-15)	25	2.5	1	18	1.8	2
Adoption applications in year (aged 0-17)	7	0.6	1	4	0.4	2
Stranger adopter applications (aged 0-17)	4	0.4	1	0	0.0	4

Clackmannanshire has one of the highest rates for child protection referrals. Although the number of children subject to a case conference and the number placed on the child protection register is relatively high, most referrals do not proceed as far as case conference. Numbers of adoption applications are low and there were no adoption applications from strangers in 1999-2000.

Between 1999 and 2001 the number of looked after children increased slightly: numbers in residential care remain low; relatively high numbers live with foster carers or friends or relatives. The Council joins Stirling and Falkirk Councils in twice-yearly campaigns to recruit foster carers.

Progress has been made in implementing the recommendations of *Learning with Care:* all looked after children now have care plans and all schools have accurate information on such children. A local review of the educational attainment of looked after children revealed low levels, in line with the national picture.

The Council is preparing to administer new arrangements for care leavers. Staff from generic child care teams are to provide specific throughcare and after care support for the three to four children who will need it each year.

4. Performance: Criminal Justice

Key Activities	1999-2000	2000-2001	2000-2001 per 10,000	Quartile
Number of social enquiry reports submitted to the courts during the year	526	509	150.8	1
Number of community service orders made during the year	65	88	26.1	1
The proportion of social enquiry reports reported to court within target time	2000-2001	Quartile		
Proportion of social enquiry reports submitted to the courts by due date	100.0	1		
The time taken to complete community service orders				
Average length of community service (hours) for orders completed during the year	175.0	1		
Average hours completed per week	5.6	1		

The rate of social enquiry reports submitted in 2000-2001 was higher than in many other authorities. All reports were submitted to courts by the due date. The rate of community service orders made was also higher than in many other authorities. The average length of orders was long, but they were completed comparatively quickly, with an average of 5.6 hours completed per week.

The Council forms with Clackmannanshire, Falkirk and Stirling the Forth Valley criminal justice grouping. They had already been working closely together, on some developments, since 1996. A review of all assessment tools and practices across the grouping, with a common framework for auditing all services, is planned for completion in autumn 2002.

Much of Clackmannanshire's work with young people who offend is delivered with partner agencies including APEX, the Community Alcohol and Drugs Service and SACRO. Through a partnership with Barnardo's, the Freagarrach Project has been extended to include 16-17 year olds, in order to maintain persistent young offenders within the children's hearing system.

Although prevalence rates are below average, staff report significant numbers of young drug and alcohol misusers. The substance misuse forum has developed an arrest referral scheme, among other measures, to tackle the consequences of misuse. The scheme supports a treatment programme involving local GPs.

The criminal justice service has achieved the international quality assurance standard ISO 9002. This has to be renewed every two years and surveillance takes place every six months.

5. Finance

Service Area (£000)	GAE 1999-2000	Final net Out turn 1999-2000	GAE 2000-2001	Final net Out turn 2000-2001
Children's Services	£1,940	£3,517	£1,948	£3,861
Community Care	£7,603	£7,191	£7,976	£7,474
Adult Offenders		£336		£617
Other SW Services	£944	£692	£946	£570
Total	**£10,487**	**£11,737**	**£10,870**	**£12,522**

Spend per head		1999-2000		2000-2001
Spend per head		£242.20		£258.39
Quartile		2		2

Criminal Justice services receive funding from the Scottish Executive, £395,686 was provided in 2000-2001. Children's services expenditure includes Family Centres for which social services had no responsibility until 1 June 2002.

Expenditure on children's services is significantly and consistently above the GAE. Expenditure on other social work services is significantly lower. Spend per head on social work services is relatively high.

6. Staffing

Staff	WTE 1999 actual	WTE 1999 per 1,000	Quartile 1999	WTE 2000 actual	WTE 2000 per 1,000	Quartile 2000
Managers & central staff	26	0.5	3	48	1.0	1
Frontline staff	176	3.6	4	162	3.3	4
Other	91	1.9	1	75	1.6	1
Total	**293**	**6.0**	**3**	**285**	**5.9**	**3**

Vacancies	Vacancies 2000	% Vacancies 2000	% Vacancies 2000 Scotland	Vacancies 2001	% Vacancies 2001	% Vacancies 2001 Scotland
SWs with adults	0	0	7.8	1	5.3	10.9
SWs with children	2	11.4	7.4	3	16.2	10.7
SWs with offenders	0	0	7.5	0	0	7.2
Generic workers	0	0	8.0	0	0	12.7
Total	**2**	**4.5**	**7.7**	**4**	**8.2**	**10.5**

Rates of front-line staff are relatively low but managerial and central staff are relatively high. The number of managers increased significantly from 1999 to 2000. The rate of 'other' staff is also high. Vacancy rates are low in most areas but high in children's services.

The difficulties in recruiting qualified social work staff for children's services have been serious, with a fifth of staff resigning in 2001. A recent reorganisation of childcare services, coupled with success in recruiting two newly qualified staff in early 2002, has improved the situation. There are no significant difficulties in recruiting staff in community care or criminal justice.

7. Modernising services

A local working group, comprising representatives of Council services and voluntary and community organisations, has examined the implications of the Race Relations (Amendment) Act and disseminated information among represented services. A local Race Equality Scheme needs to be prepared as part of implementing the legislation.

The Council subscribes to Citizen Focus, the Modernising Government funded project operated by a number of Scottish authorities. The Services to People Department is involved in a customer relationship management system being developed over the next three years.

8. The Future

The Council is working closely with the Health Board in establishing and bringing into operation joint management and budgeting arrangements, in order to realise the objectives of community care. Specific aspects of implementing community care which call for early attention are:

- strengthening partnership with carers and with people using services in planning services, particularly in mental health;
- giving greater priority services to meet the needs of people with sensory impairment, there is an urgent need to take forward the recommendations of *Sensing Progress* in collaboration with health and education services; and
- establishing a system of needs assessment for those with learning difficulties and to build further on earlier progress in improving services for those with learning difficulties.

The low level of educational provision for children in the residential home should be addressed as a matter of urgency. The combination of education and child care services in one department of a small authority creates the potential to tailor services to the needs of looked after children. The Council needs to promote good practice on exclusions, enable the smooth exchange of information about looked after children and promote joint professional development for teaching and social work staff.

Aftercare of young people is a particularly difficult function for smaller Councils to discharge effectively, in view of the variety of needs which can arise and the specialist skills required to deal with them. The Council has placed working responsibility on generic social workers but it should make efforts to ensure that they have access to specialist knowledge and practice to support them in their work.

Deciding and implementing standard procedures and systems for the new Forth Valley criminal justice group is now a matter of some urgency, so that the flow of referrals can be dealt with smoothly and consistently.

The Council continues to have significant problems in terms of childcare staffing and there is recent evidence to suggest that criminal justice services are also starting to experience difficulty in recruitment. The Council should adopt measures specifically designed to retain and recruit social work staff, based on best practice.

Established client information systems for adults and children need to be reviewed in order to establish better links with health and education: linking data systems is vital to support positive developments such as single shared assessment.

1. Profile for 2002

A predominantly rural authority, Dumfries & Galloway has a population of 145,800.

The population is set to drop by 7% over the next 14 years, particularly in the under 15's and 30-44 age group. The proportion of households with pensioners is already high and the number of people aged over 75 is set to increase by almost a third.

At 3.7%, the unemployment rate is lower than for Scotland as a whole, but unemployment amongst 18-24s has risen over 600% in the last year.

The drug misuse rate is below average (1.6% of 15 to 54 year olds).

The rate of recorded crime has fallen slightly to 528 per 10,000 of population in 2001. Relatively high offending among women and young people is a constant local feature, which may be associated with increased misuse of drugs.

The Council has recently reorganised both its committee and management arrangements. The Council is strengthening the role of its 4 Area Committees, and developing a more strategic and corporate approach at the centre of its activities. The interests of children and older people are seen to cut across all Council business, and will have their own sub-committees.

One of three corporate directorates, Education and Community Services embraces all services delivered by the council to individuals, including social services. The Chief Social Work Officer post is to lie with either the Head of Children's Services or the Head of Community Care.

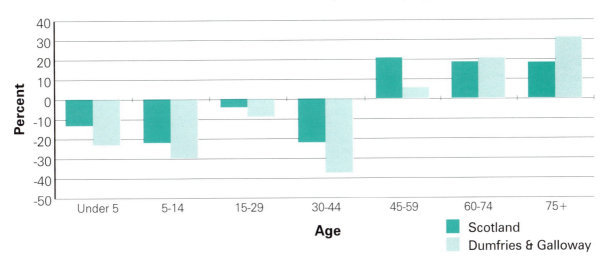

Expected % change in population, 2000-2016, local and national comparisons by age band

2. Performance: Community Care

Balance of care (aged 65+)	1999 actual	1999 per 1,000	Quartile	2000 actual	2000 per 1,000	Quartile
Older people in residential care homes	615	22	2	668	24	1
Older people in private nursing homes	456	16	4	401	15	4
Older people receiving home care	1,545	56	3	1,455	52	4
Older people in special needs housing	1,581	57.2	4	1,599	57.4	4
People receiving a community care service	1999-2000 actual	1999-2000 per 1,000	Quartile	2000-2001 actual	2000-2001 per 1,000	Quartile
Older people (aged 65+)	6,504	233.4	2	5,620	201.7	3
For mental health problems/dementia (aged 18-64)	146	1.7	4	147	1.7	4
For physical disabilities (aged 18-64)	1,592	18.4	1	1,116	12.9	3
For learning disabilities (aged 18-64)	355	4.1	2	135	1.6	4
For drug/alcohol abuse problems (aged 18-64)	26	0.3	3	20	0.2	4

Dumfries and Galloway has a higher rate of older people living in residential care homes than many other authorities and a lower rate of people living in special needs housing. Fewer older people receive home care than many other authorities, but the service is provided for longer hours than in most, because the Council has targeted services on older people with more complex needs who often require personal care. The service is both provided and purchased, but does not include overnight care. Social work teams (outwith Stewartry where there is a joint management pilot) have close links with GP practices and primary care teams. The Nithsdale Rapid Response Team and the Dumfries Community Rehabilitation Team are jointly managed.

A joint board produced the Partnership in Practice Agreement (PiP) and is responsible for its implementation. An integrated learning disability service is being put in place, with community learning disability teams of social workers, community learning disability nurses and occupational therapists working together in a shared base. The council is working towards integrating administrative systems, wherever possible. Work is ongoing to agree a way of sharing some common information held by Social Services and the Primary Care Trust on its separate IT systems. Integrated teams will each have one manager that comes from either a social work or health background.

A learning plan sets out the training and development needs of local authority and NHS staff. The local authority and the NHS are developing a single quality assurance system linking clinical governance and best value. This will help to make sure that services are effective and good value for money. People with learning disabilities and their families have been consulted in a series of workshops. A small transition project in one area of Dumfries and Galloway helps young people with a learning disability into jobs or further education.

Mental health services are similarly organised, with a joint board giving a lead in planning and implementation. Five multi-disciplinary community mental health teams serve adults and similar teams are being developed for older people. A joint training plan sets out the training needs of social work and NHS staff and includes a current programme on the Adults with Incapacity (Scotland) Act 2000.

A multi-agency group oversees the development and implementation of single shared assessment. Carenap E is being piloted for older people and is to be adapted for other care groups. Protocols have still to be agreed on IT and information sharing, including issues of client consent.

Initiatives have been taken to develop services for people with a sensory impairment:

- direct input into the future needs assessment process;
- improved links with ophthalmologists and low vision clinics;
- consultation with service users;
- close working with education, health and voluntary organisations to improve the procedures for certifying and registering people with a visual impairment; and
- training for specialist staff and sensory awareness training for all staff.

The local joint management and resourcing agenda is well established. The Local Partnership Agreement for older peoples services incorporates health, social services, housing and the voluntary sector. A joint board, jointly chaired by the chief executive in the NHS and the social services chief officer, gives a strategic focus.

Health and social services teams are being integrated and managed in localities, under integrated management arrangements and with combined budgets.

3. Performance: Children and families

Balance of care – Looked after children (aged 0-17)	1999-2000 actual	1999-2000 per 1,000	Quartile	2000-2001 actual	2000-2001 per 1,000	Quartile
At home	124	3.9	2	113	3.6	2
With friends/relatives/other community	35	1.1	2	42	1.3	1
With foster carers/prospective adopters	114	3.6	1	141	4.5	1
In residential accommodation	34	1.1	2	28	0.9	4
Total	**307**	**9.8**	**2**	**324**	**10.3**	**2**

Key performance indicators	1998-1999 actual	1998-1999 per 1,000	Quartile	1999-2000 actual	1999-2000 per 1,000	Quartile
Child protection (CP) referrals (aged 0-15)	226	7.8	2	160	5.7	3
Children subject to a CP case conference (aged 0-15)	127	4.6	1	94	3.4	1
Children placed on CP register (aged 0-15)	98	3.5	1	63	2.3	2
Adoption applications in year (aged 0-17)	11	0.3	3	16	0.5	1
Stranger adopter applications (aged 0-17)	5	0.2	3	10	0.3	1

After a steep increase between 1998 and 1999, the number of children on the child protection register has now reduced; but its rate remains relatively high. A high rate of referrals proceed to a case conference. Numbers of adoptions are high.

The social services department is implementing an action plan which takes forward the lessons learned from the death of a three-year-old child:

- retraining staff;
- revising child protection procedures;
- regular audits of casework practice and recording;
- stronger screening, assessment and overview of key decision-making.

The rate of looked after children has increased, with high rates living with foster carers or friends or relatives. An external audit of foster care resulted in recruitment targeted in specific geographic areas, and among a younger group of carers. Subsequently, placement breakdowns have been reduced by 55%. There are relatively few children in residential care, including residential schools. This is partly attributable to the Crannog Project (see below) which has halved the number of young people placed in residential schools.

The number of referrals to the Reporter has increased partly because of an increase in the misuse of drugs and alcohol. 44% of recent referrals in Stranraer are alleged to relate to the misuse of heroin.

Arrangements and expectations for the education of looked after children are detailed in an education/social work protocol. Several children in residential homes do not have full-time education, and alternative arrangements do not provide full-time provision. Children in the three residential homes have study areas and computer hardware and software for educational purposes; foster children have similar facilities; all looked after children have an e-mail account. The dispersed rural areas do not allow library access for all children.

An assessment and support service working with young people at risk of exclusion from school, Crannog is operated by Aberlour Child Care Trust in partnership with education and social services. It achieved national recognition by winning the 2001 Community Care award for inter-agency working. The project forges links between home, school and community, and has won the confidence of young people, their families, and the children's hearing system. It provides an initial assessment and comprehensive plan to the area review group (which makes decisions about young people at risk), and offers support both in and outside school.

A care leavers team, involving the Benefits Agency, health, education, housing providers and homeless advice workers, was established following an audit which revealed that all those who left care over a five-year period experienced a period of homelessness. The team trains staff and provides care leavers with information. Supported accommodation is provided by Loreburn Housing Association.

The social services and education departments are gradually integrating services e.g. strengthening family support services through multi-disciplinary teams in four localities and in family centres in Dumfries and Stranraer. A respite unit for children with disabilities has been developed with the health service.

4. Performance: Criminal Justice

Key Activities	1999-2000	2000-2001	2000-2001 per 10,000	Quartile
Number of social enquiry reports submitted to the courts during the year	789	751	75.3	2
Number of community service orders made during the year	181	189	18.9	1
The proportion of social enquiry reports reported to court within target time	**2000-2001**	**Quartile**		
Proportion of social enquiry reports submitted to the courts by due date	Not reported	4		
The time taken to complete community service orders				
Average length of community service (hours) for orders completed during the year	100	4		
Average hours completed per week	2.7	4		

The rate of social enquiry reports submitted in 2000-2001 was relatively high.

The rate of community service orders made was higher than in many other authorities. The average length of orders completed in 2000-2001 was shorter than in most other authorities but the orders took longer to complete. An average of just 2.7 hours were completed per week.

As a stand-alone authority for criminal justice services Dumfries and Galloway, one of the three Pathfinder projects sponsored by the Getting Best Results initiative, committed to introducing service-wide quality assurance practices and procedures and subject to external evaluation. Staff input their own data to the SWIS information system, which is used for case-work and for staff supervision. The system is also used for workload management including managing high-risk cases, and for aggregate information which is fed back to staff.

There is a "getting best results" quality assurance group and staff have received quality assurance training which will be integrated into practice. All staff – both operational and support – have been involved in the development of the Pathfinder pathway, beginning with a review of effective practice research and of organisational culture. The Intranet allows staff access to procedures, standards and legislation.

5. Finance

Service Area (£000)	GAE 1999-2000	Final net Out turn 1999-2000	GAE 2000-2001	Final net Out turn 2000-2001
Children's Services	£4,405	£7,530	£4,386	£8,179
Community Care	£23,541	£23,587	£24,796	£23,418
Adult Offenders		£38		£59
Other SW Services	£2,818	£3,084	£2,838	£3,016
Total	**£30,764**	**£34,239**	**£32,021**	**£34,673**

Spend per head		1999-2000		2000-2001
Spend per head		£234.83		£237.81
Quartile		2		2

Criminal Justice services receive funding from the Scottish Executive, £1,267,535.76 was provided in 2000-2001.

The Community Care budget was overspent significantly in 1999-2000. Since that time a combination of improved financial control, targeting of and charging for services has brought expenditure within budget. The Council spent significantly above GAE on children's services. Spend per head on social work services is relatively high.

6. Staffing

Staff	WTE 1999 actual	WTE 1999 per 1,000	Quartile 1999	WTE 2000 actual	WTE 2000 per 1,000	Quartile 2000
Managers & central staff	79	0.5	3	82	0.6	3
Frontline staff	503	3.4	4	242	1.7	4
Other	152	1.0	3	129	0.9	3
Total	**733**	**5.0**	**4**	**453**	**3.1**	**4**

Vacancies	Vacancies 2000	% Vacancies 2000	% Vacancies 2000 Scotland	Vacancies 2001	% Vacancies 2001	% Vacancies 2001 Scotland
SWs with adults	2	4.5	7.8	8	13.3	10.9
SWs with children	6	12.4	7.4	9	14.6	10.7
SWs with offenders	1	7.2	7.5	4	20.2	7.2
Generic workers	0	0	8.0	0	0	12.7
Total	**9**	**8.3**	**7.7**	**21**	**14.3**	**10.5**

The Council has far lower rates of managerial and front-line staff than many other authorities. The number of front-line staff, already low in 1999, has more than halved since then. In 2001 vacancy levels were high in all areas except for generic workers, but the Council is not experiencing the severe recruitment and retention problems affecting some other councils.

Local difficulties include the recruitment of childcare social workers in more isolated areas and of mental health specialists. The problem manifests itself in high turnover and in poor responses to advertising.

The Council has worked with their advertising agents on style of information to candidates and enhanced relocation packages. Advertising on a recruitment website yielded good results. The ability to seize on all expressions of interest requires specialist training and support which the advertising agency is to supply. The Council is also working with health colleagues on joint advertisement of posts, in order to save on costs, and in the hope of appealing to couples in related professions considering a move to the area.

7. Modernising services

Dumfries and Galloway has small and dispersed Asian and Chinese communities. Travelling communities are a significant part of the landscape, and more recently asylum seekers, travelling via Ireland and Stranraer, have presented themselves for assistance. The social services department has sought to address the needs of elderly Chinese people.

The Council has promoted the use of information kiosks to improve access to service information in rural areas, but with little direct involvement from social services. The department has a well-established client information system, which is currently being upgraded to include care assessment and management information. Plans for improved integration with health systems awaits funding. E-mail is a key tool for staff in the dispersed rural areas in which most of them operate.

8. The Future

The Council has pursued a range of community care initiatives, which have created a platform for improvement to meet changing needs. Specific areas for attention are:

- expansion of home care for older people, as their numbers grow;
- full implementation of integrated learning disability services through multi-disciplinary teams based in the community;
- similar full implementation of mental health services; and
- improvement of services for sensory impairment through closer joint working with education and health.

The provision of full-time education for looked after children in residential care is now an urgent priority.

Aftercare services for young people should be further developed to meet their often complex needs. A useful starting point would be to establish a database to track care leavers.

Criminal justice services stand to derive real benefits from involvement in the Pathfinder Initiative; management should implement service improvements as soon as practicable, based on that experience.

The Council has yet to take a proactive approach to implementing the Race Relations (Amendment) Act 2000. Given the evidence of endemic racism in rural areas more attention needs to be given to this area of work.

1. Profile at 2002

Dundee is a medium sized urban authority with a population of 142,700. While working hard to regenerate it continues to have significant areas of deprivation.

The population continues to decline at a substantial rate. Proportionately Dundee has the highest loss of all Scottish cities, with deaths exceeding births. The proportion of households with dependent children is below average (27% compared to 30% nationally). The authority faces a larger than average reduction in the number of children and younger adults.

The number of jobs in Dundee City has decreased by 6% between 1995 and 2000. Dundee has a high rate of unemployment (5.9% in January 2002).

The drug misuse rate is the second highest in Scotland (3.5 % of 15-54 year olds).

The crime rate is the fourth highest of all local authorities (1,130 crimes were recorded per 10,000 population in 2001).

Social work services are delivered by a social work department under a director, who is also chief social work officer.

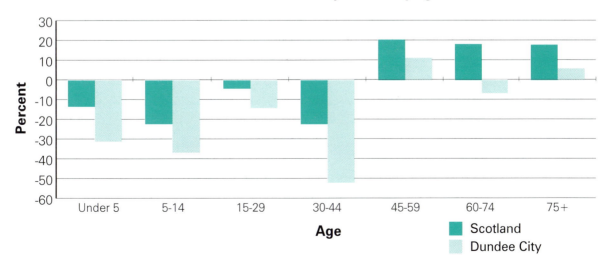

Expected % change in population, 2000-2016, local and national comparisons by age band

2. Performance: Community Care

Balance of care (aged 65+)	1999 actual	1999 per 1,000	Quartile	2000 actual	2000 per 1,000	Quartile
Older people in residential care homes	402	16	3	408	16	3
Older people in private nursing homes	556	22	3	610	24	3
Older people receiving home care	2,610	103	1	2,586	102	1
Older people in special needs housing	5,559	218.5	1	5,449	215.2	1
People receiving a community care service	1999-2000 actual	1999-2000 per 1,000	Quartile	2000-2001 actual	2000-2001 per 1,000	Quartile
Older people (aged 65+)	4,237	167.3	3	4,052	160	4
For mental health problems/dementia (aged 18-64)	204	2.3	3	236	2.7	3
For physical disabilities (aged 18-64)	902	10.3	3	825	9.5	3
For learning disabilities (aged 18-64)	421	4.8	1	415	4.8	1
For drug/alcohol abuse problems (aged 18-64)	128	1.5	1	96	1.1	2

Relatively few older people live in residential or nursing home care. A high proportion of older people live in special needs housing. The Council has consistently provided more older people with home care support than most other mainland authorities. Care services have been re-organised to provide a more efficient re-distribution of resources. This has involved developing the level and range of practical suport while maintaining a steady increase in the number of people with complex and personal care needs accessing appropriate levels of support.

The Council is implementing an older people's strategy, which incorporates new approaches to delivering home care and extra care housing. Its key features are:

- home support services divided between domestic or practical support and personal care;
- social care officers working to neighbourhood teams to provide the personal care between 7:00 a.m. and 10:00 p.m., 7 days a week with management support; and
- day care services to be redeveloped, particularly for older people with dementia: a model of provision which integrates health and social care is being rolled out.

The Dundee Partnership in Practice (PiP) with NHS Tayside allows for systematic assessment of local needs and prominent consultation with people with a learning disability and their carers. Social work and health jointly lead integrated community learning disability teams. The social work department is introducing a range of initiatives as alternatives to traditional day services. With Sense Scotland, it has developed a weekend respite service for 13 adults.

It was recognised that work had to be done to identify the needs and provide locally based services for mentally disordered offenders. Processes have been put in place to achieve this.

There have been Tayside-wide difficulties in progressing the strategic agenda for community mental health services. A Tayside-wide accountability steering group has been charged with formulating strategic priorities and more recently a mental health review group, with an external facilitator, has been established.

Dundee is participating in a jointly funded review of community mental health teams (CMHTs), which is co-led by social work and health.

A single shared assessment tool, produced by a project team and developed after consultation with staff, users and carers, is being introduced from summer 2002, in conjunction with staff training. A joint staff development programme will be developed for all staff implementing the single shared assessment tool. Ultimately the assessment process will be supported by shared protocols.

Dundee does not have an over-arching strategy group for sensory impairment services, embracing service providers, health and education. The Council has recently renewed service level agreements with its two principal providers of sensory impairment services: Tayside Association for the Deaf and Dundee Society for the Visually Impaired, who work closely with children's services, who also work closely with education. Services for deaf-blind people are provided by a range of providers.

The Council and its partners are adopting a joint management approach to community care, and are revising committee and senior management structures. The partners are identifying services and associated resources for inclusion in aligned budgets, initially for older people. There is an agreement to establish a joint staff forum, which will have a lead role in the progression of a joint development and training plan and a statement of intent detailing staff involvement. The partners have an implementation action plan and a set of agreed outcomes against which to monitor progress.

3. Performance: Children and Families

Balance of care – Looked after children (aged 0-17)	1999-2000 actual	1999-2000 per 1,000	Quartile	2000-2001 actual	2000-2001 per 1,000	Quartile
At home	136	4.4	2	152	5.0	2
With friends/relatives/other community	70	2.3	1	65	2.1	1
With foster carers/prospective adopters	151	4.9	1	122	4.0	1
In residential accommodation	53	1.7	2	53	1.7	1
Total	**410**	**13.4**	**1**	**392**	**12.8**	**1**

Key performance indicators	1998-1999 actual	1998-1999 per 1,000	Quartile	1999-2000 actual	1999-2000 per 1,000	Quartile
Child protection (CP) referrals (aged 0-15)	245	8.9	2	166	6.1	3
Children subject to a CP case conference (aged 0-15)	120	4.4	1	91	3.3	1
Children placed on CP register (aged 0-15)	66	2.4	2	67	2.5	1
Adoption applications in year (aged 0-17)	14	0.5	2	15	0.5	1
Stranger adopter applications (aged 0-17)	4	0.1	3	8	0.3	2

The rate of child protection referrals is relatively low but a high rate of children who are investigated are subject to a case conference and are placed on the child protection register. The adoption rates are relatively high.

Run by NCH in partnership with the housing and social work departments, the Dundee Families Project helps families who have exhibited anti-social behaviour and have lost their home or are at risk of eviction. The aim is to avoid eviction or achieve satisfactory tenancy arrangements, and to prevent the breakdown of vulnerable families. Services consist of individual and couple counselling, family support and groupwork. An external evaluation identified as the Project's success factors:

- commitment to inter-agency partnership;
- supportive yet challenging nature of its direct work;
- flexible range of interventions; and
- good management.

There is a high rate of looked after children. Numbers increased from 1999 to 2000 but fell again in 2001. A high proportion of those children and young people who are looked after and accommodated are cared for in foster homes. This is a creditable achievement in a city with high levels of deprivation and unemployment. While progress has been made in reducing the numbers of children in residential homes, the rate remains high.

The recommendations of *Learning with Care* which cover assessment, care planning, the provision of full-time education, and statistical monitoring have been implemented. In addition, every school has a designated teacher to oversee progress of looked after children, and some individual learning plans contain educational targets. A link teacher (co-located with the childcare review team) inspects and reports on the educational environment of each accommodated child. There is a homework base in every establishment, and an educational resource pack for foster carers.

The Council has a throughcare and aftercare strategy. A lead officer has been appointed to ensure the successful implementation of the strategy and of the new responsibilities. The care and assessment teams are arranging joint training for relevant staff. An implementation group has been set up to consider issues including local payment methods, data collection and a system for representation.

In a Council response to 'For Scotland's children', an action team consisting of the Directors of Social Work and Education, the Commissioner for Child Health and a representative from the Voluntary Sector is planning a single system for the planning and delivery of children's services. It is charged with securing:

- improved co-ordination in the planning, development and delivery of services;
- partnership of health, voluntary sector services, educational and housing services to support the most vulnerable children;
- much improved information-sharing between agencies; and
- enhancement of the skills of staff in working with families.

With Sense Scotland, the Social Work Department has developed a flexible respite service for the carers of 5 young people with complex health and care needs. A multi-agency review is currently being undertaken on Tayside Child and Adolescent Mental Health Services. As part of this CAMHS review a study of needs assessment has been carried out and a CAMHS strategy and action plan will be produced by Spring 2003.

4. Performance: Criminal Justice

Key Activities	1999-2000	2000-2001	2000-2001 per 10,000	Quartile
Number of social enquiry reports submitted to the courts during the year	2,294	2,514	253.8	1
Number of community service orders made during the year	483	508	51.3	1
The proportion of social enquiry reports reported to court within target time	2000-2001	Quartile		
Proportion of social enquiry reports submitted to the courts by due date	97.4	3		
The time taken to complete community service orders				
Average length of community service (hours) for orders completed during the year	156	2		
Average hours completed per week	2.7	4		

The Council is part of a criminal justice grouping with Angus and Perth and Kinross. Criminal justice services are delivered in Dundee against a background of acute poverty, unemployment and drug use. Drug and alcohol issues affect almost two thirds of offenders on whom a social enquiry report is prepared.

As the demand for social enquiry reports continues to rise, so do the numbers of probation and community service orders. The Council is able to report meticulously on targeting in terms of the likelihood of re-conviction in the next 18 months.

Numbers of offenders completing statutory orders without breach have improved significantly, from under 40% to a reported 75%. Since 2001 all offenders subject to probation orders participate in groupwork, starting with an induction module. This is followed by a menu of structured interventions. Evaluation is built in at the end of each session and programme.

Youth Justice work continues to be taken forward through the CHOICE project, based within Children's Services, aimed at reducing the number of young people progressing from the children's hearing system into the adult court system. Criminal Justice Services support the CHOICE project by way of funding a social work post.

Management information is used to improve performance at all levels. There is prompt feed-back to workers, and the supervision of potentially dangerous offenders, including sex offenders, is subject to annual external audit. However, unified management information will not be easily achieved across the three partner authorities, as Dundee continues its long-standing commitment to in-house development, and at least one other authority is moving to a commercial software provider. It is, however, recognised that the use of OASys and the wider issue of delivering accredited programmes will attract significant costs. Dundee is in the process of agreeing a common assessment and evaluation process with partners.

When Criminal Justice Social Work moves back to refurbished accommodation a team of two police officers will move to this office. This will strengthen links with the police, particularly with regard to both registered and non-registered sex offenders. The Tay Project is also based in Dundee and offers personal change programmes to adult sex offenders. One such programme has won a national award for work with sex offenders who have an intellectual difficulty.

5. Finance

Service Area (£000)	GAE 1999-2000	Final net Out turn 1999-2000	GAE 2000-2001	Final net Out turn 2000-2001
Children's Services	£8,910	£13,658	£8,870	£14,844
Community Care	£25,962	£25,578	£26,912	£26,470
Adult Offenders		£63		£44
Other SW Services	£3,103	£2,942	£3,075	£3,022
Total	**£37,975**	**£42,240**	**£38,858**	**£44,380**

Spend per head		1999-2000		2000-2001
Spend per head		£296		£311
Quartile		1		1

Criminal Justice services receive funding from the Scottish Executive, £2,089,458 was provided in 2000-2001.

Dundee spends significantly above GAE on children's services. The number of children in residential schools bears particularly heavily on a hard-pressed Children and Families budget. The overall spend on social work services per head is higher than in many other authorities.

6. Staffing

Staff	WTE 1999 actual	WTE 1999 per 1,000	Quartile 1999	WTE 2000 actual	WTE 2000 per 1,000	Quartile 2000
Managers & central staff	93	0.6	2	117	0.8	2
Frontline staff	834	5.8	1	878	6.2	1
Other	315	2.2	1	196	1.4	1
Total	**1,242**	**8.6**	**1**	**1,190**	**8.3**	**1**

Vacancies	Vacancies 2000	% Vacancies 2000	% Vacancies 2000 Scotland	Vacancies 2001	% Vacancies 2001	% Vacancies 2001 Scotland
SWs with adults	0	0	7.8	0	0	10.9
SWs with children	0	0	7.4	4	5.0	10.7
SWs with offenders	2	7.5	7.5	0	0	7.2
Generic workers	0	0	8.0	0	0	12.7
Total	**2**	**1.5**	**7.7**	**4**	**2.4**	**10.5**

Dundee City Council has a high rate of staff, particularly frontline staff, in comparison with many other authorities. There are currently no care management and social work vacancies in community care or criminal justice and the number of vacancies in children's services is lower than in many other authorities.

Committed to the belief that "if you don't get it right for staff, you don't get it right for the users", Dundee has not experienced the same staffing crises as other authorities, partly because of strong local links with academic institutions which provide a steady flow of qualified applicants and partly due to relatively cheap housing. However, there are now problems in recruiting social care staff, as a result of competition from, for example, call centres.

A new handbook on "Effective Support to Staff and Good Practice in Management" provides a policy and practice framework for induction, supervision and employee development and review. It sets out the elements of good practice which all staff employed within the department can expect. Innovative routes to improving the career options for departmental staff are planned, including taster sessions in other areas of the department, short secondments, (especially from residential childcare) and shadowing the director.

7. Modernising services

Approximately 3,000 people are from minority ethnic groups, which represents a higher proportion of the population than in many other authorities.

Dundee first published a race equality scheme in 1994. It is proposed this will form part of a wider Equality Scheme. Having significant Asian and Chinese communities, the City has responded to the cultural needs of their older people with the provision of specialist day services and sheltered housing. The home care workforce includes ethnic minority employees. Each department in the Council will identify actions to be taken to ensure that the standards set out in the Equality Schemes are complied with. An inter-agency anti-racist working group has been formed to identify and address gaps in provision for ethnic minorities within the criminal justice system.

A Modernising Government funded project, Dundee.Com, aims to provide a digital information facility for citizens and visitors alike. Current work focuses on provision of customer centres, to reduce the number of telephone calls citizens have to make to access council services, including social work.

The existing social work information system is being developed with case notes designed to help practitioners improve assessment and delivery of care for children, adults and offenders. It is to "talk" to health information systems. Criminal justice links are to be made with Perth and Kinross Council, but not with Angus, which is adopting a different information system.

8. The Future

Dundee City Council has made great strides in shifting provision for older people and people with learning disabilities, from residential to home care and in improving other aspects of community care. To compliment these achievements it should tackle a number of outstanding priorities in other areas:

- the Social Work Department has participated in a review of forensic services and will play its part in implementing the outcome of the review;
- with health partners, identify priorities for development of community-based mental health services – including services for children and young people – and prepare a realistic implementation plan within the agreed financial framework and resource distribution;
- develop the single assessment tool for community care services, introduce it and monitor its effectiveness; and
- with health, education and voluntary organisation partners, carry out a strategic overview of sensory impairment services and identify priorities for improvement.

To build on and maintain momentum for progress achieved in the education of looked after children, the Council should develop joint training and development opportunities for social work and education staff who work with those children.

If the grouping with partner councils is to achieve lasting improvement in delivery of criminal justice services, it will be necessary to harmonise systems, procedures and practice. But a prerequisite will be harmonisation of information systems. Renewed efforts should be made to work out a standard system which benefits all three partner councils.

1. Profile at 2002

East Ayrshire has a population of 120,600 over a diverse area.

The population is set to drop by almost 8.5% over the next 14 years, a higher rate than average. A steep reduction is likely in the 30-44 age group. The decrease in the number of children and young people is expected to be greater than the national average.

The unemployment rate is falling but is still one of the highest in Scotland (5.7% in January 2002). Two thirds of working age people are in employment, compared to a Scottish average of 73%.

The drug misuse rate is below average (1.6% of 15-64 year olds).

The local crime rate is below the national average (780 per 10,000 population in 2001).

The Council has retained a traditional service committee structure with a separate Social Work Committee. Seven local committees reflect the interests of different localities.

Social work services are provided by an Educational and Social Services Department under a director, with a separate head of social work, who is also the chief social work officer.

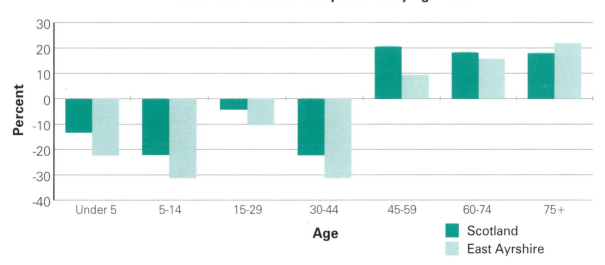

Expected % change in population, 2000-2016, local and national comparisons by age band

2. Performance: Community Care

Balance of care (aged 65+)	1999 actual	1999 per 1,000	Quartile	2000 actual	2000 per 1,000	Quartile
Older people in residential care homes	333	17	3	291	15	3
Older people in private nursing homes	459	24	2	472	25	2
Older people receiving home care	1,287	67	3	1,187	61	3
Older people in special needs housing	1,465	76.3	4	2,990	154.4	1
People receiving a community care service	**1999-2000 actual**	**1999-2000 per 1,000**	**Quartile**	**2000-2001 actual**	**2000-2001 per 1,000**	**Quartile**
Older people (aged 65+)	4,713	243.4	2	4,222	218.1	3
For mental health problems/dementia (aged 18-64)	516	6.9	1	489	6.6	1
For physical disabilities (aged 18-64)	1,557	21	1	1,514	20.5	1
For learning disabilities (aged 18-64)	332	4.5	1	313	4.2	2
For drug/alcohol abuse problems (aged 18-64)	685	9.3	1	530	7.2	1

East Ayrshire has a higher rate of older people in special needs housing than many other authorities. Home Care Services are targeted on the most vulnerable older people, with older people in receipt of a service being more likely to receive an intensive service (more than 10 hours per week) in East Ayrshire compared to many other authorities. The rate of older people in residential care is relatively low. A best value review of residential care for older people is not yet concluded. The Council will continue to support some continuing residential provision whilst increasingly targeting people with dementia.

After a home care review the Council is matching the profile of social care staff more closely to the needs of service users. It is in the process of introducing a new grade of staff, a Personal Carer, whose tasks will be wider and whose hours will be more flexible than those worked by traditional home help staff.

The Rowallan Day Care Centre was short-listed for a Community Care Award in 2001. A joint venture with Alzheimer Scotland Action on Dementia, the Centre provides a wide range of social and therapeutic activities including light exercises and musical therapy. Up to 16 people can attend during six sessions a week during the day, with plans to move towards continental hours in order to offer more flexible supports.

The Council subscribes to a joint Partnership in Practice Agreement (PiP) for learning disability services, applying to councils and the NHS across Ayrshire. People with learning disabilities and their families are involved in its implementation. East Ayrshire also submitted a PiP Agreement specifically for its own area. East Ayrshire has a joint education and social services department. Education is an active partner in the implementation of the PiP Agreements. People with learning disabilities are given help with literacy and numeracy skills and a social worker is based in each of the four special educational needs schools. A review of day opportunities is under way. Local area co-ordination for people with learning disabilities is being planned at the present time.

The Council has employment initiatives that help people with learning disability to get jobs.

The pan-Ayrshire mental health strategy is being reviewed, underpinned by a separate but co-ordinated joint strategy for East Ayrshire. The Council and its NHS partners are gradually co-locating social work and mental health teams. Links with GPs and local health care co-operatives are strong. A jointly commissioned Community Guides service supports people with mental health problems to get involved in community activities. There is a joint training programme to support the implementation of the Adults with Incapacity (Scotland) Act 2000.

East Ayrshire and its health partners are leading the development in Ayrshire of a single shared assessment tool. Having piloted the tool, the process is being rolled out for older people. It is to be extended to all care groups during 2003-2004. Housing has been involved in the development process.

The three councils are working to improve sensory impairment services. Links with voluntary organisations, Visual Impairment Ayrshire and the Ayrshire Mission for the Deaf, have added value to the professional practice delivered by the local authorities. There is an opportunity to enhance guide/communicator services jointly with Deafblind Scotland. The Council is in the process of reviewing its future needs assessment procedures for children with sensory impairment.

The Council is developing the Joint Future agenda at a local level. Its focus is on promoting joint working rather than changing structures. Social work boundaries have been aligned with GP practices. Integrated working is well developed and is overseen by the East Ayrshire Joint Future Implementation Group. Elements of the joint resourcing pot have been agreed and listed.

3. Performance: Children and Families

Balance of care – Looked after children (aged 0-17)	1999-2000 actual	1999-2000 per 1,000	Quartile	2000-2001 actual	2000-2001 per 1,000	Quartile
At home	158	5.8	1	142	5.2	1
With friends/relatives/other community	8	0.3	4	2	0.1	4
With foster carers/prospective adopters	56	2.1	3	72	2.6	2
In residential accommodation	27	1.0	3	39	1.4	2
Total	**249**	**9.1**	**2**	**255**	**9.3**	**2**

Key performance indicators	1998-1999 actual	1998-1999 per 1,000	Quartile	1999-2000 actual	1999-2000 per 1,000	Quartile
Child protection (CP) referrals (aged 0-15)	64	2.6	4	40	1.6	4
Children subject to a CP case conference (aged 0-15)	14	0.6	4	16	0.7	4
Children placed on CP register (aged 0-15)	10	0.4	4	12	0.5	4
Adoption applications in year (aged 0-17)	8	0.3	3	9	0.3	2
Stranger adopter applications (aged 0-17)	2	0.1	4	5	0.2	2

The rates of child protection referrals, children subject to a case conference and children placed on the child protection register are all low, compared to other local authorities. Numbers have however increased since 2000.

Drug abuse is a serious problem, especially in North Kilmarnock, and exerts a continuing and increasing demand on child care services. Almost half of children on the child protection register are there as a result of drug misuse. With support from the Children's Challenge Fund and Lloyds TSB Foundation, the Council has appointed 3 new members of staff working with children misusing drugs and parents who misuse drugs. In addition the Children and Families Fieldwork Service Unit has taken on 5 drug misuse workers to enhance assessment and care management.

Relatively high rates of children are looked after in East Ayrshire, following increases since 1999. The rate of looked after children who are living at home is high. The rate of looked after children living with friends or relatives is very low.

Recommendations in *Learning with Care* for multi-disciplinary assessment, care planning, and full-time education for looked after children have been fully implemented. A designated senior manager in every school ensures that each looked after child has a personal education plan containing specific targets. The implementation group will develop an integrated policy and joint training for social work and education staff, audit practice and keep parents informed about their child's educational progress.

A link teacher monitors and reports on the quality of provision in the Council's two residential units, which have been equipped with new computers and other educational aids; children in foster care have been provided with similar equipment. An independent reviewing officer is to be appointed to monitor and report on all aspects of the care of looked after children. The Council plans to introduce a computerised system incorporating fuller information on the education of looked after children.

The three Ayrshire councils and other key agencies have devised new arrangements for care leavers. A joint working group is implementing a detailed action plan. A local budget has yet to be formulated for East Ayrshire. Joint training has been provided for staff in the agencies involved.

The Council is committed to improved integration of children's services. An Integration Services Manager, funded from the New Community School programme, will develop and train multi-disciplinary teams. The three Ayrshire councils and the health service are working towards a common assessment process, supported by a pooled budget from the Changing Children's Services Fund and by common electronic communication.

4. Performance: Criminal Justice

Key Activities	1999-2000	2000-2001	2000-2001 per 10,000	Quartile
Number of social enquiry reports submitted to the courts during the year	639	681	81.0	2
Number of community service orders made during the year	172	195	23.2	1
The proportion of social enquiry reports reported to court within target time	2000-2001	Quartile		
Proportion of social enquiry reports submitted to the courts by due date	97.5	3		
The time taken to complete community service orders				
Average length of community service (hours) for orders completed during the year	152	3		
Average hours completed per week	4.3	2		

The Council delivers criminal justice services in partnership with North and South Ayrshire. Despite different management information systems, the partnership is expected to develop a consistent quality assurance system and bench-marking across the grouping. The partners, in conjunction with SACRO, have developed a pan-Ayrshire reparation and mediation scheme. A wider range of community-based disposals has yet to be achieved across the partner councils.

5. Finance

Service Area (£000)	GAE 1999-2000	Final net Out turn 1999-2000	GAE 2000-2001	Final net Out turn 2000-2001
Children's Services	£5,472	£5,640	£5,533	£6,256
Community Care	£19,249	£14,371	£20,142	£15,700
Adult Offenders		£131		£80
Other SW Services	£2,391	£4,318	£2,397	£4,190
Total	**£27,113**	**£24,459**	**£28,072**	**£26,226**
Spend per head		1999-2000		2000-2001
Spend per head		£202.76		£217.40
Quartile		4		3

Criminal Justice services receive funding from the Scottish Executive, £888,902 was provided in 2000-2001.

The Council's social work budget has been consistently below GAE. In 2001-2002 the Council spent 64% of GAE for Community Care, above GAE on children's services (but significantly less than in most other authorities) and above GAE on other social work services. The overall social work spend per head was less than in most other authorities.

6. Staffing

Staff	WTE 1999 actual	WTE 1999 per 1,000	Quartile 1999	WTE 2000 actual	WTE 2000 per 1,000	Quartile 2000
Managers & central staff	117	1.0	1	112	0.9	1
Frontline staff	545	4.5	2	542	4.5	3
Other	162	1.3	2	127	1.1	2
Total	**823**	**6.8**	**2**	**782**	**6.5**	**2**

Vacancies	Vacancies 2000	% Vacancies 2000	% Vacancies 2000 Scotland	Vacancies 2001*	% Vacancies 2001	% Vacancies 2001 Scotland
SWs with adults	3	9.4	7.8	–	–	10.9
SWs with children	8	19.0	7.4	–	–	10.7
SWs with offenders	0	0	7.5	–	–	7.2
Generic workers	0	0	8.0	–	–	12.7
Total	**11**	**12.6**	**7.7**	**–**	**–**	**10.5**

* East Ayrshire did not submit staffing figures for 2001

There is a relatively high ratio of managerial staff to front-line staff. In 2000 vacancy levels were below average, levels have increased subsequently and significant difficulties were reported in recruiting and retaining particular staff for children's services, where the vacancy rate in spring 2002 was 25%. The situation is likely to deteriorate with the increasing demand on services. Difficulties with recruitment have also been experienced for staff working in residential homes for older people.

The Council has re-introduced a secondment scheme for access to DipSW training by distance learning and made additional responsibility payments for student practice supervisors and mental health officers. There is a commitment to the appointment of senior practitioners, across all care groups, open to all staff of three years' experience or more who are able to display additional competencies.

7. Modernising services

The educational and social services departments are awaiting publication of codes of guidance from the Commission for Racial Equality before preparing a Race Equality Scheme.

The Council has been developing the infrastructure to improve access to public services by:

- creating access points at which residents can obtain information in person, by telephone or online; and
- co-locating services where appropriate: e.g. the Dalmellington area centre combines police, council, health and voluntary sector services under one roof.

Work has commenced on an information sharing protocol for mental health services and an Ayrshire-wide bid has been made for Modernising Government second round funding to develop an electronic information system.

8. The Future

If the Council is to build on what has already been achieved in community care, priority attention is likely to be required for the following developments:

- a re-shaped out of hours service allowing greater flexibility with extended 24 hour cover; it is anticipated this will be in place by autumn 2002;
- planning more and better targeted community-based services for older people in East Ayrshire, particularly at a time when their number is increasing;
- developing and expanding local area co-ordination for adults and children with learning disabilities within a set timescale;
- formulating with partners, plans for progressive improvement of mental health services across the communities of East Ayrshire; and
- preparing a scheme for the progressive improvement of sensory impairment services across the area.

It would consolidate and enhance the improvements made in the education of looked after children if the Council were to develop training and development opportunities for the social work and education staff who work with those children.

To achieve the reality of an effective aftercare service for young people, the Council with its partners, should implement within the next year the action plan which has been formulated.

If the benefits of partnership in provision of criminal justice services are to be realised within measurable time greater priority needs to be given to harmonising systems, procedures and practice. The development of a common information system is vital to underpin these developments.

The Council, with its criminal justice partners, should develop for early implementation a wider range of community-based disposals.

The significant difficulties in attracting social work staff, particularly for children's services, demand special effort, and the Council could benefit from following the example of those authorities who have established a sustained policy and practice of "growing their own" social work staff.

In preparation for preparing a Race Equality Scheme, the Educational and Social Services Departments would benefit from undertaking an audit of the needs of black and ethnic minorities using the Department's services, particularly social work services.

EAST DUNBARTONSHIRE COUNCIL

1. Profile at 2002

Geographically East Dunbartonshire is one of Scotland's smallest authorities, with a population of 110,800.

The population includes a high percentage of households with dependent children – 37% compared to a Scottish average of 30%. The number of households with pensioners is below the national average but is set to increase dramatically over the next 14 years. The increase in the number of people over 75 will be especially steep. The decrease in under 5s is expected to be far smaller than the national average; the decrease in 15-29 year olds is expected to be far larger than the national average.

Unemployment rates are low (2.2% in January 2002).

The drug misuse rate is half the national average rate (1.0% of 15-54 year olds).

The local crime rate is well below average for Scotland at 462 recorded crimes per 10,000 population in 2001.

The Council reorganised late in 2000. Social Work and Joint Ventures, led by the Head of Service, who is also the Chief Social Work Officer, is a part of a Community Services Directorate which embraces social inclusion, education and housing.

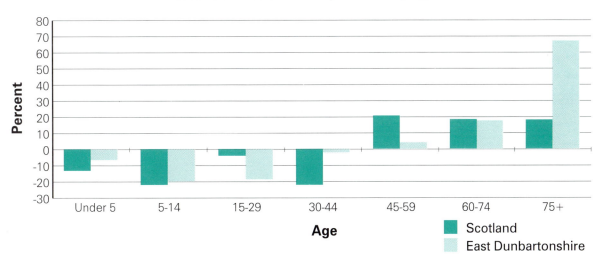

Expected % change in population, 2000-2016, local and national comparisons by age band

2. Performance: Community Care

Balance of care (aged 65+)	1999 actual	1999 per 1,000	Quartile	2000 actual	2000 per 1,000	Quartile
Older people in residential care homes	130	8	4	104	6	4
Older people in private nursing homes	337	21	3	314	19	4
Older people receiving home care	832	51	4	839	51	4
Older people in special needs housing	487	30	4	664	40	4
People receiving a community care service	**1999-2000 actual**	**1999-2000 per 1,000**	**Quartile**	**2000-2001 actual**	**2000-2001 per 1,000**	**Quartile**
Older people (aged 65+)	4,225	254.7	1	4,326	260.8	2
For mental health problems/dementia (aged 18-64)	291	4.1	2	373	5.3	1
For physical disabilities (aged 18-64)	1,423	20	1	1,552	21.9	1
For learning disabilities (aged 18-64)	200	2.8	3	112	1.6	4
For drug/alcohol abuse problems (aged 18-64)	75	1.0	2	303	4.3	1

Lower rates of older people receive residential care, nursing home care, special needs housing and home care than in most other authorities. To increase residential and nursing home places the Council recently commissioned an additional private provider to provide nursing and respite care. Older people receiving home care are more likely to receive periods of support of less than 10 hours per week than in most other authorities.

The Council has recently enhanced day care provision, established a dedicated team of Personal Home Carers to facilitate hospital discharges and embarked on a best value review of services for older people.

Following a joint occupational therapy study, the council developed a Joint Occupational Therapy Service (JOTS), in partnership with the Primary Care Trust and North Glasgow Trust. Whilst this service was initially to serve Strathkelvin, the development has now been extended to cover the whole East Dunbartonshire area. The implementation of has begun on a phased basis.

Learning disability services are provided in collaboration with NHS partners, under a Partnership in Practice Agreement (PiP). A joint learning disability team has been established for some months, with social work and health staff based in one place under a single operational manager. The Council has agreed to appoint at least one local area co-ordinator for people with learning disabilities and then evaluate the model.

Education and housing contribute to implementation of the PiP. They aim to ensure that:
- young people with learning disabilities experience a seamless transition between children's services and services for adults; and
- people with learning disabilities get appropriate tenancies.

A former residential home for people with learning disabilities has been refurbished to provide a good quality home for people with learning disabilities. A Disability Employment Unit is being established by a partnership between the Council and the independent sector. The unit will help people with disabilities (including learning disabilities) to get jobs.

A multi-disciplinary social work and health team is to be established to provide a primary care mental health service for people with mild to moderate mental health problems. This team will undertake single shared assessments and provide services linked to GPs and local health care co-operatives (LHCCs).

East Dunbartonshire Association for Mental Health has been commissioned to provide a range of services including individual focused support, social support groups, befriending, training, and advice and information.

Good progress has been made on single shared assessment unusually across all care groups. It is in place for people with learning disabilities and dementia, about to be implemented for adult mental health, and under development for carers' assessments. A screening tool and common data sets are in place, and there is already more direct access to services (respite, day care, and home care).

Sensory impairment services are provided by a small team and a number of voluntary service providers. Future needs assessments have been reviewed and are the subject of a pilot study commissioned from the Profound and Multiple Impairment Service.

The number of people receiving a community care service for drug and alcohol abuse problems increased fourfold between 1999 and 2001.

The Council and partners are progressing towards the Bottom Line. The joint management structure and the scope of the resources pot have been discussed but not yet agreed with health service partners. Budgets will be aligned.

3. Performance: Children and Families

Balance of care – Looked after children (aged 0-17)	1999-2000 actual	1999-2000 per 1,000	Quartile	2000-2001 actual	2000-2001 per 1,000	Quartile
At home	68	2.9	4	46	2.0	4
With friends/relatives/other community	22	1.0	3	12	0.5	3
With foster carers/prospective adopters	10	0.4	4	12	0.5	4
In residential accommodation	25	1.1	2	26	1.1	2
Total	**125**	**5.4**	**4**	**96**	**4.1**	**4**

Key performance indicators	1998-1999 actual	1998-1999 per 1,000	Quartile	1999-2000 actual	1999-2000 per 1,000	Quartile
Child protection (CP) referrals (aged 0-15)	68	3.3	4	48	2.3	4
Children subject to a CP case conference (aged 0-15)	24	1.2	4	12	0.6	4
Children placed on CP register (aged 0-15)	18	0.9	4	10	0.5	4
Adoption applications in year (aged 0-17)	7	0.3	3	8	0.3	2
Stranger adopter applications (aged 0-17)	3	0.1	3	5	0.2	2

The rates of looked after children (low in 1999-2000), have reduced still further, with the exception of those living in residential accommodation. The reduction has been marked in those living at home and those living with friends and relatives. The rate of those living with foster carers is low.

Rates of child protection referrals, numbers of children subject to a case conference and numbers on the child protection register are all very low compared to other local authorities. Adoption rates are relatively high.

Children and young people's services have recently been reorganised. Teams specialising in working with children according to age or disability have replaced generic teams. Child protection procedures have been revised and training in risk assessment developed. Fieldwork Assistants now support qualified staff and numbers of staff in residential units have increased.

Improvements have been introduced in the education of looked after children, led by a task force responsible for implementing an action plan. Most of the *Learning with Care* recommendations have been implemented: the learning environment in children's and foster homes has been improved by links with library services; IT equipment is being purchased for children's units and foster homes; and a bank of laptops is available for use by children and carers. Seconded staff visit all residential schools to assist in formulating individual education plans. Training in care planning has been given to residential and fieldwork staff and to foster parents. Further progress has to be achieved in delivering joint staff training and shared information systems.

A dedicated throughcare team has been expanded to provide new services for care leavers. Further progress has to be achieved in developing inter-agency arrangements, for instance with housing, and securing the active involvement of the voluntary sector (NCH). A register of care leavers has been established.

A youth housing support initiative is being launched with NCH to provide temporary accommodation and support in a hostel and independent bedsits for eight vulnerable homeless young people. It will include provision for disabled people and young parents. The aim is to develop independence and budgetary and tenancy skills, so that people can move on to less supported resources in shared and individual tenancies. The initiative is closely linked to the throughcare team.

4. Performance: Criminal Justice

Key Activities	1999-2000	2000-2001	2000-2001 per 10,000	Quartile
Number of social enquiry reports submitted to the courts during the year	311	276	34.4	4
Number of community service orders made during the year	69	56	7.0	4
The proportion of social enquiry reports reported to court within target time	2000-2001	Quartile		
Proportion of social enquiry reports submitted to the courts by due date	99.3	2		
The time taken to complete community service orders				
Average length of community service (hours) for orders completed during the year	167	2		
Average hours completed per week	3.7	3		

The Council is part of a criminal services grouping which includes West Dunbartonshire and Argyll and Bute. Its advantages lie in creating a larger pool of offenders and making it possible to work in more specialised ways with specific groups. The grouping is working towards consistency in the development of assessment tools, intervention programmes and evaluation arrangements.

In East Dunbartonshire feedback from the IT system is used in the supervision of front-line workers, covering variances between preferred option and disposal, targets and profiles. All social enquiry reports are quality assured.

A local key performance indicator has been introduced for contact within seven days with all those who received custodial sentences, following a social enquiry report. This is a foundation for voluntary aftercare and can help to establish a non-offending lifestyle.

Though services for adults are provided across the grouping, youth justice arrangements vary between the authorities. In East Dunbartonshire a youth justice forum carries forward developments.

5. Finance

Service Area (£000)	GAE 1999-2000	Final net Out turn 1999-2000	GAE 2000-2001	Final net Out turn 2000-2001
Children's Services	£1,624	£3,214	£1,872	£3,523
Community Care	£13,152	£10,485	£13,746	£11,284
Adult Offenders		£390		£61
Other SW Services	£1,876	£2,160	£1,881	£2,246
Total	**£16,652**	**£16,248**	**£17,499**	**£17,114**

Spend per head		1999-2000		2000-2001
Spend per head		£146.69		£154.51
Quartile		4		4

Criminal Justice services receive funding from the Scottish Executive, £346,707 was provided in 2000-2001.

Community Care expenditure has been consistently and significantly below GAE. The Council spent nearly £5m below GAE levels in 2001-2002, reflecting low levels of residential and nursing home provision. Spending on children's services has significantly exceeded GAE. The overall social work spend per head is less than in most other authorities.

6. Staffing

Staff	WTE 1999 actual	WTE 1999 per 1,000	Quartile 1999	WTE 2000 actual	WTE 2000 per 1,000	Quartile 2000
Managers & central staff	60	0.5	3	59	0.5	4
Frontline staff	324	2.9	4	378	3.4	4
Other	129	1.2	3	58	0.5	4
Total	**513**	**4.6**	**4**	**494**	**4.5**	**4**

Vacancies	Vacancies 2000	% Vacancies 2000	% Vacancies 2000 Scotland	Vacancies 2001*	% Vacancies 2001	% Vacancies 2001 Scotland
SWs with adults	0	0	7.8	–	–	10.9
SWs with children	1	5.9	7.4	–	–	10.7
SWs with offenders	2	40.0	7.5	–	–	7.2
Generic workers	1	16.7	8.0	–	–	12.7
Total	**4**	**9.8**	**7.7**	**–**	**–**	**10.5**

*East Dunbartonshire did not submit staffing vacancy figures for 2001

Rates of managerial and front-line social work staff are low, in comparison to many other authorities. The number of front-line staff increased between 1999 and 2000 while the number of 'other' staff more than halved. The latest restructuring – the second in 3 years- caused senior and middle managers prolonged uncertainty.

Vacancy levels were higher than average in 2000. Four vacant posts amounted to a 40% vacancy rate in criminal justice.

The staffing problems have been noticeably different to those in many other authorities – numbers of workers in the planned workforce were insufficient. This had been a legacy from local government reorganisation when too few workers were allocated to the new authority. Following creation of a joint social work and human resources task force, additional managerial and front-line posts were created and career grading was introduced, with front line workers given the opportunity to become senior practitioners.

7. Modernising services

Asian and Chinese communities in the area use the services and resources of their own communities in Glasgow. The Council aims to provide culturally sensitive services for those who choose to seek support locally, or who are unable to travel to Glasgow.

The Council has not been at the forefront of the modernising agenda and understandably continues to rely on developments in larger local authorities and in consortia of authorities.

Social work is in the process of introducing client information systems. CareFirst has been purchased as the software package, and is being implemented on a modular basis. IT support has made an impact on the implementation of *Learning with Care*. IT is viewed as the backbone to these developments, with the provision of e-mail, educational software, links to libraries and training support for children and staff.

All staff have individual desk-top PC access, with e-mail and Internet link-up opportunities. Partnership and consortium bids for Modernising Government Funds are in progress, in order to develop the shared information agenda further, both with adult and children services.

8. The Future

The future range, quantity and quality of services for older people need to be addressed urgently, considering the present comparatively limited provision and the projected growth in the elderly population. Home support for older people with complex needs calls for particular attention. The best value review which has been undertaken needs to be completed as a matter of urgency, so that the Council can make well-informed decisions on priorities for service development.

The Council should develop and expand local area co-ordination for adults and children with learning disabilities.

The Council and partners should build on current progress to reach agreement on comprehensive joint management and joint resourcing frameworks, and develop firm implementation plans for both that and single shared assessment.

To consolidate and maintain progress in developing mental health services, information-sharing, which takes place in pockets, needs to be systematised and extended across the board.

Services for people with a sensory impairment call for higher priority in future. The department needs to establish joint working with health and education. To chart the way ahead, the Council might establish with partners a strategy and resource group for people with a sensory impairment.

The Council's commitment to community planning and joint ventures has led to successful pilot developments such as occupational therapy services and a joint equipment store. As a smaller Council it should seek opportunities to adopt joint ventures and joint resourcing more generally.

To maintain the momentum behind improvements in the education of looked after children, action is required to extend joint staff training, deliver shared information systems and notify parents and carers about the educational progress of looked after children.

If the benefits of the grouping of criminal justice services is to be realised within measurable time, sustained effort is required with partner councils to harmonise systems, procedures and practice.

1. Profile at 2002

With a population of 91,300, East Lothian is one of Scotland's smaller rural mainland authorities.

It is a growth area and the population is expected to increase by 10.9% over the next 14 years. There will be a rise in the under fives, this is in contrast to Scotland as a whole. The 60-74 age group is expected to increase more rapidly than for Scotland as a whole.

At 2.2% (January 2002), unemployment is one of the lowest in the country.

The drug misuse rate is below average (1.6% of 15-54 year olds).

The crime rate is very low – only 439 crimes were recorded by police per 10,000 population, in 2001.

East Lothian Council has an Executive Committee and a set of Performance Review Panels organised around the business groups of the council, of which housing and social work is one. Reporting arrangements, including use of the balanced scorecard, have ensured that members are increasingly well informed about social work matters.

The joint housing and social work department, which recently gained responsibility for social inclusion, has a Director and 4 heads of service one of whom is the Chief Social Work Officer.

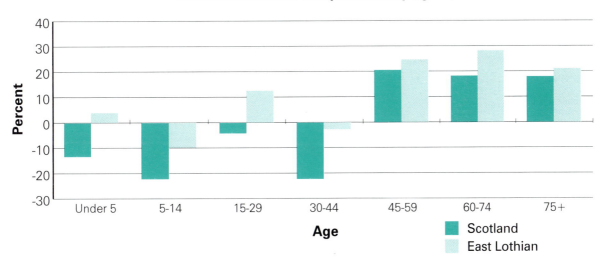

Expected % change in population, 2000-2016, local and national comparisons by age band

2. Performance: Community Care

Balance of care (aged 65+)	1999 actual	1999 per 1,000	Quartile	2000 actual	2000 per 1,000	Quartile
Older people in residential care homes	270	18	2	242	16	3
Older people in private nursing homes	313	21	3	455	30	1
Older people receiving home care	1,148	77	2	1,130	75	2
Older people in special needs housing	1,918	127.8	2	1,859	123.6	2
People receiving a community care service	1999-2000 actual	1999-2000 per 1,000	Quartile	2000-2001 actual	2000-2001 per 1,000	Quartile
Older people (aged 65+)	1,853	123.1	4	2,385	158.6	4
For mental health problems/dementia (aged 18-64)	64	1.1	4	83	1.5	4
For physical disabilities (aged 18-64)	539	9.6	4	605	10.8	3
For learning disabilities (aged 18-64)	225	4.0	2	239	4.3	2
For drug/alcohol abuse problems (aged 18-64)	13	0.2	4	20	0.4	3

The rate of older people in residential care is fairly high, as is the rate in special needs housing. The number of older people receiving home care is also relatively high but fewer hours of support are received than in many other authorities. This may change, depending on the outcome of the current Domiciliary Care Review. The number of older people in private nursing homes has increased significantly between 1999 and 2000, and the rate of such residents is now high, compared with many other authorities.

A joint Discharge Response Team has been developed in response to growing numbers waiting in hospital for permanent care or intensive community care packages. The pathway from hospital to home has been enhanced, with intensive care packages provided at home for up to six weeks following discharge. Extension of the service to seven days per week is planned, with a single access point, a discharge liaison nurse, care management and improved carer support.

Learning disability services have been examined in a best value review, but the resources for making changes are tight, in view of rising demand and chronic overspends in recent years. The local health care cooperative (LHCC) has reviewed transitional arrangements from children's to adult services. Care packages for young people with complex needs are adding to the demand on resources.

Day services are both provided by the Council and purchased from other providers. The East Lothian Vocational Occupation Service, which is provided in-house, helps find work placements and employment for people with learning disability.

A limited number of people receive a community care service for mental health problems in East Lothian, with social work and health staff working closely together and maintaining links with users. Following a review of mental health services, a small social work team is to become part of the integrated mental health service. In future, decisions related to mental health specific grant are to be taken jointly.

The Council and its partners have a good infrastructure and relationships on which to build the Joint Future agenda, but all Lothian issues can complicate reaching conclusions. The Council and its partners are to appoint a Joint Future implementation/change manager to lead progress.

On single shared assessment, the partners have decided on Carenap E as the assessment tool, and Lothian-wide systems are now being developed to apply it. Information sharing is part of this development. Having progressed towards, rather than met, the Bottom Line, implementing single shared assessment across all community care will require firm planning.

On joint resourcing and joint management, the partners had made considerable progress towards but had not met the Bottom Line. The Joint Future steering group has yet to agree the management structure and resources pot. Budgets will initially be aligned. Single management in local care teams will need to be harmonised with higher level integrated service management. The Council and partners envisage extending joint resourcing and joint management to all community care services by 2004.

Services for people with sensory impairments are under review, which should lead to future improvements. All assessments and services are commissioned from voluntary organisations: Visual Impairment Services South East Scotland and Edinburgh and East of Scotland Deaf Society. Health staff take the lead on future needs assessment – which is also being reviewed.

3. Performance: Children and families

Balance of care – Looked after children (aged 0-17)	1999-2000 actual	1999-2000 per 1,000	Quartile	2000-2001 actual	2000-2001 per 1,000	Quartile
At home	67	3.3	3	58	2.9	3
With friends/relatives/other community	3	0.2	4	0	0.0	4
With foster carers/prospective adopters	65	3.2	2	79	3.9	1
In residential accommodation	18	0.9	3	21	1.0	3
Total	**153**	**7.6**	**3**	**158**	**7.8**	**3**

Key performance indicators	1998-1999 actual	1998-1999 per 1,000	Quartile	1999-2000 actual	1999-2000 per 1,000	Quartile
Child protection (CP) referrals (aged 0-15)	183	10.1	2	150	8.3	2
Children subject to a CP case conference (aged 0-15)	52	2.9	2	55	3.0	2
Children placed on CP register (aged 0-15)	38	2.1	2	46	2.5	1
Adoption applications in year (aged 0-17)	11	0.5	1	9	0.5	2
Stranger adopter applications (aged 0-17)	5	0.3	1	6	0.3	1

The Council has a fairly low rate of looked after children and currently none live with friends or relatives. A high rate of looked after children live with foster carers and a relatively low rate are in residential accommodation.

The two six-bedded residential units have been refurbished with single rooms. The service to young people extends to independent flats, aftercare and outreach work, and benefits from ongoing consultancy from external organisations, Who Cares? Scotland and Children 1st.

A high rate of children are placed on the child protection register although numbers have fallen since 1999. The rate of stranger adoptions is relatively high.

Led by an inter-departmental working group, progress has been made with six of the recommendations of *Learning with Care*. An audit of children's and foster homes has been completed and joint training for teachers, social workers, and carers is well under way. A database has been established, but further work is required for information to be shared between education and social work. All looked after and accommodated children of school age are receiving full-time education.

A lead officer – assisted by a sub-group comprising representatives of key agencies – has been nominated for new arrangements for care leavers. It is anticipated that an additional member of staff will be required, who will need appropriate training.

4. Performance: Criminal Justice

Key Activities	1999-2000	2000-2001	2000-2001 per 10,000	Quartile
Number of social enquiry reports submitted to the courts during the year	307	306	48.4	4
Number of community service orders made during the year	83	108	17.1	2
The proportion of social enquiry reports reported to court within target time	**2000-2001**	**Quartile**		
Proportion of social enquiry reports submitted to the courts by due date	80.1	4		
The time taken to complete community service orders				
Average length of community service (hours) for orders completed during the year	148	3		
Average hours completed per week	3.7	3		

The rate of social enquiry reports submitted to courts is lower than in many other authorities and is a reflection of the low crime rate. The Council is able to submit only 80.1% of social enquiry reports by the due date. The number of community service orders made has increased and the rate is now relatively high. The average length of community service orders completed in 2000-2001 was relatively short. The time taken to complete the orders was relatively long – an average of 3.7 hours were completed per week.

The Council forms part of a partnership with Edinburgh City, Midlothian, West Lothian and the Scottish Borders. Their aim is to achieve:

- set shared service standards;
- consistency of provision and practice;
- consistent application of performance measures, monitoring and evaluation of outcomes, collective planning; and
- involvement of independent sector organisations.

The Council currently uses a range of quality assurance mechanisms for criminal justice services, including case reviews. They are moving towards more outcome/output based methods. All criminal justice work is to be monitored using an OLM database which went live early in 2002. The new system covers risk assessment, action planning, service inputs, breaches and reviews, targets and outcomes. It will produce a range of management reports and allow individual feedback to workers.

Breaking the Cycle, East Lothian's youth crime initiative, co-ordinates work with young people in transition between the children's hearings and criminal justice social work services. It links children and families and criminal justice social work teams, the Reporter, the Procurator Fiscal and independent agencies. A criminal justice social worker has been seconded to the project since 2001 dealing with all 16-18 year olds referred to the diversion scheme. The project is being externally evaluated.

5. Finance

Service Area (£000)	GAE 1999-2000	Final net Out turn 1999-2000	GAE 2000-2001	Final net Out turn 2000-2001
Children's Services	£2,491	£3,696	£2,538	£4,422
Community Care	£13,990	£13,493	£14,665	£13,565
Adult Offenders		£77		-£31
Other SW Services	£1,687	£1,683	£1,705	£2,096
Total	**£18,168**	**£18,949**	**£18,907**	**£20,051**
Spend per head		1999-2000		2000-2001
Spend per head		£207.59		£219.66
Quartile		3		3

Criminal Justice services receive funding from the Scottish Executive, £464,829 was provided in 2000-2001.

East Lothian spent more than GAE on Social Work Services in 1999-2000 and 2000-2001. The overall social work spend per head is relatively low.

6. Staffing

Staff	WTE 1999 actual	WTE 1999 per 1,000	Quartile 1999	WTE 2000 actual	WTE 2000 per 1,000	Quartile 2000
Managers & central staff	37	0.4	4	36	0.4	4
Frontline staff	365	4.0	3	389	4.3	3
Other	84	0.9	4	59	0.6	4
Total	**486**	**5.4**	**4**	**483**	**5.3**	**4**

Vacancies	Vacancies 2000	% Vacancies 2000	% Vacancies 2000 Scotland	Vacancies 2001	% Vacancies 2001	% Vacancies 2001 Scotland
SWs with adults	0	0	7.8	0	0	10.9
SWs with children	0	0	7.4	2	4.7	10.7
SWs with offenders	0	0	7.5	0	0	7.2
Generic workers	0	0	8.0	0	0	12.7
Total	**0**	**0**	**7.7**	**2**	**3.3**	**10.5**

East Lothian have relatively low rates of all staff. The number of 'other' staff – already low in 1999 – was further reduced in 2000. There are just two vacancies in children's services, none in the other areas of social work.

East Lothian is an area of high employment, and local competition for unqualified staff has created recruitment and retention problems, particularly in day care services. The Council is enhancing personal social services as a career by offering SVQ level 2 to all domiciliary staff and by enriching the work of social work assistants.

Professional staffing is stable, as is the staffing in residential childcare units, partly a result of the investment in training and professional development that was made before reorganisation. Budgetary restrictions could put this situation at risk, especially as older staff begin to leave the department.

7. Modernising services

The Council has improved its race equality practice, prompted partly by work with asylum seekers, coming mainly from Kosovo, and partly by work with travellers. There is a strong corporate lead for race equality under a generic Equal Opportunities Committee, and preparations for a Race Equality Scheme are well advanced. The Council has access to an East Lothian Ethnic Minority Forum for consultative purposes.

East Lothian had a modest participation in the first round of the Modernising Government financed projects, but is preparing a series of bids for the second round.

Social work services are implementing the CareFirst suite of information systems, which should all be in place by the end of 2002. Management reports from the systems are fed directly into the quarterly production of balanced scorecards. Communication between social work and education information systems is rudimentary, but the interface with health is better developed and will support the use of single shared assessment.

8. The Future

There is an urgent need:

- to review the balance of community care for the elderly in the light of future population projections; and
- in particular, to determine changes required in the packages of home care to be offered in future and their quality, in light of the recommendations of the current review of domiciliary care.

In response to the best value study of learning disability services, the Council will have to plan with health partners for their progressive improvement and to determine resource priorities for implementation. Plans should allow for short breaks and services for people with challenging behaviour. The opportunity should be taken to clarify and co-ordinate the roles of the joint learning disability team and the social work community care team.

In response to the review of sensory impairment services, the Council should plan and determine resource priorities, as suggested for learning disability.

Building on progress to date and their aspirations for the longer term, the Council and partners will need to project manage the next steps towards full implementation of the Joint Future agenda next April.

To consolidate the progress made in improving education for looked after children, it is necessary to improve the flows of information about these children between education and social work.

In criminal justice services the main priority will be to participate in harmonising systems, procedures and practice, so that the benefits of the new grouping can be realised as early as possible without prejudice to standards of service.

Access to the internet is available for specific research and training uses, but is not available to all staff. An e-culture still needs to be introduced and maintained within the housing and social work department.

1. Profile at 2002

East Renfrewshire has a largely suburban population of 89,800.

The local population is predicted to rise by 9.6% over the next 14 years, compared with a decline for Scotland as a whole. The number of older people is to rise dramatically by more than a third. There will also be increases in the under fives and 15-29 populations, in contrast with national predictions.

The rate of unemployment is low (2.4% in January 2002).

East Renfrewshire has a lower than average rate of problem drugs misuse (1.3% of 15-54 year olds).

The rate of recorded crime has fallen and at 433 per 10,000 population in 2001 is significantly lower than the national average.

The Council maintains a separate social work department led by a Director, and following a management review, a Head of Strategy and Development. The Director also carries out the responsibilities of Chief Social Work Officer.

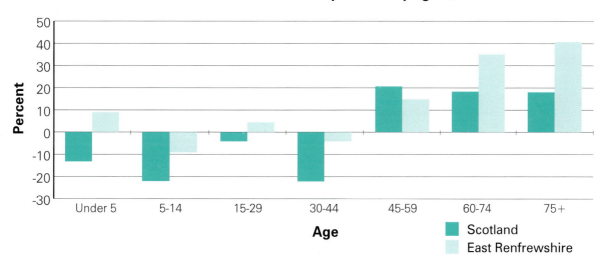

Expected % change in population, 2000-2016, local and national comparisons by age band

2. Performance: Community Care

Balance of care (aged 65+)	1999 actual	1999 per 1,000	Quartile	2000 actual	2000 per 1,000	Quartile
Older people in residential care homes	200	15	3	192	14	4
Older people in private nursing homes	415	31	1	332	25	2
Older people receiving home care	693	52	4	715	53	4
Older people in special needs housing	1,289	97.4	3	1,295	96.3	3
People receiving a community care service	1999-2000 actual	1999-2000 per 1,000	Quartile	2000-2001 actual	2000-2001 per 1,000	Quartile
Older people (aged 65+)	2,529	188.1	3	1,772	131.8	4
For mental health problems/dementia (aged 18-64)	146	2.6	3	158	2.8	3
For physical disabilities (aged 18-64)	652	11.6	3	321	5.7	4
For learning disabilities (aged 18-64)	152	2.7	3	178	3.2	3
For drug/alcohol abuse problems (aged 18-64)	57	1.0	2	59	1.1	2

The rate of older people receiving a community care service is lower than in most other authorities, having fallen considerably from 1999 to 2001. There are comparatively low rates of older people in residential care homes and of older people receiving home care, although the number of the latter increased slightly between 1999 and 2000.

The Council is reconfiguring its services for older people. Day care has expanded to seven days a week, and includes evening opening hours. Use of both the day centre and the community alarm scheme is now non-assessable. Bonnyton House, a residential unit, has been substantially refurbished to provide dementia care. The home support service now includes a "Mr Fixit" service, a laundry service, and a shopping service in partnership with a supermarket.

Support to people with more complex needs has been improved by the introduction of a Rapid Response team, an intensive personal care and bathing service (jointly with Argyll & Clyde Health Board), and a short-term care and rehabilitation team (jointly with Greater Glasgow Health Board).

However, the number of people receiving a community care service for physical disabilities more than halved between 1999 and 2001.

East Renfrewshire has a Partnership in Practice Agreement which is directed to improving accommodation and social support for people with learning disabilities. Current priorities are refurbishment of Atholl House as a learning disability facility and the move of former residents to their own homes. In addition, properties are being purchased for re-provisioning, and 9 houses have been purchased to be turned into 20 houses through Home Link.

Provision of mental health services varies across East Renfrewshire, according to the priority afforded by the two Health Boards concerned – Argyll and Clyde and Greater Glasgow. The Council aims to achieve comparability of mental health services across the localities, in conjunction with voluntary organisations and its health partners.

A shared assessment tool, agreed with health partners, is being implemented with the aim of speeding up people's access to services. Its use is being monitored and is being reviewed in summer 2002.

A small sensory impairment team is based in a Disability Information Centre, and works in collaboration with local and national voluntary organisations. There are few formal links with health services, although more are planned. Links with education focus on future needs assessments and the work of the children with disabilities team. Referrals for an assessment for people with a hearing impairment can take up to four months to attract a response. There are no specific services for the deaf-blind.

A structure has been developed to take forward the Joint Future agenda. This includes a high level policy group including elected members and NHS Board representatives; a joint steering group; locality planning groups for both Health Board areas, and client group focused strategy and implementation groups.

3. Performance: Children and Families

Balance of care – Looked after children (aged 0-17)	1999-2000 actual	1999-2000 per 1,000	Quartile	2000-2001 actual	2000-2001 per 1,000	Quartile
At home	60	3.0	3	34	1.7	4
With friends/relatives/other community	9	0.5	3	16	0.8	3
With foster carers/prospective adopters	7	0.4	4	6	0.3	4
In residential accommodation	5	0.3	4	6	0.3	4
Total	**81**	**4.0**	**4**	**62**	**3.1**	**4**

Key performance indicators	1998-1999 actual	1998-1999 per 1,000	Quartile	1999-2000 actual	1999-2000 per 1,000	Quartile
Child protection (CP) referrals (aged 0-15)	51	2.8	4	61	3.4	4
Children subject to a CP case conference (aged 0-15)	36	2.0	3	40	2.2	3
Children placed on CP register (aged 0-15)	26	1.4	3	28	1.6	3
Adoption applications in year (aged 0-17)	6	0.3	3	8	0.4	2
Stranger adopter applications (aged 0-17)	5	0.3	1	6	0.3	1

The rates of child protection referrals and children subject to a case conference and on the child protection register are low compared to many other authorities. Numbers of adoption applications are relatively high.

The rate of looked after children is lower than in most other authorities, and numbers continue to fall.

Education and social work collaborated to implement the recommendations of *Learning with Care:* joint assessment arrangements for children in residential care are well established; all children in residential care receive full-time education and education reports are available to social work staff for all those children.

Social work, health and education have jointly prepared a scheme under the changing children's services fund, for a pilot project for children with special educational needs within Neilston schools, which will deliver person-centred planning together with multi-agency assessment and co-ordination.

A throughcare team is well established. The financial framework and administrative support necessary for the new arrangements for care leavers are not yet in place, but the department expects to be in a position to deliver the full service required for looked after children.

4. Performance: Criminal Justice

Key Activities	1999-2000	2000-2001	2000-2001 per 10,000	Quartile
Number of social enquiry reports submitted to the courts during the year	226	248	39.3	4
Number of community service orders made during the year	70	56	8.9	4

The proportion of social enquiry reports reported to court within target time	2000-2001	Quartile		
Proportion of social enquiry reports submitted to the courts by due date	96.1	3		
The time taken to complete community service orders				
Average length of community service (hours) for orders completed during the year	168	1		
Average hours completed per week	4.7	2		

Though the number of social enquiry reports submitted to courts in a year has increased, it is still relatively lower than in many other authorities, reflecting the low crime rate in the area. But 4% are not submitted by the due date. The number of community service orders made reduced between 1999 and 2001. The average length of community service orders in 2000-2001 was longer than in many other authorities. Orders were completed relatively quickly.

With its partners in a criminal justice grouping – Renfrewshire and Inverclyde – undertook a best value review of probation, social enquiry reports and community service. Different existing information systems limit the availability of consistent information across the grouping and development of joint approaches has still to be progressed.

A Youth Justice Team has been operating since March 2002. Work with sex offenders focuses on harm reduction and managing risk. All reports on sex offenders are prepared on the basis of joint assessment with the inter-authority Pathways Project.

5. Finance

Service Area (£000)	GAE 1999-2000	Final net Out turn 1999-2000	GAE 2000-2001	Final net Out turn 2000-2001
Children's Services	£1,709	£2,464	£1,805	£2,322
Community Care	£11,336	£9,894	£11,933	£10,759
Adult Offenders		£33		£77
Other SW Services	£1,548	£2,179	£1,556	£2,228
Total	**£14,593**	**£14,570**	**£15,293**	**£15,386**

Spend per head		1999-2000		2000-2001
Spend per head		£162.26		£171.35
Quartile		4		4

Criminal Justice services receive funding from the Scottish Executive, £333,931 was provided in 2000-2001.

Expenditure on children's services has been above GAE levels. Spend per head on social work services is low compared to many other authorities.

6. Staffing

Staff	WTE 1999 actual	WTE 1999 per 1,000	Quartile 1999	WTE 2000 actual	WTE 2000 per 1,000	Quartile 2000
Managers & central staff	73	0.8	1	60	0.7	2
Frontline staff	244	2.7	4	292	3.3	4
Other	54	0.6	4	76	0.8	4
Total	**371**	**4.2**	**4**	**428**	**4.8**	**4**

Vacancies	Vacancies 2000	% Vacancies 2000	% Vacancies 2000 Scotland	Vacancies 2001	% Vacancies 2001	% Vacancies 2001 Scotland
SWs with adults	2	8.7	7.8	0	0	10.9
SWs with children	2	7.1	7.4	1	4.5	10.7
SWs with offenders	1	22.2	7.5	1	22.2	7.2
Generic workers	0	0	8.0	1	50.0	12.7
Total	**5**	**8.9**	**7.7**	**3**	**5.8**	**10.5**

There are lower rates of social work staff than in most other authorities. The rate of managerial and central staff was high in 1999, but due to the reconfiguration of the service, the rate is now relatively low. There were just three social work vacancies in 2001. In March 2002 there were no social worker vacancies, but the Council reported that fewer people were applying for vacant posts. Vacancies among social care staff are few.

After a staff turnover study, the Council has taken a proactive approach to recruitment and retention, including promoting a public image for social work and the Council, and enhancing the quality of student placements. The Council supports two secondees through the Open University's Diploma in Social Work, and is raising its training budget to ensure that SVQ training is available for care staff.

7. Modernising services

From the 1991 census 2.4% of local population were from black and ethnic minority communities, double the Scottish average. That percentage has subsequently increased. Jewish people account for some 7% of the population.

Social work has contributed to the corporate preparation of a Race Equality Scheme. The Council aims to provide services within East Renfrewshire accessible to the local black and ethnic minority communities, acknowledging that many Indian and Pakistani residents travel to Glasgow for culturally sensitive services. The Council mainstreams its work on equality, and develops cultural awareness among employees.

The Council contracts with Jewish Care to provide a social work service to Jewish people who choose to use it. The partnership, which provides comprehensive services including assessment, is based at a purpose-built centre in Giffnock, which provides a model for the joint development of culturally sensitive services.

The Council has established a Customer First project, funded by the Modernising Government programme. The project is intended to enhance the electronic delivery of services. It is at an early stage in identifying the uses social work services might make of the new systems.

The CareFirst social work information system is being introduced in phases, and will be linked to a joint assessment tool. A bid is being made for e-government funding for software which will bring together the health and social work IT systems.

8. The Future

The Council spends above the Scottish average on all community care services for older people, which suggests scope for shifting services for older people towards more community-based support. This shift was endorsed in a best value review for older people undertaken jointly with Argyll & Clyde health agencies. To maintain momentum behind what has already been done to develop community-based services, the Council could take opportunity to review future needs in the light of population projections and identify resource priorities for further improvement, for example, strengthening the capacity of the home care service.

The quality and range of local services for older people and adults with a mental health problem vary within East Renfrewshire according to the partnership arrangements with health. This seems the right time to initiate with health partners a strategic review of future needs for mental health services and the resources required to achieve services of consistent quality.

Services for people with a sensory impairment are not well developed, particularly for people who are deaf-blind. There is a need for improved links with health services. The situation seems to call for searching review of service and resource priorities by the community care joint planning group and a strategic plan for future improvement.

The Council and its health partners should build on the progress to date on joint management arrangements for community care – for example, development of joint service teams to deliver day care, a joint equipment store, joint training for council, health and voluntary sector staff and shared information systems, in preparation for joint developments of computerised information systems.

To sustain the progress made in implementing improvements in the education of looked after children, the Council should formulate a scheme for the joint professional development and training of teachers and social workers who deal with those children.

Now that a throughcare team has been established, the Council should set in place the financial framework and administrative support necessary to bring into full operation the new arrangements for care leavers.

The Council should take action urgently with its criminal justice partners to harmonise systems, procedures and practice, in order to produce a seamless and efficient service. Work should be started urgently on, for example, joint quality assurance; a single Drug Treatment and Testing Orders scheme; bail provision; and shared group work with women offenders.

1. Profile at 2002

With 453,400 people, the City of Edinburgh Council has the second largest population of all local authorities in Scotland.

By 2016, the Council will face a smaller decrease of children under 5 and in the 5-14 age group. The increase in the number of 45-59 year olds will be significantly above the national average. The older population is expected to increase but at a rate less than the national projection.

Unemployment is low (3% in January 2002).

The drug misuse rate is high (2.2% of 15-54 year olds), the 6th highest rate of all authorities.

Edinburgh has the third highest rate of crime, with 1148 crimes recorded per 10,000 population in 2001.

The Council is a leading member of the Edinburgh Partnership, which consists of senior representatives of Edinburgh's public, private and community organisations. The Partnership has had the responsibility for monitoring *onecity*, the report of the Lord Provost's Commission on Social Exclusion in Edinburgh, which addresses many of the issues facing social work services.

These services are organised in a single department under a director, who is also the chief social work officer. The department commissions voluntary and private organisations to provide approximately half of the services for which it is responsible, a proportion higher than average in Scotland. The new scrutiny panels have increased oversight of services and knowledge of social work among Council members.

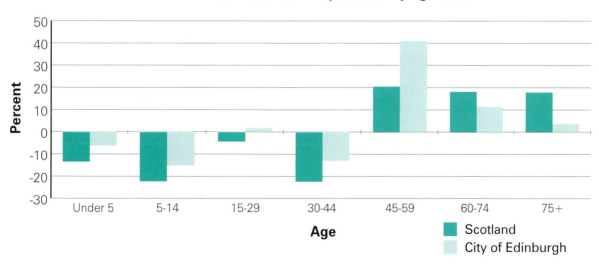

Expected % change in population, 2000-2016, local and national comparisons by age band

2. Performance: Community Care

Balance of care (aged 65+)	1999 actual	1999 per 1,000	Quartile	2000 actual	2000 per 1,000	Quartile
Older people in residential care homes	1,214	18	2	1,167	17	2
Older people in private nursing homes	1,893	28	2	1,876	27	2
Older people receiving home care	5,958	87	2	5,237	77	2
Older people in special needs housing	5,095	74.3	4	5,095	74.8	4
People receiving a community care service	1999-2000 actual	1999-2000 per 1,000	Quartile	2000-2001 actual	2000-2001 per 1,000	Quartile
Older people (aged 65+)	18,114	265.7	1	15,707	230.5	2
For mental health problems/dementia (aged 18-64)	1,743	5.8	1	1,662	5.6	1
For physical disabilities (aged 18-64)	3,799	12.7	3	3,158	10.6	3
For learning disabilities (aged 18-64)	1,142	3.8	2	1,359	4.6	1
For drug/alcohol abuse problems (aged 18-64)	461	1.5	1	554	1.9	2

The rate of older people receiving a community care service has reduced in the last 2 years. The rate of older people living in special needs housing is low. On the other hand, a relatively high rate of older people live in residential and nursing homes. The rate of people receiving home care remains fairly high compared with many other authorities, though it has reduced since 1999.

The Home Care Service is being gradually reshaped to provide higher levels of personal care, and to cover evenings and weekends. Plans are in hand to enhance the shopping and domestic service and greater use of the independent sector form a part of the City's developing services for older people.

A significant reduction in the supply of places in nursing homes in the last 2 years has contributed to delays in discharging older people from hospital. The Council and NHS Lothian have agreed a range of measures to relieve these pressures, including:

- developing housing with extra care services;
- using new technology to promote independent living;
- speeding up assessments and discharge arrangements; and
- ensuring that aids to daily living and equipment are more readily available.

Learning Disability services are provided in collaboration with NHS partners, under a Partnership in Practice Agreement (PiP). With the agreement of health partners, resources from the Change Fund have been used to enhance services for people with learning difficulties, in particular to:

- improve services for 80 people with complex needs;
- replace the Burdiehouse hostel with supported accommodation; and
- fund a new post of joint programme manager.

The Engine Shed training project has helped 80% of its service users to move into paid work.

Two local co-ordinators (whole time equivalents) will be appointed for people with learning disabilities by Autumn 2002.

The joint mental health plan shared with health is to be linked to the joint future agenda, and will be overseen by a joint programme manager. All the Lothian councils and the Health Board area have agreed to base single shared assessment on the Carenap E tool. A joint services manager is responsible for implementation.

A multi-agency group develops strategy for sensory impairment services and an all-Lothian initiative co-ordinates strategy, develops user involvement, and shares good practice. Visual Impairment Services South East Scotland, Edinburgh and East of Scotland Deaf Society, and Deafblind UK are contracted to provide services, including assessments. Voluntary sector staff share training with the Council and are involved in new initiatives, such as single shared assessment.

All offices have loop systems, and training has been carried out to improve communications with people with sensory impairment. Translating and interpreting services are provided through corporate services. Community education has lip speaking classes for people who are losing or have lost their hearing.

The Council and Lothian Health Board have made an early start on developing their Local Partnership Agreement. This will identify the range of jointly managed and resourced services for older people. Budgets are likely to be aligned rather than pooled initially. The joint management structures envisaged are a joint committee of the Council and the NHS Board and a joint senior officers group. The joint action plan will cover a joint performance framework and joint development priorities and targets.

3. Performance: Children and Families

Balance of care – Looked after children (aged 0-17)	1999-2000 actual	1999-2000 per 1,000	Quartile	2000-2001 actual	2000-2001 per 1,000	Quartile
At home	486	5.6	1	450	5.2	2
With friends/relatives/other community	46	0.5	3	87	1.0	2
With foster carers/prospective adopters	343	3.9	1	354	4.1	1
In residential accommodation	169	1.9	1	172	2.0	1
Total	**1,044**	**12**	**1**	**1,063**	**12.2**	**1**

Key performance indicators	1998-1999 actual	1998-1999 per 1,000	Quartile	1999-2000 actual	1999-2000 per 1,000	Quartile
Child protection (CP) referrals (aged 0-15)	576	7.4	3	641	8.2	2
Children subject to a CP case conference (aged 0-15)	194	2.5	3	209	2.7	2
Children placed on CP register (aged 0-15)	178	2.3	2	185	2.4	2
Adoption applications in year (aged 0-17)	34	0.4	2	23	0.3	3
Stranger adopter applications (aged 0-17)	17	0.2	2	11	0.1	3

The rate of children on child protection registers is relatively high but has reduced since 1999. Numbers of adoption applications are relatively low.

Edinburgh has a high rate of looked after children; numbers have increased by almost a fifth between 1998 and 2000. The rate of looked after children away from home has also increased; precise reasons for this increase are not known but may relate to factors as diverse as drug misuse and improved assessment procedures. The demand for foster care placements now outstrips the resources of Edinburgh and the surrounding areas and a similar pattern is indicated for adoption. The rate of children in residential accommodation is high and the Council report a marked increase in demand for residential school and secure accommodation places.

The Council has reconfigured children's services through a range of initiatives including targeted foster care recruitment, enhanced outreach services, weekend respite and more flexible residential service support.

By autumn 2001 some 80% of the City's looked after children had their educational needs identified in care plans. A small minority of those children received only six hours of education each week. The Council has an action plan to improve performance, which includes:

- provision of a new off-site educational provision for girls;
- carer support in primary schools;
- sessional tutoring; homework support; and
- link teachers for all residential units.

There are arrangements to collate the examination results of looked after children, through manual systems. Recently resources have been earmarked to upgrade the educational environment of residential units and foster care placements.

It is estimated that 150 children each year need support under the new arrangements for care leavers. Edinburgh provides a range of employment and educational opportunities for care leavers. A specialist team is to provide support and build on links with partners in housing and education.

4. Performance: Criminal Justice

Key Activities	1999-2000	2000-2001	2000-2001 per 10,000	Quartile
Number of social enquiry reports submitted to the courts during the year	2,102	2,257	68.5	3
Number of community service orders made during the year	549	549	16.7	2
The proportion of social enquiry reports reported to court within target time	2000-2001	Quartile		
Proportion of social enquiry reports submitted to the courts by due date	83.3	4		
The time taken to complete community service orders				
Average length of community service (hours) for orders completed during the year	146	3		
Average hours completed per week	2.5	4		

Edinburgh submitted a relatively low rate of social enquiry reports to courts during 2000-2001. A low proportion of reports was submitted by the due date in comparison with other authorities. A relatively high rate of community service orders was made during 2000-2001. The average length of orders was relatively low, but they took a comparatively long time to complete, with just 2.5 hours being completed on average per week.

Edinburgh forms part of a grouping with the three Lothian councils and Scottish Borders. It has an established system for monitoring criminal justice social work, concentrating primarily on key performance indicators. Quarterly reports are available for managers. However, there are limitations to data collection across the city due to the nature of the data systems and the availability of clerical time. A programme of service improvement is planned across the grouping, although the use of different management information systems in individual authorities is likely to be a complicating factor.

After a best value audit of hostel accommodation, to address the over-provision of unsuitable accommodation, the Council has now identified providers for a service for women and young offenders needing additional support, and is seeking funding for a high-risk offender service including follow-on accommodation. Service profiles will be developed to facilitate monitoring.

5. Finance

Service Area (£000)	GAE 1999-2000	Final net Out turn 1999-2000	GAE 2000-2001	Final net Out turn 2000-2001
Children's Services	£18,060	£36,519	£18,989	£39,018
Community Care	£70,815	£68,911	£74,068	£71,858
Adult Offenders		£222		£261
Other SW Services	£8,742	£11,770	£8,818	£13,647
Total	**£97,618**	**£117,422**	**£101,875**	**£124,784**

Spend per head		1999-2000		2000-2001
Spend per head		£258.96		£275.20
Quartile		1		1

Funding for criminal justice services is paid directly to the Council by the Scottish Executive, and was £3,693,483 in 2000-2001.

The growth in the numbers of looked after children who are accommodated in either foster homes or residential accommodation has placed significant pressures on the social work budget and Edinburgh spends significantly above GAE on children's services. Social work spend per head is higher than in most other authorities.

6. Staffing

Staff	WTE 1999 actual	WTE 1999 per 1,000	Quartile 1999	WTE 2000 actual	WTE 2000 per 1,000	Quartile 2000
Managers & central staff	208	0.5	3	303	0.7	2
Frontline staff	2,681	5.9	1	2,652	5.8	1
Other	760	1.7	1	808	1.8	1
Total	**3,649**	**8.1**	**1**	**3,763**	**8.3**	**1**

Vacancies	Vacancies 2000	% Vacancies 2000	% Vacancies 2000 Scotland	Vacancies 2001	% Vacancies 2001	% Vacancies 2001 Scotland
SWs with adults	0	0	7.8	2	1.8	10.9
SWs with children	0	0	7.4	18	8.3	10.7
SWs with offenders	0	0	7.5	0	0	7.2
Generic workers	0	0	8.0	7	7.1	12.7
Total	**0**	**0**	**7.7**	**26**	**5.0**	**10.5**

Edinburgh has a high rate of social work staff compared with most other authorities but has a fairly low rate of managers and central staff. Vacancy levels are generally low, although there are at present 18 vacant posts in children's services. The Council has experienced difficulty in recruiting home helps and unqualified care workers, and in retaining staff within childcare.

Recruitment procedures were radically overhauled to address the shortage of home helps. Recruitment was centralised and the Council hired external premises as a single venue for giving presentations to the large number of applicants, and for conducting interviews. To speed up the process, extra clerical staff were appointed and interviewers received additional training. From 1000 applicants, 200 were interviewed and 146 were appointed – triple the return from a previous exercise at no greater unit cost.

Measures have been taken to retain staff. The Council has established a Trainee Social Worker Scheme, which supports up to five staff through training, and a bursary scheme to subsidise up to ten students.

7. Modernising services

The ethnic population (almost 10,000 in 1991) is above the average rate for Scotland, particularly for people of Pakistani or Chinese origin. There are also around 2,000 refugees from a wide variety of cultures, religions, nationalities and ethnic backgrounds.

The Council, both corporately and within social work, has a well-developed platform for race equality work. A black and ethnic minorities consultation group is consulted regularly on service developments and there is an active black workers support group. A minority ethnic carers project was launched after a successful pilot stage in 2001. The Khandan Initiative (Barnardo's family placement service) won a Community Care award in the same year. The social work department, jointly with housing colleagues, work to support up to 300 asylum seekers.

Citizen Focus, a major project resourced by the Modernising Government fund and based on a partnership with BT, is designed to support online service delivery and a council-wide customer/property database. The social work department is negotiating improvement of outdated and fragmented client information systems within these corporate developments.

All social work services, including residential children's homes and residential schools, will be linked with PCs by the end of 2002, and there is provision for non-networked PCs for foster children. Work in progress includes:

- a study of the feasibility of linking the information systems of health, education and social work for looked after children; and
- development of an online joint aids and equipment store with three other authorities and health, involving online self-assessment.

8. The Future

Through its *onecity* report the Council has demonstrated a readiness to tackle major issues facing vulnerable adults and children in Edinburgh. It brought to the task an improved corporate approach and closer partnership working with both statutory and independent sectors. It now needs to devote attention to consolidating progress and to planning to meet changing needs in the light of demographic changes.

Meeting the needs of older people depends critically on partnership working between the Council and NHS Lothian. The Council could build on past achievements in partnership working in order to achieve workable solutions and better services sooner for older people.

To build on its programme of service improvements being introduced into home care, the Council should review the scope for other supportive measures, for example, enhancing shopping and domestic services and harnessing the independent sector more closely in plans to develop local services for older people.

In the longer term the council seeks to shift the balance of care away from care home placements towards housing with extra care.

There is scope for further improving learning disability services by establishing a joint commissioning team and by raising standards of assessment and care planning.

To complement its services for people with sensory impairments, the Council should review the future needs of children with sensory impairments and how it analyses them, with a view to planning the future pattern of services for children and the resource priorities required to achieve it.

Increasing numbers of looked after children are challenges to the Council and a heavy drain on the resources on which it can call. While the Council is bound to maintain a high standard of services for the children for which it has a care responsibility, it seems prudent to give increasing priority to prevention and to mobilising the efforts of staff in social work, education and health and also voluntary organisations to this end.

To consolidate the progress in improving the education of looked after children included in its action plan, the Council should formulate joint training and development opportunities for staff who work with those children

A programme of service improvement is planned across the grouping for criminal justice services, but fundamental to success in achieving the full benefits of grouping services is a common system of information for practice and management. The Council should take the initiative in undertaking or commissioning with its partners a review of information needs for criminal justice services and the options for developing a standard system to meet them.

COMHAIRLE NAN EILEAN SIAR

1. Profile at 2002

Eilean Siar has a population of 27,200 scattered over a number of mainly small island communities.

41% of households include pensioners, the highest proportion in Scotland, and numbers are predicted to increase by 2016, though at a lower rate than the national average. The overall population is expected to decline by 17.4%. Decreases are expected in all age groups under 60.

At 5.2% (January 2002) the unemployment rate is higher than Scotland as a whole.

The area has a very low level of drug misuse (0.5% of 15-54 year olds), but the incidence of alcohol misuse is high.

The recorded crime rate has gone up slightly, but at 237 per 10,000 population was the second lowest of all local authorities in 2001.

The Council is in the process of reviewing its committee and management arrangements for social work services. This review was prompted by the formation of the NHS Western Isles and Comhairle Joint Committee for Community Care.

At spring 2002 all social services were provided by a social work department under a director, supported by 2 senior managers. The director carries out the responsibilities of chief social work officer.

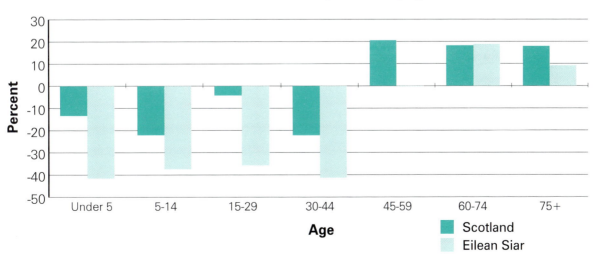

Expected % change in population, 2000-2016, local and national comparisons by age band

2. Performance: Community Care

Balance of care (aged 65+)	1999 actual	1999 per 1,000	Quartile	2000 actual	2000 per 1,000	Quartile
Older people in residential care homes	159	31	1	164	32	1
Older people in private nursing homes	62	12	4	62	12	4
Older people receiving home care	796	154	1	735	143	1
Older people in special needs housing	220	42.6	4	211	41.1	4
People receiving a community care service	**1999-2000 actual**	**1999-2000 per 1,000**	**Quartile**	**2000-2001 actual**	**2000-2001 per 1,000**	**Quartile**
Older people (aged 65+)	1,001	194.9	3	1,036	200.8	3
For mental health problems/dementia (aged 18-64)	38	2.4	3	34	2.1	4
For physical disabilities (aged 18-64)	36	2.2	4	29	1.8	4
For learning disabilities (aged 18-64)	48	3	3	51	3.2	3
For drug/alcohol abuse problems (aged 18-64)	19	1.2	2	20	1.2	2

The Council has a higher rate of older people in residential care homes than most other authorities but a lower rate of older people in nursing homes. There are plans to increase the number of single status beds to address the deficit in nursing home places, as part of a programme of replacement or refurbishment of residential homes. The Comhairle has an effective Care & Repair scheme which, together with OT provision, ensures older people do not need to enter residential care because their homes are not in a suitable condition. The number of people in special needs housing is low.

A high rate of older people receive a home care service, but the service received is more likely to be of a shorter duration than in the other island authorities and is focused on morning hours. The Comhairle has embarked on a programme of introducing contracts for home care workers, with guaranteed working hours, based on a flexible system of employment through annualised hours. This is to address the fact that recruitment and retention has been hampered seriously by the insecurity of employment, despite many other aspects of care work proving to be very attractive to employees. The Comhairle is using their success within recruitment, retention and training in its residential care settings as a template for home care developments.

In partnership with the NHS Board, the Comhairle has started an overnight support service, addressing the acknowledged deficit in services available for personal care at unsocial hours. One team is fully operational, and another due to start in autumn 2002. The Comhairle and NHS Board jointly fund the overnight support service.

The Comhairle and NHS Western Isles work in partnership with Alzheimer Scotland and Crossroads Scotland to provide community care services throughout the Western Isles. Through a network of locally based organisations (Cobhair Barraigh, Tagsa Uibhist, Harris Crossroads, Lewis Crossroads and the Lewis and Harris Alzheimers Service), a home based support service for carers and people with dementia ensures they can be supported in their own homes for as long as possible. It also provides home based respite for carers of people with a wide range of support and care needs.

The Western Isles Learning Disability Partnership, comprising NHS Western Isles, the Council, voluntary organisations and user groups, has a key role in producing the strategic direction of services for people with learning difficulties, living in scattered communities throughout the Western Isles.

The Council provides assessment and care management, five day centres, and residential and supported accommodation, and educational support for children with learning disabilities. Two learning disability nurses with a Western Isles remit, are attached to the PMS Plus Project based in North Harris. In-patient care is provided in Inverness. NCH Scotland has been commissioned to provide advocacy and also provide residential and respite service for children with special needs. An area co-ordinator in the Southern Islands helps people with leaning disabilities and their carers to access services, and there is a new jointly funded advocacy service being developed in partnership with the Western Isles Community Care Forum.

The Comhairle and the NHS Board have agreed to establish a joint committee and a locality management framework with single managers who have operational management responsibility for integrated community care teams. Initially, a joint development manager is to be recruited to develop the framework. Operational budgets will be aligned in the first place but pooled in due course and some aspects of these will be devolved.

The Opportunities for Training Towards Independence has been initiated by the Council, with support from Lews Castle College and funding from the European Social Fund. Based at Lews Castle College in Stornoway (OFTTI Project), it provides educational, training and employment opportunities for adults with a range of disabilities, including learning disabilities. The Project can be accessed throughout the Western Isles.

Mental health services involve two consultant psychiatrists who use video-conferencing for outpatient appointments across the Islands, and there are in-patient facilities in Stornoway. Community services are provided by community psychiatric nurses, an addiction worker and appropriate social work staff, three of whom are mental health officers. The I-Reach Project, funded by the NHS Board and administered by the Social Work Department, provides tailored grants to fund articles or services to help individuals with recovery following a period of severe mental illness.

Joint working is driven by the Western Isles Mental Health Partnership, comprising NHS Western Isles, the Council, voluntary organisations and a user group. The Partnership have agreed to implement joint assessment arrangements to complement the established use of the care programme approach.

The partners have agreed to apply single shared assessment procedures incrementally to all client groups. Both Carenap E and Carenap D are being piloted as assessment tools. They will be rolled out to all areas during 2002, alongside the development of integrated locality-based community care teams and specialist support services. Single shared assessment tools are also being developed for learning disability and for children and young people with special needs.

For people who have a sensory impairment (who tend to be in the older age group) a specialist worker provides a support service, maintaining a network of resources including day centres and occupational therapy. She carries out assessments and provides equipment as necessary. Any registration procedure for people who are blind or partially sighted is initiated by a visiting ophthalmologist, though delays can follow in providing significant support. Specialist rehabilitation services for people with a visual impairment are purchased from Guide Dogs for the Blind.

The Comhairle and NHS Western Isles have made significant steps towards joint resourcing and joint management, based on a tradition of joint working and the positive approach of staff. The joint resourcing pot has been scoped and will include most community care and some hospital services for older people.

The Comhairle and NHS Board have agreed to establish a joint committee, and a locality management framework with joint managers who will have overall responsibility for integrated community care teams. Initially, a joint development manager is to be recruited to develop the framework. Operational budgets – aligned in the first place but pooled in due course – will be devolved. A joint staff forum will finalise the partners' statement of intent. Joint training and team building is to be developed in 2002, including training for staff engaged in single shared assessments.

3. Performance: Children and Families

Balance of care – Looked after children (aged 0-17)	1999-2000 actual	1999-2000 per 1,000	Quartile	2000-2001 actual	2000-2001 per 1,000	Quartile
At home	23	3.8	2	36	5.9	1
With friends/relatives/other community	11	1.8	1	9	1.5	1
With foster carers/prospective adopters	10	1.7	4	8	1.3	4
In residential accommodation	5	0.8	4	7	1.2	2
Total	**49**	**8.1**	**2**	**60**	**9.9**	**2**

Key performance indicators	1998-1999 actual	1998-1999 per 1,000	Quartile	1999-2000 actual	1999-2000 per 1,000	Quartile
Child protection (CP) referrals (aged 0-15)	17	3.1	4	23	4.3	4
Children subject to a CP case conference (aged 0-15)	7	1.3	4	9	1.7	4
Children placed on CP register (aged 0-15)	3	0.6	4	8	1.5	3
Adoption applications in year (aged 0-17)	5	0.8	1	1	0.2	4
Stranger adopter applications (aged 0-17)	5	0.8	1	0	0.0	4

Eilean Siar has low rates of child protection referrals and a relatively low rate of children on child protection registers. There were no stranger adoption applications in 1999-2000.

There is relatively high rate of looked after children and most live at home or with friends or relatives. Very few live with foster carers.

Residential services for children and young people are provided locally on behalf of the Comhairle by NCH Scotland. NCH also provides a family support project to prevent children going into care, a respite scheme for children with disabilities, an Independent Living Project and a multi-disciplinary assessment and therapy and support service to children with special needs and their families.

The social work and education departments have been taking forward the *Learning with Care* recommendations. Most of the recommendations have been implemented but further work is required in relation to the development and implementation of a joint policy; staff/carer training and developing the Children's services plan.

There are good links with throughcare agencies on the mainland. Further progress is required in establishing an inter-agency approach and in consulting young people. Particular strengths include the NCH Independent Living Project, which provides supported accommodation, independent living and practical support to young people leaving care.

Joint funded by the Comhairle and NHS Board, respite care is provided by NCH for children and young people with special needs in both residential and outreach settings. The outreach care may take place at home, to allow parents to have some time to themselves, or may involve the child in an activity away from the home. A part-time co-ordinator links with families, supports the sessional outreach staff and provides training.

The Comhairle's 2002 review of committee and management arrangements for social work services is directed towards:

- integrated working between education and child care services; and
- consultation of children and their families about the development of integrated services.

4. Performance: Criminal Justice

Key Activities	1999-2000	2000-2001	2000-2001 per 10,000	Quartile
Number of social enquiry reports submitted to the courts during the year	84	73	39.7	4
Number of community service orders made during the year	16	16	8.7	4
The proportion of social enquiry reports reported to court within target time	2000-2001	Quartile		
Proportion of social enquiry reports submitted to the courts by due date	98.6	2		
The time taken to complete community service orders				
Average length of community service (hours) for orders completed during the year	171	1		
Average hours completed per week	5.4	1		

A low rate of social enquiry reports were submitted in 2000-2001 – a reflection of the very low crime rate. A relatively high proportion were submitted by the due date. A low rate of community service orders were made during the year. The average number of hours of orders was high compared to many other authorities, but orders were completed relatively quickly with an average of 5.4 hours completed per week.

Though not part of a formal grouping, the Council maintains links with the Northern Partnership. The small numbers of offenders create some difficulties for specialist service delivery. Alcohol abuse is linked to more than half of requests for social enquiry reports. Given the small numbers, monitoring is a relatively simple manual process.

New funding for a criminal justice manager post – to be filled by autumn 2002 – will enhance management capacity to meet complex needs. Increasing use of specialisation within a necessarily generic framework is being fostered. Partnership arrangements include peer review with Orkney and Shetland, supported by the installation of a video link; opting into training arrangements with Highland Council; using a consultant to support work with sex offenders; and importing a drink-driving scheme developed by Orkney Islands Council and SACRO.

A partnership approach is taken to delivery of all criminal justice services. For example, all domestic abuse cases automatically trigger a child protection enquiry. The youth justice strategy focuses on early intervention with a range of tailored responses delivered by NCH, aimed at limiting the chances of troubled children entering the adult criminal justice system.

5. Finance

Service Area (£000)	GAE 1999-2000	Final net Out turn 1999-2000	GAE 2000-2001	Final net Out turn 2000-2001
Children's Services	£525	£1,056	£523	£997
Community Care	£5,649	£8,638	£5,830	£8,421
Adult Offenders		£113		£119
Other SW Services	£573	£551	£570	£562
Total	**£6,747**	**£10,359**	**£6,923**	**£10,099**

Spend per head		1999-2000		2000-2001
Spend per head		£381.12		£371.55
Quartile		1		1

The Council receives funding direct from The Scottish Executive for criminal justice services, and it received £118,048 in 2000-2001.

Eilean Siar spent more than GAE on social work services in 1999-2000 and 2000-2001. Spend per head on social work services is high. Expenditure on children's services was around twice as high as GAE and expenditure on community care was also above GAE (more on community care per head of population than Orkney or Shetland).

6. Staffing

Staff	WTE 1999 actual	WTE 1999 per 1,000	Quartile 1999	WTE 2000 actual	WTE 2000 per 1,000	Quartile 2000
Managers & central staff	24	0.9	1	24	0.9	1
Frontline staff	298	10.8	1	283	10.4	1
Other	62	2.2	1	62	2.3	1
Total	**384**	**13.9**	**1**	**368**	**13.5**	**1**

Vacancies	Vacancies 2000	% Vacancies 2000	% Vacancies 2000 Scotland	Vacancies 2001	% Vacancies 2001	% Vacancies 2001 Scotland
SWs with adults	0	0	7.8	0	0	10.9
SWs with children	0	0	7.4	0	0	10.7
SWs with offenders	0	0	7.5	0	0	7.2
Generic workers	0	0	8.0	0	0	12.7
Total	**0**	**0**	**7.7**	**0**	**0**	**10.5**

Eilean Siar has a high rate of social work staff, particularly frontline staff, mainly home carers, although the number reduced between 1999 and 2000. In 2001, There were no vacant posts. The Council has not encountered the same acute problems as other authorities, but they have had difficulties in recruiting to specific posts, and experienced pressure on home care posts. A shift to annualised hours will make the Council competitive with other available jobs. Improved training for residential care staff has enhanced staff morale and service standards.

Despite the huge financial and personal premium on off-islands training, the Council has maintained its commitment to training and workforce development. SVQs have been used extensively, because they can be delivered without recourse to the mainland.

A supervision contract deployed in fieldwork services has been welcomed and extended to the residential sector which received Investors in People status some 18 months ago. Technological solutions to training needs are particularly attractive.

7. Modernising services

The majority Gaelic-speaking population has cultural traditions which are reflected strongly in both public services and community life. There is also a small Asian community. By spring 2002 a race equality plan had yet to be started. The Council has an equal opportunities policy but has not embraced race equality as a significant theme. It does not deal with the very significant problems that are being faced elsewhere, although people do have a strong sense of cultural differences.

The Council was an early beneficiary of upgraded telecommunications in the 90s. This allowed the development of technologies such as video conferencing and alarm systems. All social workers have mobile phones. The council has no existing Modernising Government projects, but has a current bid submitted to the MGF for the development of electronic monitoring of home-based care.

The introduction of client information systems remains at an early stage. The home care service apart, managers have not considered it a priority, given the number of service users. The social work department is exploring an off-the-shelf system for children and criminal justice services.

8. The Future

In addressing the future growth in numbers of older people, the Council recognises the need to consider urgently greater emphasis on community-based support and improvements in the flexibility and quality of the home care service. In drawing resource priorities in the future, development of services will need to assess the pressure of rising costs, against its present high expenditure on community care per head of population.

Specific action which calls for continued attention includes:

- a programme of replacement or refurbishment of residential homes;
- implementation of a home care contracted workforce; and
- providing services during unsocial hours through the overnight support service.

For future improvements across community care, the Council should continue with health partners to work out and implement joint assessment and care management arrangements, to complement the established use of the care programme approach.

There are no organisations for people with a sensory impairment. Demand for services is low but highly volatile, and the Council faces real practical difficulties in funding and staffing a professional service. To address the problem and bring together realistic proposals for development the Council could commission a multi-disciplinary group to carry out a strategic review of options for the future.

The shortage of foster carers remains a shortcoming in the services for looked after children, and the Council should seek the advice of specialist agencies in planning future diverse efforts to boost the numbers of carers.

To consolidate the progress made in improving the education of looked after children, the Council should press ahead with:

- developing and implementing a joint strategy to be followed by social work and education for implementing the range of recommendations of *Learning with Care;*
- devising joint development and training opportunities for staff who work with those children; and
- making, as soon as possible, an appointment to the new post of development officer for children and families to support work on child protection.

In order to establish the ground for a throughcare service for young people the Council should consider:

- forming a suitable type of inter-agency mechanism to oversee the planning and implementation of vital services; and
- establishing reliable communication means for consulting young people about services.

As a working priority, the Council should prepare a race equality plan appropriate to its needs and circumstances.

To give greater focus to and to enhance its various services, the Council should implement mutually consistent client information systems, which have clear service links. A possibility is to acquire off-the-shelf systems of the kind which the social work department is exploring for children and criminal justice services.

COMHAIRLE NAN EILEAN SIAR

1. Cunntas aig 2002

Tha 27,200 neach a' fuireach anns na h-Eileanan Siar, sgapte air feadh grunn choimhearsnachdan eileanach.

'S e luchd-peinnsean a th' ann an 41% de dhachaighean, an àireamh is mòtha an Alba, agus tha dùil gun èirich na h-àireamhan sin ro 2016, ach aig ìre nas lugha na an àireamh nàiseanta. Tha dùil gun tuit an àireamh-sluaigh 17.4%. Tha dùil ri lùghdachadh anns gach buidheann fo aois 60.

Aig 5.2% (Faoilleach 2002), tha ìre cion-cosnaidh nas àirde na Alba gu lèir.

Tha ìre glè ìseal mì-ghnàthachadh dhrugaichean san sgìre (0.5% eadar 15-54 bliadhna a dh'aois), ach tha tachartasan mì-ghnàthachadh deoch-làidir nas àirde.

Tha an ìre eucoir clàraichte air a dhol suas beagan, ach aig 237 mu choinneamh gach 10,000 neach, b' e an dara fear is ìsle airson gach ùghdarras ionadail ann an 2001.

Tha a' Chomhairle a' dèanamh ath-bhreithneachadh air solarachadh comataidh agus stiùiridh airson seirbheisean obair shòisealta. Chaidh an ath-bhreithneachadh seo a chur air bhonn as dèidh NHS nan Eilean Siar agus Co-chomataidh na Comhairle air Cùram Coimhearsnachd a stèidheachadh.

San Earrach 2002 bha na seirbheisean sòisealta gu lèir air an lìbhrigeadh le roinn obair shòisealta le stiùiriche agus 2 àrd-stiùiriche. Tha an stiùiriche a' gabhail uallaichean àrd oifigear obair shòisealta.

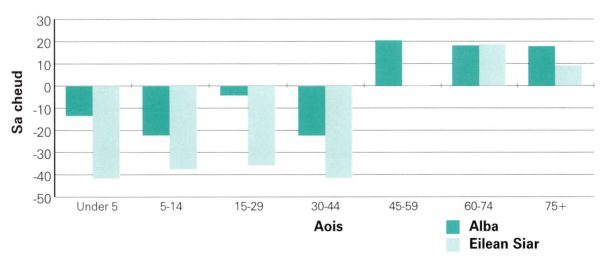

% atharrachadh-sluagh ris a bheil dùil, 2000-2016, coimeasan ionadail agus nàiseanta le bann aoise

2. Coileanadh: Cùram Coimhearsnachd

Cothromachadh cùraim (aois 65+)	1999 àireamh	1999 gach 1,000	Gach ràith	2000 àireamh	2000 gach 1,000	Gach ràith
Seann daoine ann an dachaighean cùraim còmhnaidh	159	31	1	164	32	1
Seann daoine ann an dachaighean nursaidh prìobhaideach	62	12	4	62	12	4
Seann daoine a' faighinn cùram dachaigh	796	154	1	735	143	1
Seann daoine ann an taigheadas feuman sònraichte	220	42.6	4	211	41.1	4
Daoine a' faighinn cùram sònraichte sa choimhearsnachd	**1999-2000 àireamh**	**1999-2000 gach 1,000**	**Gach ràith**	**2000-2001 àireamh**	**2000-2001 gach 1,000**	**Gach ràith**
Seann daoine (aois 65+)	1,001	194.9	3	1,036	200.8	3
Airson trioblaidean inntinn/dementia (aois 18-64)	38	2.4	3	34	2.1	4
Airson ciorramachd corporra (aois18-64)	36	2.2	4	29	1.8	4
Airson ciorramachd ionnsachaidh (aois18-64)	48	3	3	51	3.2	3
Airson trioblaidean dhrugaichean/ deoch-làidir (aois 18-64)	19	1.2	2	20	1.2	2

Tha àireamh nas àirde de sheann daoine ann an dachaighean cùraim còmhnaidh aig a' Chomhairle seach a' mhòr-chuid de dh'ùghdarrais eile ach àireamh nas ìsle airson daoine ann an dachaighean nursaidh. Tha planaichean san amharc airson àireamh nas motha de leapannan singilte mu choinneamh a' ghainnid de dh'àiteachan ann an dachaighean nursaidh, mar phàirt de chlàr-obrach togail agus càraidh air dachaighean cùraim. Tha sgeama Cùraim agus Càraidh èifeachdach aig a' Chomhairle a tha, còmhla ri solarachadh OT, a' dèanamh cinnteach nach fheum seann daoine an dachannan fhèin fhàgail ma tha iad ann an staid mi-fhreagarrach. Tha an àireamh dhaoine ann an taigheadas feuman sònraichte ìseal.

Tha àireamh àrd de sheann daoine a' faighinn seirbheis cùram san dachaigh, ach tha an t-seirbheis nas giorra seach coimhearsnachdan eileanach eile agus ag amas air uairean na maidne. Tha a' Chomhairle air tòiseachadh air cùmhnantan a thoirt do luchd-obrach cùram dachaigh, le uairean obrach air an gealltainn, stèidhichte air siostam cosnaidh subailte le uairean bliadhnail. Tha seo airson dèiligeadh ris na trioblaidean a th' air a bhith ann a' cumail agus a' fastadh luchd-obrach air sàilleibh mì-chinnt na h-obrach, ged a tha mòran eile co-cheangailte ri obair cùraim a tha tarraingeach cuideachd. Tha a' Chomhairle a' cleachdadh an cuid soirbheachais ann a bhith a' fastadh, a' cumail agus a' trèanadh san raon seo mar shlàt-tomhais airson leasachaidhean cùraim dachaigh eile.

Ann an com-pàirt ri Bòrd an NHS, tha a' Chomhairle air seirbheis taic oidhche a thoiseachadh, mar sin a' dèiligeadh ris a' bheàrn ann an seirbheisean cùram pearsanta aig uairean mi-shòisealta. Tha aon sgioba ag obair mar-thà, agus dùil gun tòisich tè eile san fhoghar 2002. Tha a' Chomhairle agus Bòrd an NHS a co-mhaoineachadh na seirbheis seo.

Tha a' Chomhairle agus NHS nan Eilean Siar ag obair ann an com-pàirt ri Alzheimers Alba agus Crossroads Alba gus seirbheisean cùram coimhearsnachd a thoirt seachad air feadh nan Eilean Siar. Tro lìonra de bhuidhnean ionadail (Cobhair Bharraigh, Tagsa Uibhist, Crossroads na Hearadh, Crossroads Leodhais agus Seirbheis Alzheimers Leodhais agus na Hearadh), tha seirbheis taic dachaigh do luchd-cùraim agus daoine le dementia a' dèanamh cinnteach gum faigh iad taic san dachaigh aca fhèin cho fad's a ghabhas. Tha e cuideachd a' toirt faochadh do luchd-cùraim dhaoine le roghainn farsaing de thaic agus feuman cùraim.

Tha àite cudromach aig Com-pàirteachas Ciorram Ionnsachaidh, a' toirt a-steach NHS nan Eilean Siar, a' Chomhairle, buidhnean saor-thoileach agus luchd-cleachdaidh, ann a bhith a' stiùireadh ro-innleachd airson seirbheisean do dhaoine le duilgheadasan ionnsachaidh, a tha a' fuireach ann an coimhearsnachdan sgapte air feadh nan Eilean Siar.

Tha a' Chomhairle a' tairgsinn stiùireadh measaidh agus cùraim, ionadan còig là, agus àiteachan còmhnaidh le taic, agus taic foghlaim airson clann le ciorram ionnsachaidh. Tha dithis nursaichean ciorram ionnsachaidh le uallach airson nan Eilean Siar gu lèir, stèidhichte aig a' Phròiseict PMS Plus ann an Ceann a Tuath na Hearadh. Tha cùram in-euslainteach air a thairgsinn ann an Inbhirnis. Chaidh NCH Alba fhastadh airson comhairle agus seirbheis dachaigh agus faochaidh a thoirt do chlann le feuman sònraichte. Tha co-òrdanaiche anns na h-Eileanan a Deas a' cuideachadh dhaoine le duilgheadasan ionnsachaidh agus an luchd-cùraim gu bhith ruighinn sheirbheisean, agus tha seirbhis comhairleachaidh ùr ga leasachadh ann an com-pàirt ri Fòraim Cùraim Coimhearsnachd nan Eilean Siar.

Tha a' Chomhairle agus Bòrd an NHS air aontachadh co-chomataidh a stèidheachadh agus frèam-obrach stiùiridh le manaidsearan singilte air am bith uallach airson sgiobannan cùram coimhearsnachd a threòrachadh. Anns a' chiad dhol a-mach, thèid manaidsear leasachaidh fhastadh airson am frèam-obrach a thoirt air adhart. Bith buidseatan obrach fa leth ann sa chiad àite ach thèid an tarraing còmhla rè ùine agus cumhachdan pàirtean dhiubh a sgaoileadh a-mach.

Chaidh Cothroman Trèanaidh gu Ruige Neo-eisimileachd a chur air bhonn leis a' Chomhairle, le taic bho Colaiste Caisteal Leodhais agus airgead bho Maoin Shòisealta na h-Eòrpa. Stèidhichte aig Colaiste Caisteal Leodhais ann an Steòrnabhagh (Pròiseact OFTI), tha e a' tabhann cothroman foghlaim, trèanaidh agus cosnaidh do dh'inbhich le deifir chiorraman, agus duilgheadasan ionnsachaidh. Tha am Pròiseact air chothrom air feadh nan Eilean Siar.

Tha seirbheisean slàinte inntinn a' gabhail a-steach dà lighiche-inntinn a tha a' cleachdadh goireasan co-labhairt bhideo airson ruighinn air euslaintich air feadh nan Eilean, agus tha goireasan airson in-euslaintich ann an Steòrnabhagh. Tha seirbheisean coimhearsnachd air an lìbhrigeadh le nursaichean coimhearsnachdan sònraichte, neach-obrach dhrugaichean agus luchd-obrach sòisealta freagarrach, triùir dhiubh a tha nan oifigearan slàinte inntinn. Tha am Pròiseact I-Reach, air a mhaoineachadh le Bòrd an NHS agus air a ruidh le Roinn na h-Obrach Shòisealta, a' tabhann taic-airgead airson artaigilean no seirbhisean a chuidicheas daoine as dèidh faighinn seachad air tinneas inntinn.

Tha co-obrachadh air a stiùireadh le Com-pàirteachas Slàinte Inntinn nan Eilean Siar, a' toirt a-steach NHS nan Eilean Siar, a' Chomhairle, buidhnean saor-thoileach agus buidheann luchd-cleachdaidh. Tha an com-pàirteachas air aontachadh dòighean-obrach co-mheasaidh a chur an sàs a thuilleadh air a' phrògraim cùraim a tha stèidhichte mar-thà.

Tha na com-pàirtichean air aontachadh dòighean-measaidh a roinn mean air mhean ri na buidhnean dèiligidh air fad. Tha an dà chuid Carenap E agus Carenap D gam feuchainn mar innealan measaidh. Thèid an sgaoileadh a-mach gu gach raon tro 2002, còmhla ri leasachadh air sgiobannan cùraim coimhearsnachd amalaichte agus seirbheisean taic sònraichte, stèidhichte sna coimhearsnachdan. Tha innealan measaidh gan leasachadh cuideachd airson ciorram ionnsachaidh agus airson clann agus daoine òga le feuman sònraichte.

Airson daoine le bacadh mothachaidh (seann daoine mar is àbhaist) tha neach-obrach sònraichte a' tairgsinn seirbheis taic, agus a' cumail suas lìonra de ghoireasan leithid ionadan là agus leasachadh obrach. Tha ise a' dèanamh measadh agus a' tairgsinn uidheamachd mar a tha feum air. Tha sùil-lighiche tadhail a' cur an gleus obair clàraidh sam bith a tha a dhìth airson daoine a tha dall no gann san fhradharc, ach faodaidh taic shusbainteach toirt nas fhaide. Tha seirbheisean sònraichte do dhaoine le gainne fradhairc air an ceannach bho Choin Treòrachaidh airson nan Dall.

Tha a' Chomhairle agus NHS nan Eilean Siar air ceumannan mòra a ghabhail gu ruige co-ghoireasachadh agus co-stiùireadh, stèidhichte air cleachdadh co-obrachadh agus dòighean adhartach an luchd-obrach. Tha sinn air tomhas a dhèanamh air na goireasan agus bheir iad a-steach a' mhòr-chuid de chùram coimhearsnachd agus cuid de sheirbheisean ospadail airson seann daoine.

Tha a' Chomhairle agus Bòrd an NHS air aontachadh co-chomataidh a stèidheachadh, a thuilleadh air frèam-obrach stiùireadh ionadail le co-mhanaidsearan air am bith uallach airson sgiobannan cùram coimhearsnachd amalaichte. Thèid buidseatan obrach – fa leth an toiseach ach air an tarraing còmhla rè ùine – an sgaoileadh a-mach. Cuiridh fòram luchd-obrach ri chèile aithris dheireannach dheth na tha san amharc aig na com-pàirtichean. Thèid trèanadh agus togail sgioba a leasachadh ann an 2002, a' toirt a-steach trèanadh airson luchd-obrach an sàs ann am measadh singilte co-roinnte.

3. Coileanadh: Clann agus Teaghlaichean

Cothromachadh cùraim – Clann (aois 0-17)	1999-2000 àireamh	1999-2000 gach1,000	Gach ràith	2000-2001 àireamh	2000-2001 gach1,000	Gach ràith
Aig an taigh	23	3.8	2	36	5.9	1
Còmhla ri caraidean/cairdean/coimhearsnachd eile	11	1.8	1	9	1.5	1
Còmhla ri luchd-cùraim altruim/uchd-mhacair ri teachd	10	1.7	4	8	1.3	4
Ann an àite-còmhnaidh	5	0.8	4	7	1.2	2
Iomlan	**49**	**8.1**	**2**	**60**	**9.9**	**2**

Prìomh chomharran coileanaidh	1998-1999 àireamh	1998-1999 gach1,000	Gach ràith	1999-2000 àireamh	1999-2000 gach1,000	Gach ràith
Iomradh Dìon chloinne (CP) (aois 0-15)	17	3.1	4	23	4.3	4
Clann le cùis co-labhairt CP (aois 0-15)	7	1.3	4	9	1.7	4
Clann air Clàr CP (aois 0-15)	3	0.6	4	8	1.5	3
Tagraidhean uchd-mhacachd sa bhliadhna (aois 0-17)	5	0.8	1	1	0.2	4
Tagraidhean uchd-mhacair ùra (aois 0-17)	5	0.8	1	0	0.0	4

Tha àireamhan coimeasach ìseal sna h-Eileanan Siar airson iomraidhean dìon chloinne agus àireamhan an ìre mhath ìseal airson clann air clàran dìon chloinne. Cha robh gin thagraidhean uchd-mhacair ùra ann airson 1999-2000.

Tha àireamh coimeasach àrd ann airson clann a tha fo chùram agus tha a' mhòr-chuid a' fuireach aig an taigh no còmhla ri caraidean no càirdean. 'S e glè bheag a tha a' fuireach comhla ri luchd-cùraim altruim.

Tha seirbheisean còmhnaidh airson clann agus daoine òga air an tairgsinn gu h-ionadail as leth na Comhairle le NCH Alba. Tha NCH cuideachd a' tairgsinn pròiseact taic teaghlaich gus clann a chumail a-mach a cùram, sgeama faochaidh airson clann le ciorramachdan, Pròiseact Beatha Neo-eisimeil agus seirbheis taic measaidh agus leasachaidh do chlann le feuman sònraichte agus an teaghlaichean.

Tha roinnean obair shòisealta agus foghlaim air a bhith a' toirt air adhart molaidhean *Ionnsachadh le Cùram*. Tha a' mhòr-chuid dheth na molaidhean air an cur an-sàs ach feumar tuilleadh obrach a dhèanamh a thaobh leasachadh agus cur an cèill co-phoileasaidh; trèanadh luchd-obrach/luchd-cùraim agus ann a bhith a' leasachadh plana seirbheisean Chloinne.

Tha ceangalan math ann ri aonadan taic air tìr-mòr. Feumar tuilleadh adhartais a dhèanamh ann a bhith a' stèidheachadh dòigh-obrach eadar-bhuidhne agus ann a bhith a' conaltradh ri daoine òga. Tha am Pròiseact Beatha Neo-eisimeil aig NCH na dheagh eiseimpleir air mar a ghabhas aite-còmhnaidh, beatha neo-eisimeil agus taic phractaigeach a thoirt do dhaoine òga a tha a' tighinn a-mach a cùram.

Air a cho-mhaoineachadh leis a' Chomhairle agus Bòrd an NHS, tha faochadh cùraim air a thoirt seachad le NCH airson clann agus daoine òga le feuman sònraichte, an dà chuid ann an àiteachan-còmhnaidh agus suidheachaidhean às-ruigsinneach. Faodar cùram às-ruigsinneach a thoirt seachad san dachaigh, gus ùine a thoirt do phàrantan dhaibh pèin, no faodar cur-seachad a chur air dòigh dhan leanabh air falbh bhon dachaigh. Tha co-òrdanaiche pàirt-ùine a' togail cheangalan ri teaghlaichean agus a' cumail taic agus trèanadh ri luchd-obrach.

Tha ath-bhreithneachadh na Comhairle 2002 air rèiteachadh comataidh agus stiùiridh airson seirbheisean obair shòisealta ag amas air:

- dòigh-obrach amalaichte eadar seirbheisean foghlaim agus cùram chloinne; agus
- co-chomhairleachadh ri clann agus na teaghlaichean aca mu leasachadh sheirbheisean amalaichte.

4. Coileanadh: Ceartas Eucorach

Prìomh ghnìomhan	1999-2000	2000-2001	2000-2001 gach 10,000	Gach ràith
Àireamh aithisgean rannsachadh sòisealta a' dol gu cùirtean tron bhliadhna	84	73	39.7	4
Àireamh òrdain seirbheis coimhearsnachd tron bhliadhna	16	16	8.7	4
Àireamh aithisgean rannsachasdh sòisealta a' dol gu cùirtean air taobh a-staigh àm sònraichte	**2000-2001**	**Gach ràith**		
Àireamh aithisgean rannsachasdh sòisealta a' dol gu cùirtean ro cheann-là sònraichte	98.6	2		
An t-àm a bheir e òrdugh seirbheis coimhearsnachd a chrìochnachadh				
Fad seirbheis coimhearsnachd sa chumantas (uairean) airson òrdain air an crìochnachadh tron bhliadhna	171	1		
Uairean crìochnaichte sa chumantas gach seachdain	5.4	1		

Chaidh àireamh ìseal de dh'aithisgean rannsachaidh sòisealta a chur a-steach airson 2000-2001 – comharra air cho fìor ìseal agus a tha ìre eucoir. Chaidh àireamh coimeasach àrd a chur a-steach ron cheann-là sònraichte. Chaidh àireamh ìseal de dh'òrdain seirbheis coimhearsnachd a thoirt seachad tron bhliadhna. Bha an àireamh uairean an uaireadair de dh'òrdain àrd sa chumantas an coimeas ri ùghdarrasan eile, ach chaidh an crìochnachadh gu luath le 5.4 uair gach seachdain sa chumantas.

Ged nach eil e mar phàirt de bhuidhean foirmeil, tha a' Chomhairle a' cumail suas cheangalan ris a' Chom-pàirteachas a Tuath. Tha na h-àireamhan beaga de chiontaich ag adhbhrachadh beagan dhuilgheadasan ann a bhith a' lìbhrigeadh seirbheis spèisealta. Tha mì-ghnàthachadh deoch-làidir a' buntainn ri còrr san dara leth de dh'iarrtasan airson aithisgean rannsachaidh sòisealta. Bhon a tha na h-àireamhan cho beag, tha e an ìre mhath sìmplidh sùil a chumail orra.

Bheir maoineachas ùr airson dreuchd manaidsear ceartas eucorach – ri lìonadh ro foghar 2002 – adhartas air coimeas stiùiridh ann a bhith coinneachadh feumalachdan toinnte. Tha sinn a' brosnachadh barrachd sgilean spèisealta air taobh a-staigh frèam-obrach coitcheann. Tha rèiteachadh com-pàirteachais a' toirt a-steach ath-bhreithneachadh comais le Arcaibh agus Sealtainn, a' cleachdadh ceangal bhideo; a' roghnachadh cothroman trèanaidh còmhla ri Comhairle na Gaidhealtachd; a' cleachdadh comhairliche airson obair taic le ciontaich feise; agus a' cleachdadh sgeama deoch-dhraibheadh a leasaich Comhairle Eileanan Shealtainn agus SACRO.

Tha dòigh-obrach com-pàirteachais ga ghabhail ann a bhith a' lìbhrigeadh gach seirbheis ceartas eucorach. Mar eiseimpleir, faodaidh cùisean mi-ghnàthachadh san dachaigh rannsachadh dìon chloinne a phriobrachadh. Tha an ro-innleachd airson ceartas òigridh a' coimhead ri dhol an sàs cho luath sa ghabhas le freagairtean iomchaidh air an lìbhrigeadh le NCH, ag amas cho fad's a ghabhas air clann ann an trioblaid a chumail air falbh bho siostam ceartas eucorach nan inbheach.

5. Ionmhas

Raon Seirbheis (£000)	CTC 1999-2000	Cosgaisean Deireannach 1999-2000	CTC 2000-2001	Cosgaisean Deireannach 2000-2001
Seirbheisean Chloinne	£525	£1,056	£523	£997
Cùram Coimhearsnachd	£5,649	£8,638	£5,830	£8,421
Ciontaich Inbheach		£113		£119
Seirbheisean Obair Shòisealta Eile	£573	£551	£570	£562
Iomlan	**£6,747**	**£10,359**	**£6,923**	**£10,099**
Cosgais gach ceann		**1999-2000**		**2000-2001**
Cosgais gach ceann		£381.12		£371.55
Gach ràith		1		1

Tha a' Chomhairle a' faighinn maoineachas airson seirbheisean ceartas eucoir direach bho Riaghaltas na h-Alba agus fhuair i £118,048 ann an 2000-2001

Chosg Comhairle nan Eilean Siar barrachd na CTC air seirbheisean obair shòisealta ann an 1999-2000 agus 2000-2001. Tha cosgaisean àrd mu choinneamh gach ceann airson seirbheisean sòisealta. Bha cosgaisean seirbheisean chloinne timcheall a dhà uiread ri CTC agus bha cosgais air cùram coimhearsnachd cuideachd os cionn CTC (barrachd air cùram coimhearsnachd mu choinneamh gach ceann seach Arcaibh agus Sealtainn).

6. Luchd-obrach

Luchd-obrach	CÙO 1999 àireamh	CÙO 1999 gach 1,000	Gach ràith 1999	CÙO 2000 àireamh	CÙO 2000 gach 1,000	Gach ràith 2000
Manaidsearan & prìomh luchd-obrach	24	0.9	1	24	0.9	1
Luchd-obrach air beulaibh sluagh	298	10.8	1	283	10.4	1
Eile	62	2.2	1	62	2.3	1
Iomlan	**384**	**13.9**	**1**	**368**	**13.5**	**1**

Dreuchdan bàn	Dreuchdan bàn 2000	% Dreuchdan bàn 2000	% Dreuchdan bàn 2000 Alba	Dreuchdan bàn 2001	% Dreuchdan bàn 2000	% Dreuchdan bàn 2001 Alba
Neach-obrach Sòisealta le inbhich	0	0	7.8	0	0	10.9
Neach-obrach Sòisealta le clann	0	0	7.4	0	0	10.7
Neach-obrach Sòisealta le ciontaich	0	0	7.5	0	0	7.2
Luchd-obrach choitcheann	0	0	8.0	0	0	12.7
Iomlan	**0**	**0**	**7.7**	**0**	**0**	**10.5**

Tha ìre àrd de luchd-obrach sòisealta aig Comhairle nan Eilean Siar, gu sònraichte luchd-obrach air beulaibh sluagh, luchd-cùraim dachaigh sa mhòr-chuid, ged a tha an àireamh air lùghdachadh eadar 1999 agus 2000. Ann an 2001, cha robh dreuchdan bàn ann idir. Chan eil na h-aon thrioblaidean air a bhith aig a' Chomhairle seach ùghdarrasan eile, ach tha duilgheadasan air a bhith aca ann a bhith a' lìonadh dreuchdan sònraichte, agus bha cuideam orra a thaobh dreuchdan cùraim dachaigh. Bi gluasad gu uairean bliadhnail a ciallachadh gun tèid aig a' Chomhairle air farpais nas fheàrr ri dreuchdan eile sa mhargaidh. Tha trèanadh nas fheàrr airson luchd-cùraim àiteachan-còmhnaidh a ciallachadh gum bheil tlachd obrach agus ìrean seirbheis nas fheàrr ann.

A dh'aindheoin a chosgais a tha an luib trèanadh air falbh bho na h-eileanan, tha a' Chomhairle air cumail ris a' ghealltanas aca a thaobh trèanadh agus leasachadh luchd-obrach. Tha SVQs air an cleachdadh gu tric, a chionn is gum faighear air an dèanamh as aonais a dhol gu tìr-mòr.

Chaidh fàilte a chur air cùmhnant stiùiridh ann an seirbheisean obair a-muigh agus a leudachadh chun an raon còmhnaidh a fhuair inbhe Investors in People bho chionn bliadhna gu leth. Tha fuasglaidhean teicnigeach airson feumalachdan trèanaidh gu sònraichte tarraingeach.

7. Ag Ùrachadh Sheirbheisean

Tha dualchas Gàidhlig sluagh na sgìre ri fhaicinn gu làidir, an dà chuid ann an seirbheisean poblach agus ann am beatha na coimhearsnachd. Tha coimhearsnachd bheag Àsianach san sgìre cuideachd. San Earrach 2002 bha obair gun tòiseachadh fhathast air plana co-ionannachd cinnidh. Tha poileasaidh co-ionannachd chothroman aig a' Chomhairle ach chan eil i air co-ionannachd cinnidh a ghabhail thuice fhèin mar chuspair cudromach fhathast. Chan eil am poileasaidh a' dèiligeadh ri na duilgheadasan cudromach a tha a' nochdadh ann an àiteachan eile, ged a tha mothachadh làidir aig daoine air eadar-dhealachadh cultarail.

Fhuair a' Chomhairle buannachd bho leasachaidhean conaltraidh fòn tràth sna 90an. Thug seo cothrom goireasan leithid co-labhairt bhideo agus siostaman rabhaidh a leasachadh. Tha fònaichean pòca aig luchd-obrach sòisealta air fad. Chan eil gin a phròiseactan Ùrachadh Riaghaltais aig a' Chomhairle an dràst, ach tha tagradh a-staigh airson leasachadh a thoirt air siostam sgrùdaidh eileagtronaigeach airson cùram dachaigh.

Tha siostaman fiosrachaidh luchd-cleachdaidh fhathast aig ìre bhunasach. A thuilleadh air an t-seirbheis cùram dachaigh, chan eil manaidsearan a' coimhead ris mar phrìomh amas, ri linn an àireamh de luchd-cleachdaidh. Tha roinn na h-obrach shòisealta a' coimhead ri siostam far-na-sgeilp airson seirbheisean chloinne agus ceartas eucorach.

8. An t-Àm ri Teachd

Ann a bhith a' dèiligeadh ris an àrdachadh ann an àireamh seann daoine, tha a' Chomhairle ag aithneachadh gum feumar cuideam a chur sa bhad air taic choimhearsnachd agus leasachadh a dhèanamh ann an subailteachd agus inbhe na seirbheis cùram dachaigh. Ann a bhith a' sònrachadh prìomh amasan ghoireasan san àm ri teachd, feumaidh leasachadh sheirbheisean tomhas a dhèanamh air cosgaisean ag èirigh, mu choinneamh a chosgais àrd a th' ann an dràst airson cùram coimhearsnachd mu choinneamh gach ceann dhen t-sluagh.

Tha na leanas am measg nan gnìomhan sònraichte a tha feumach air aire leantainneach:

- pròiogram airson dachaighean còmhnaidh a thogail no a chàradh;
- luchd-obrach cùram dachaigh chùmhnantaichte a stèidheachadh; agus
- seirbheisean a thoirt seachad aig uairean mi-shòisealta tro sheirbheis taic oidhche.

Airson leasachaidhean air feadh cùram choimhearsnachd, bu chòir dhan Chomhairle leantail ri com-pàirtichean slàinte agus dòighean co-mheasaidh agus stiùireadh cùraim obrachadh a-mach agus a chur an gnìomh, a thuilleadh air a' phrògraim cùram stèidhichte.

Chan eil gin de bhuidhnean ann airson daoine le bacadh mothachaidh. Tha iarrtas airson seirbheisean ìseal ach uamhasach sradagach, agus tha fìor dhuilgheadasan practaigeach aig a' Chomhairle ann a bhith a' maoineachadh agus a' frithealadh seirbheis phroifeiseanta. Gus dèiligeadh ris an trioblaid agus molaidhean ciallach a thoirt air adhart, dh'fhaodadh a' Chomhairle buidheann ioma-chuspaireach fhastadh a dhèanadh ath-bhreithneachadh ro-innleachdail air roghainnean airson an àm ri teachd.

Tha gainne luchd-altruim na dhuilgheadas airson seirbheisean cùraim chloinne, agus bu chòir dhan Chomhairle comhairle a ghabhail bho bhuidhnean spèisealta ann a bhith a' dealbh oidhirpean gus barrachd luchd-cùraim a thaladh.

Gus adhartas a dhaingneachadh ann a bhith a' leasachadh foghlam airson clann ann an cùram, bu chòir dhan Chomhairle cumail orra le bhith:

- a' leasachadh agus a' cur an gnìomh ro-innleachd airson obair shòisealta agus foghlam airson a bhith a' cur an gnìomh roghainn de mholaidhean *Ionnsachadh le Cùram;*
- a' dealbh co-leasachadh agus cothroman trèanaidh do luchd-obrach a tha ag obair leis a chlann sin; agus
- ag ainmeachadh, cho luath sa ghabhas, cuideigin airson dreuchd oifigear leasachaidh airson clann agus teaghlaichean gus taic a thoirt do dh'obair dìon chloinne.

Mar dhòigh air seirbheis cùram-leantaileach a stèidheachadh airson daoine òga bu chòir dhan Chomhairle beachdachadh air:

- innleachd eadar-bhuidhne a stèidheachadh gus coimhead ri planadh agus cur an gnìomh seirbheisean deatamach; agus
- dòigh conaltraidh sheasmhach a stèidheachadh airson beachdan a thrusadh bho dhaoine òga mu sheirbheisean.

Mar phrìomh amas obrach, bu chòir dhan Chomhairle plana co-ionannachd cinnidh a dheasachadh a tha a' freagairt feumalachd agus suidheachadh na Comhairle.

Airson aire nas fheàrr agus na seirbheisean aice a thoirt air adhart, bu chòir dhan Chomhairle siostaman fiosrachaidh luchd-cleachdaidh a chur an gnìomh, le ceangalan seirbheis follaiseach. Dh'fhaodadh i 's docha coimhead ri siostaman far-na-sgeilp dhen t-seòrsa ris a bheil roinn na h-obrach shòisealta a' coimhead airson clann agus seirbheisean ceartas eucorach.

1. Profile at 2002

A medium-sized mainly urban authority, Falkirk has a population of 144,300.

The over 75 population is projected to increase by over a quarter. The number of under 5s is predicted to decline by more than the Scottish average.

At 4.5% (January 2002), the local rate of unemployment, though falling, is above the Scottish average.

The drug misuse rate is low at 1.4% of 15-54 year olds.

The local recorded crime rate is below the national average (603 per 10,000 of population in 2001).

The Council operates a Scrutiny Committee, which has permitted wider debate of social work issues and created more support for social work within the Council.

Social work services are part of a joint department with housing. The Department has had a new Director since January 2002.

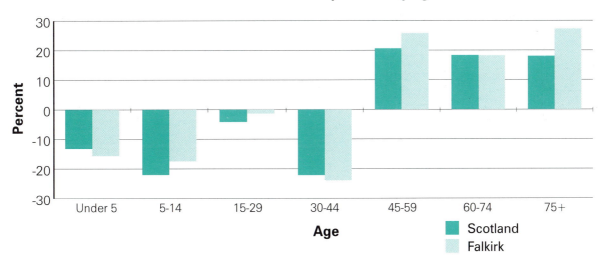

Expected % change in population, 2000-2016, local and national comparisons by age band

2. Performance: Community Care

Balance of care (aged 65+)	1999 actual	1999 per 1,000	Quartile	2000 actual	2000 per 1,000	Quartile
Older people in residential care homes	273	13	4	258	12	4
Older people in private nursing homes	431	20	4	470	22	3
Older people receiving home care	2,111	98	1	1,966	91	2
Older people in special needs housing	1,770	82.6	3	1,770	82.1	3
People receiving a community care service	**1999-2000 actual**	**1999-2000 per 1,000**	**Quartile**	**2000-2001 actual**	**2000-2001 per 1,000**	**Quartile**
Older people (aged 65+)	6,479	300	1	6,737	312.5	1
For mental health problems/dementia (aged 18-64)	215	2.4	3	214	2.4	3
For physical disabilities (aged 18-64)	1,579	17.4	2	1,671	18.4	2
For learning disabilities (aged 18-64)	353	3.9	2	369	4.1	2
For drug/alcohol abuse problems (aged 18-64)	63	0.7	2	61	0.7	3

A higher rate of older people receive a community care service than in most other authorities. The rate of older people in residential and nursing home care is lower than many other authorities. A relatively high rate of older people receive a home care service, but most receive the service only in the morning or at lunch time.

Following a joint best value review of services for older people the Council and health partners have acted:

- to redesign residential care in order to increase services available to older people with dementia and with functional mental illness; and
- to redevelop and make more flexible the home care service.

The redevelopment of the home care service was to be completed by mid 2002, as part of a range of initiatives to improve services for older people and to enable more to be cared for at home. They include:

- provision of personal care;
- integration with sheltered housing;
- shift patterns that allow delivery of home care at more flexible hours;
- a shopping scheme; and
- extension of the Mobile Emergency Care Service to fit more closely with a developing rapid response/crisis care service.

The Council is part of the joint Forth Valley Partnership in Practice agreement, which builds on a pre-existing strategy for learning disability services. An implementation group set up to progress the strategy includes representatives of primary care and education services and users and carers. Local area co-ordination pilot schemes are to be resourced by the Change Fund. An integrated health and social work team focuses on people with complex needs.

The Council led the joint preparation for retraction of the Royal Scottish National Hospital (RSNH). Forty people are still to move out. Those who first moved out into the community found it hard to make friends. The Council has to balance resources between the RSNH retraction and clients already in the community.

Existing integrated teams for adults with mental health problems are to be reshaped from five to three, matching the boundaries of community care teams and primary care. Each team is to have a single manager and a devolved budget. However, integrated management is not anticipated in the near future. There is a joint resource panel for supported accommodation and residential rehabilitation for mental health, and similar panels for learning disability and elderly services. Caledonia House works effectively on the clubhouse model, although its many services need to be integrated and linked to other services.

The development of the single shared assessment process is building on partnership working between social work and the local health care co-operative. The single shared assessment tool has been agreed, and a separate tool has been piloted for people with learning disabilities. Accessing resources across agency boundaries is an area to be addressed.

The Council is developing a multi-agency resource centre for people with sensory impairment. Resources and partnerships with health and the RNIB are in place but a site has still to be identified. A senior social worker co-ordinates sensory impairment services; she is to co-ordinate the register, manage staff and be involved in training. Other aspects of the local sensory impairment services are:

- an intake service in the eye clinic and good joint working with ophthalmology;
- a service user group which meets six weekly; and
- deafblind communicators (10 in-house, with further service available from Deafblind Scotland).

The Council and the Health Board have agreed to establish 'aligned budgets', although 'pooled budgets' are anticipated in the future. A high-level joint management group has been established. A financial management group will identify the resources as part of aligned budgets. A fundamental redesign of services is being examined, including residential care homes for older people and sheltered housing.

3. Performance: Children and Families

Balance of care – Looked after children (aged 0-17)	1999-2000 actual	1999-2000 per 1,000	Quartile	2000-2001 actual	2000-2001 per 1,000	Quartile
At home	84	2.6	4	75	2.4	4
With friends/relatives/other community	33	1.0	2	33	1.0	2
With foster carers/prospective adopters	94	3.0	2	104	3.3	2
In residential accommodation	30	0.9	3	32	1.0	3
Total	**241**	**7.6**	**3**	**244**	**7.7**	**3**

Key performance indicators	1998-1999 actual	1998-1999 per 1,000	Quartile	1999-2000 actual	1999-2000 per 1,000	Quartile
Child protection (CP) referrals (aged 0-15)	420	14.8	1	259	9.1	2
Children subject to a CP case conference (aged 0-15)	30	1.1	4	49	1.7	4
Children placed on CP register (aged 0-15)	30	1.1	4	49	1.7	2
Adoption applications in year (aged 0-17)	8	0.3	4	4	0.1	4
Stranger adopter applications (aged 0-17)	3	0.1	3	4	0.1	4

The rate of looked after children is lower than in many other authorities. A fairly high rate of looked after children are living with foster carers. A Foster Carer Payment for Skills project has been introduced and the child care resources team is working to recruit and support more foster carers.

There is a relatively high rate of child protection referrals, but only a low rate proceed to a case conference. The number of referrals were particularly high in 1998-1999. The names of all the children who were subject to a case conference were placed on the child protection register in 1999-2000. The rate of children on the child protection register has increased significantly since 1998-1999. Rates of adoption applications are low.

The Council, in partnership with Barnardos, has set up the Cluaran project as a multi-disciplinary alternative to care placements. This provides an integrated service to reduce the risk of young persons being excluded from school and/or being accommodated.

A dedicated throughcare and aftercare team is in place to provide services for care leavers. It is anticipated that additional staff will be appointed to the team. The Council is designing a system to track and monitor young people's progress, and to monitor payment arrangements. Further progress has to be achieved in securing the active involvement of the voluntary sector.

The Council has put in place a joint monitoring group to monitor progress in implementing policy and assist in the co-ordination of services to looked after children. In addition, every school has a designated looked after children co-ordinator to maintain a register of looked after and accommodated pupils, and ensure that appropriate measures are in place for supporting the children.

4. Performance: Criminal Justice

Key Activities	1999-2000	2000-2001	2000-2001 per 10,000	Quartile
Number of social enquiry reports submitted to the courts during the year	599	609	59.4	3
Number of community service orders made during the year	129	134	13.1	3
The proportion of social enquiry reports reported to court within target time	2000-2001	Quartile		
Proportion of social enquiry reports submitted to the courts by due date	92.4	4		
The time taken to complete community service orders				
Average length of community service (hours) for orders completed during the year	169	1		
Average hours completed per week	4.1	2		

A relatively low rate of social enquiry reports was submitted during 2000-2001 and a lower proportion was submitted to courts by the due date than in most other authorities. A relatively low rate of community service orders was made in the year. The average length of orders was longer than in many other authorities, but the orders were completed relatively quickly.

The Council is part of the Forth Valley criminal justice grouping, which includes Stirling and Clackmannanshire. The grouping has formalised the joint working already taking place between the authorities. Each council has its own IT system but management information is integrated across all three. The Falkirk system is geared towards providing management information but allows for case notes to be entered directly by staff. The IT that supports community service is more developed, tracking the progress of orders and generating reports to assist in supervision.

The quality of statutory reports is monitored through routine sampling. The last year has seen a 42% increase in the use of probation – believed related to an escalating drug problem – whilst the use of community service has stayed constant.

Procedures are in place to allow 16-18 year olds to be dealt with flexibly, either by the children and families teams or by the criminal justice team. Wherever possible young people are diverted away from the criminal justice system: capacity to do this has been extended by the Connect Project, which since autumn 2001, has provided services for young people who offend or have become involved in substance misuse, and for their carers and parents. It uses a multi-disciplinary approach, bringing together secondees from nursing, community education, social work, and housing services. Assistance offered includes providing information, support and programmes delivered to families and groups, including programmes exclusively for young women.

5. Finance

Service Area (£000)	GAE 1999-2000	Final net Out turn 1999-2000	GAE 2000-2001	Final net Out turn 2000-2001
Children's Services	£5,561	£9,263	£5,683	£10,239
Community Care	£21,153	£19,040	£22,356	£19,585
Adult Offenders		-£26		-£90
Other SW Services	£2,720	£2,627	£2,756	£2,640
Total	**£29,435**	**£30,904**	**£30,795**	**£32,375**
Spend per head		**1999-2000**		**2000-2001**
Spend per head		£214.13		£224.32
Quartile		3		3

Criminal Justice services receive funding from the Scottish Executive, £969,250 was provided in 2000-2001.

Spending on children's services is significantly higher than GAE. Community care expenditure has been consistently lower than GAE. Spend per head on social work services is relatively low.

6. Staffing

Staff	WTE 1999 actual	WTE 1999 per 1,000	Quartile 1999	WTE 2000 actual	WTE 2000 per 1,000	Quartile 2000
Managers & central staff	85	0.6	2	99	0.7	2
Frontline staff	650	4.5	2	706	4.9	2
Other	148	1.0	3	130	0.9	3
Total	**884**	**6.1**	**3**	**935**	**6.5**	**2**

Vacancies	Vacancies 2000	% Vacancies 2000	% Vacancies 2000 Scotland	Vacancies 2001	% Vacancies 2001	% Vacancies 2001 Scotland
SWs with adults	1	2.6	7.8	7	12.8	10.9
SWs with children	4	6.0	7.4	6	10.6	10.7
SWs with offenders	0	0	7.5	2	11.0	7.2
Generic workers	0	0	8.0	0	0	12.7
Total	**5**	**4.1**	**7.7**	**15**	**11.6**	**10.5**

The Council has an overall lower rate of staff than many other authorities, although total numbers increased between 1999 and 2000. Vacancy levels are fairly close to the Scottish average. Criminal justice was affected by posts being kept vacant to cope with a possible influx of workers deployed in prison social work service, but this has now been resolved. The most acute pressure is now within community-based children and families teams, unavoidably compounded by significant change in the management team. In January 2002 there were 10 vacancies in childcare.

Recruitment and retention are reviewed every three months by the department management team. Since student placements are an effective way of recruiting newly qualified social workers, the Council provides a disproportionate and significant number of practice teaching placements. It is examining the possibility of a traineeship scheme, enabling unqualified social care staff to become qualified through full-time or part-time courses.

Major emphasis is placed on staff development. This includes support for post-qualifying staff development, assisting staff through child protection, criminal justice, social work management, mental health officer and PQ1 programmes. Pressure on qualified staff is being addressed flexibly through the use of social work assistant posts and an increased use of administrative staff. The Council has concentrated on marketing its reputation as a good employer with flexible and improved employment conditions.

7. Modernising services

The Council has a corporate approach to the development of a Race Equality Scheme, taking full account of the resource implications, particularly in relation to education policy, but to a lesser extent to housing and social work. The Council's Race Equality Advisory Forum has started to audit procedures and practices within the Council.

As a partner in Central Scotland's Racist Attacks and Harassment Strategy Group, the Council is enhancing translation and interpreting services, and it produced guidelines in 2001 for staff who were communicating with ethnic minority communities and people with a sensory impairment.

There is a Modernising Government funded Citizen Focus project, organised around a known high use of the phone to contact Council staff, and a network of one-stop shops. 8-10% of customer contact is online. The next phase is to include division of routine enquiries from the specialist or professional tasks.

Client information systems have been completely re-designed and have the capacity to link with health for single shared assessment.

8. The Future

After the best value review and the redevelopment of the home care service the Council has a sound basis for planning and implementing progressive improvement of home care to meeting the developing needs and numbers of older people.

The Council should follow up the progress already made in learning disability services by determining the criteria for introducing direct payments.

The effectiveness of the integrated mental health teams would be enhanced by closer working links with education services.

In order to enable single shared assessment to work to its full potential for service users, the Council and its health partners should establish arrangements to allow assessors to access resources directly across agency boundaries.

Agreed information requirements and information-sharing protocols are crucial to developing joint services. The Council and its partners should agree and implement protocols – particularly for different aspects of community care – as soon as practicable.

Training and support for social work staff expected to use IT systems is essential if the benefits of using new technology are to be secured for improvements in services.

To ensure further progress is made in improving the education of looked after children, the council should:

- ensure there is a standard format for all care plans, based on assessments which include suitable educational targets;
- link information systems so that information can be shared;
- put in place quality assurance systems;
- complete audits of educational environments; and
- finalise a joint social work and education policy for looked after and accommodated children.

1. Profile at 2002

With a population of 350,400 Fife has the third highest population of all Scottish local authorities.

Numbers of children are expected to fall by 2016, as is the proportion of working age population, but numbers of older people are set to increase at a faster than average rate.

At 5.1% (January 2002) the unemployment rate is above that of the Scottish average. The rate has increased since 2000.

Fife has a lower than average rate of problem drug misuse (1.5% of 15-54 year olds).

The crime rate is below average (788 crimes recorded per 10,000 population in 2001).

Community planning encompasses all the major public, private and voluntary agencies in Fife. The development of strategic partnerships and the assumption of responsibility for cross-cutting issues underpin the community plan.

Social Work is part of the Adult and Children Sector in Fife Council, alongside Education, Housing and Community Services. Social work has its own head of service, who is also chief social work officer.

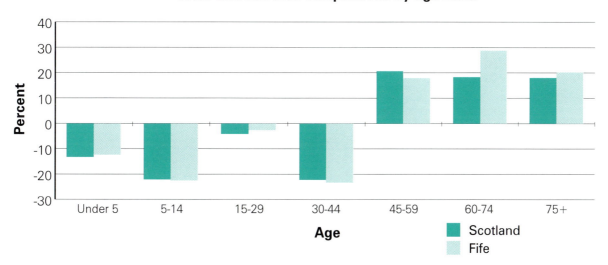

Expected % change in population, 2000-2016, local and national comparisons by age band

2. Performance: Community Care

Balance of care (aged 65+)	1999 actual	1999 per 1,000	Quartile	2000 actual	2000 per 1,000	Quartile
Older people in residential care homes	881	16	3	881	16	3
Older people in private nursing homes	1,218	22	3	1,213	22	3
Older people receiving home care	6,375	115	1	5,486	99	1
Older people in special needs housing	4,820	87.3	3	4,993	89.8	3
People receiving a community care service	**1999-2000 actual**	**1999-2000 per 1,000**	**Quartile**	**2000-2001 actual**	**2000-2001 per 1,000**	**Quartile**
Older people (aged 65+)	14,673	263.9	1	14,640	263.3	2
For mental health problems/dementia (aged 18-64)	822	3.8	2	807	3.7	3
For physical disabilities (aged 18-64)	3,048	14.1	2	2,849	13.2	2
For learning disabilities (aged 18-64)	1,026	4.7	1	965	4.5	1
For drug/alcohol abuse problems (aged 18-64)	145	0.7	2	176	0.8	3

The rates of older people living in residential or nursing homes or in special needs housing are relatively low. Although Fife provides home care services to more older people than most other authorities, it provides fewer hours per week than many others. Some of its services, for example, shopping delivery and meals on wheels are provided without using home carers.

The Council has made a number of changes by investing in:

- improvements in home care services, in equipment and in adaptations;
- more nursing home places; and
- (in collaboration with the health board) integrated response teams, which have begun to have an impact on the relatively high numbers of older people unable to be discharged from hospital.

The Oakley integrated team is a pilot project designed to enhance the care provided by home carers, to assist with hospital discharges and avoid the need for admissions. Trained home carers provide the service and are supported by nursing staff to deal with problems such as eye care, dermatology, sensory loss, continence and dementia. Professional nursing staff can concentrate on higher-level tasks. The project evaluation has confirmed that key objectives have been achieved and older people now have the kind of service they want. In addition, the work of home carers is now more highly valued and they manage personal care tasks with greater confidence.

Learning disability services are underpinned by a Partnership in Practice Agreement (PiP) between the Council and the NHS and by joint decision-making on the allocation of Change Fund resources. Responsibility for implementing the review of services for people with learning disabilities, 'The same as you?' rests with senior managers from social work and from Fife NHS. People with learning disabilities and their families are well engaged in planning and implementation, through stakeholder conferences, membership of all 11 implementation groups, and employment in the implementation project (SAY project). Fifteen people with learning disabilities receive direct payments to pay for their own services.

Through a partnership between the Council and Fife College, the services of the Woodlands Day Centre are to be relocated to 10 community bases across West Fife, with opportunities for college attendance and jobs. Local area co-ordinators are to be appointed to work with people with learning disabilities and their families within their local communities.

Under a joint strategy for mental health services three area redesign teams, involving the Council, health, independent sector providers, users and carers, lead the development of services. They support GP practices and tertiary services, and develop co-ordinated local mental health teams. There is a joint training programme in place to support the implementation of the Adults with Incapacity (Scotland) Act 2000.

A single shared assessment tool is ready to pilot. The development of processes is well under way but ways of integrating specialist inputs have yet to be concluded. An information-sharing protocol has yet to be completed.

A joint working group on sensory impairment with social work, education, health and voluntary sector representation is central to taking forward the recommendations of Sensing Progress. Voluntary organisations work alongside social work and health services to provide a one-stop shop, "Fife Sensory Impairment Centre", for people with a sensory impairment. The RNIB, in partnership with Fife Society for the Blind and the Council, have set up a facility within the new centre for people with a learning disability who have a sensory impairment.

Annual multi-disciplinary panels for all children with a sensory loss are led by the education service. Social work has commissioned the RNIB pathways unit in the centre to provide 20 sessions a week to young people with a learning disability and a visual impairment who are leaving school.

With its commitment to community planning, the Council is strongly placed to develop the Joint Future agenda. There are already many practical examples of joint working. The Council and its health partners are working towards the Bottom Line. They have discussed but not yet agreed the joint management structures and joint resourcing pot. They are exploring how to assimilate existing locality based joint teams into an integrated service management structure, with devolved budgets and providing access to services across the sector at their heart.

On single shared assessment, a local tool is ready to pilot. The development of processes is well under way but ways of integrating specialist inputs have yet to be concluded. An information sharing protocol has yet to be completed.

3. Performance: Children and Families

Balance of care – Looked after children (aged 0-17)	1999-2000 actual	1999-2000 per 1,000	Quartile	2000-2001 actual	2000-2001 per 1,000	Quartile
At home	148	1.9	4	126	1.6	4
With friends/relatives/other community	65	0.8	3	70	0.9	2
With foster carers/prospective adopters	164	2.1	3	198	2.5	3
In residential accommodation	51	0.7	4	63	0.8	4
Total	**428**	**5.5**	**4**	**457**	**5.8**	**4**

Key performance indicators	1998-1999 actual	1998-1999 per 1,000	Quartile	1999-2000 actual	1999-2000 per 1,000	Quartile
Child protection (CP) referrals (aged 0-15)	481	6.9	3	485	7.0	3
Children subject to a CP case conference (aged 0-15)	135	1.9	3	143	2.1	3
Children placed on CP register (aged 0-15)	101	1.5	3	97	1.4	3
Adoption applications in year (aged 0-17)	51	0.6	1	32	0.4	2
Stranger adopter applications (aged 0-17)	16	0.2	2	15	0.2	2

The rate of children who are looked after is low compared to most other authorities, although numbers have increased. The rate of looked after children living with foster carers is fairly low, but did increase between 1999 and 2001. Though the number of children living in residential accommodation increased recently, the rate remains low compared to most other authorities.

Rates of child protection referrals, of children subject to a case conference and of children on the child protection register are all relatively low. The number of adoption applications is relatively high.

After a former Fife Regional Council employee was convicted of sexual abuse the Council commissioned an independent inquiry. Its report made recommendations – heavily influenced by the views of the survivors – about the safety and well being of children looked after away from home. The Council has implemented the recommendations in its own residential homes, to improve children's safety and quality of care.

The Council has implemented the main recommendations of *Learning with Care* to improve the education of looked after children. A self-evaluation protocol has been developed and piloted for assessing whether residential units provide an educationally rich environment. Further progress needs to be achieved in adjusting information systems so that information can be shared; and in issuing a joint circular setting out educational targets and arrangements for monitoring progress.

The Council has made its management arrangements for its services for care leavers, and a working group with representatives from key agencies is to help with implementation. Fife has made some investment to allow it to look at the shape of future throughcare services corporately which takes account of new responsibilities and young people are being consulted by Who Cares? about future needs and services.

In a move to integrate children's services Fife Council has established a Children's committee. A recent HMI report commented that the Education Service had made good progress in promoting joint working with other services, particularly Social Work. The quality and range of support for pupils with special educational needs was said to be a strong feature.

4. Performance: Criminal Justice

Key Activities	1999-2000	2000-2001	2000-2001 per 10,000	Quartile
Number of social enquiry reports submitted to the courts during the year	1,891	1,836	75.1	3
Number of community service orders made during the year	331	306	12.5	3
The proportion of social enquiry reports reported to court within target time	2000-2001	Quartile		
Proportion of social enquiry reports submitted to the courts by due date	96.3	3		
The time taken to complete community service orders				
Average length of community service (hours) for orders completed during the year	154	2		
Average hours completed per week	3.7	3		

The rate of social enquiry reports submitted to courts was relatively low in 2000-2001; the proportion of reports which were submitted by the due date was lower than in many other authorities. The rate of community service orders made was also relatively low. The average length of hours for orders was relatively long and they took longer to complete than in many other authorities.

The Council has systems in place to monitor the performance of its criminal justice service and adherence to national standards. It has recently appointed a planning and performance officer, and intends to:

- improve co-ordination of information;
- use the LSI-R risk assessment tool to monitor change in offender characteristics and evaluate the impact of its services;
- provide all workers with feedback on their performance; and
- develop a database to capture information from the risk assessment framework, so that risk analysis can be monitored.

The Council has established a specialist project to work with sexually aggressive young people. It has two specialist workers located within the community protection team and managed jointly by the criminal justice and children and families services. It provides joint risk assessment with the police and develops personal change programmes for the young people, based on good practice in Scotland and abroad.

As one of two pilot sites in Scotland, the Drug Treatment and Testing Team is being externally evaluated in order to help inform the future of the Drug Treatment and Testing Order.

5. Finance

Service Area (£000)	GAE 1999-2000	Final net Out turn 1999-2000	GAE 2000-2001	Final net Out turn 2000-2001
Children's Services	£12,549	£11,333	£12,855	£11,880
Community Care	£54,898	£54,964	£57,825	£53,607
Adult Offenders		£171		£247
Other SW Services	£6,714	£7,347	£6,777	£7,603
Total	**£74,161**	**£73,814**	**£77,457**	**£73,337**

Spend per head		1999-2000		2000-2001
Spend per head		£210.65		£209.29
Quartile		3		4

Funding for criminal justice services comes direct from the Scottish Executive and amounted to £3,088,130 in 2000-2001.

All social work expenditure, including that on children's services, was below GAE in 2000-2001. A significant increase in high cost placements has put pressure on the children and families budget. Spend per head on social work services is comparatively low and decreased between 1999 and 2001.

6. Staffing

Staff	WTE 1999 actual	WTE 1999 per 1,000	Quartile 1999	WTE 2000 actual	WTE 2000 per 1,000	Quartile 2000
Managers & central staff	193	0.6	2	224	0.6	3
Frontline staff	1,918	5.5	2	1,922	5.5	2
Other	512	1.5	2	443	1.3	2
Total	**2,622**	**7.5**	**1**	**2,589**	**7.4**	**2**

Vacancies	Vacancies 2000	% Vacancies 2000	% Vacancies 2000 Scotland	Vacancies 2001	% Vacancies 2001	% Vacancies 2001 Scotland
SWs with adults	4	4.8	7.8	21	19.5	10.9
SWs with children	0	0	7.4	14	14.3	10.7
SWs with offenders	6	11.2	7.5	4	7.0	7.2
Generic workers	3	18.2	8.0	0	0	12.7
Total	**13**	**5.4**	**7.7**	**39**	**13.8**	**10.5**

Fife has a relatively high rate of staff. The number of managers and central staff has increased but the rate of such staff remains relatively low. Vacancy levels are above the Scottish average and are especially high in community care and children's services. The Council has recently had to undertake multiple advertising to attract middle managers and centre managers.

The main focus is on staff retention. A comprehensive workforce strategy confirms the importance of induction, individual learning, and health and safety for all staff. There are also examples of job enhancement- piloting of specially trained homecare staff who can undertake some of the work of auxiliary nurses, thus freeing up nurse time and reducing the number of staff going into clients' homes.

7. Modernising services

Fife has significant Asian and Chinese populations, and in addition the Council has a commitment to support up to 100 families seeking asylum. Experience in working with different communities has promoted an awareness of the extensive work necessary to engage with and provide culturally sensitive services. A race equality strategy for health and social care was put in place late in 2001. When implemented, the strategy should meet the requirements of a Race Equality Scheme.

A developing framework of information systems embraces a range of corporate and social work service initiatives. Social work is participating in a Council-wide Modernising Government funded project to address the information needs of older people. The existing social work information system will be replaced by the end of 2002 by a new system designed to serve the business needs of different social work staff, particularly practitioners. The Council plans to help children and young people gain ICT skills. The eMPOWER project focuses on educational, recreational and therapeutic uses of IT.

The new systems will interface with both health and education systems, although practical links can be established only when agreement is reached on information-sharing.

8. The Future

Joint working is well established between social work, health and education, to promote the interests of both adults and children. Wider practical benefits should follow, once the parties conclude an agreement about information sharing.

The Council and its health partners need to build on the progress to date and agree joint management arrangements, the resource pot and arrangements for integrated service management, and a firm implementation plan.

Similarly, they will want to agree outstanding aspects of the single shared assessment agenda, and agree an implementation plan for full application next April.

To complement the progress made in improving the education of looked after children, the Council needs to:

- secure full-time educational places for children in residential units;
- prepare and issue a joint circular on educational targets and arrangements for monitoring progress; and
- adjust and align databases so that information can be shared.

In operating its own criminal justice services, the Council has set itself a testing agenda for improvement and should bring within a single implementation plan the extensive work required on information co-ordination, assessment of services and risk analysis.

1. Profile at 2002

With 609,400 people Glasgow has the largest urban population of all Scottish local authorities. Whilst the total population is declining at a greater rate than the Scottish average, the 45-59 population is projected to increase substantially.

At 5.9% (January 2002) unemployment is high, though it has decreased by 10.4% over the last ten years - much faster than the fall for Scotland as a whole. However, the employment rate has only risen by 1% in Glasgow over that period compared with a 10% rise in Scotland as a whole.

The 1991 census showed that Glasgow had the second highest rate of households with no earner in the UK. The incidence of deprivation is very high in Glasgow which impacts heavily on social work services. For example, 52 of the 90 most deprived postcode areas in Scotland are in Glasgow. 42.3% of Glaswegian school children receive free school meals compared with a Scottish average of 20.3%.

In Glasgow the prevalence of problematic drug misuse is nearly twice that of Scotland as a whole (3.8% compared with 2% of the adult population). The estimated 55,800 problematic drug misusers in Glasgow represents 24.7% of the Scottish total.

1,398 crimes were recorded by the police per 10,000 of the population in 2001. Although the rate has fallen since 2000, it is the highest recorded in Scotland.

The Director heads the Department of Social Work, with a chief social work officer at depute level exercising professional social work responsibilities. The director is part of the Strategic Management Team of the City Council.

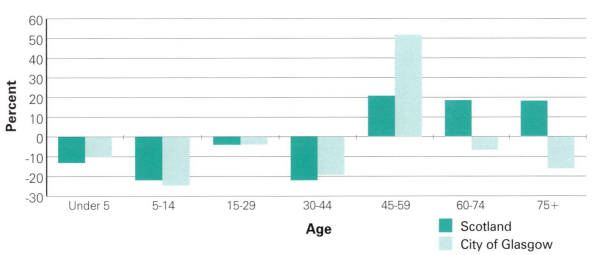

Expected % change in population, 2000-2016, local and national comparisons by age band

2. Performance: Community Care

Balance of care (aged 65+)	1999 actual	1999 per 1,000	Quartile	2000 actual	2000 per 1,000	Quartile
Older people in residential care homes	1,711	19	2	1,601	18	2
Older people in private nursing homes	2,594	29	2	2,524	28	1
Older people receiving home care	8,283	91	2	8,326	93	1
Older people in special needs housing	18,473	203.7	1	17,758	198.6	1
People receiving a community care service	**1999-2000 actual**	**1999-2000 per 1,000**	**Quartile**	**2000-2001 actual**	**2000-2001 per 1,000**	**Quartile**
Older people (aged 65+)	14,314	160	3	23,046	254.2	2
For mental health problems/dementia (aged 18-64)	2,444	6.3	1	2,267	5.8	1
For physical disabilities (aged 18-64)	5,921	15.2	2	8,570	22.1	1
For learning disabilities (aged 18-64)	1,814	4.7	1	1,658	4.3	2
For drug/alcohol abuse problems (aged 18-64)	4,017	10.3	1	4,349	11.2	1

Between 1999 and 2001 the number of older people receiving a community care service climbed steeply; the number has almost doubled since 1998-1999. The rate of older people living in residential accommodation is relatively high but has reduced since 1999. Rates of older people in nursing homes, in special needs housing and receiving home care are higher than in many other authorities.

In relation to hospital discharge, since 1999, hospital nursing staff have been able to order home care directly. Home care services are now constructed to meet more evenly the needs of older people in terms of both personal and enhanced care. A joint equipment store, with the Primary Care Trust, has been established. Proposals for a unified occupational therapy service across Health and Social Work Services are well advanced.

Close joint working across all Community Care client groups is evident. In Learning Disability Services, single management arrangements have been established, single service arrangements have been developed and aligned budgets are in place. Lennox Castle Hospital has been closed within the agreed timescale and all residents have been resettled in the community. A major review of day services has been completed and new service arrangements based on integrated care management teams have been set up.

In Mental Health, single commissioning arrangements have been established under a joint commissioning manager. Proposals are under consideration to develop an integrated mental health network at a locality level across health and social care. This includes developing new primary care services with LHCCs.

In Addiction Services, a major review of provided services has been concluded and addiction teams have been established as a core element of every Social Work Services Area Team. In addition proposals have been agreed to develop new joint community addiction teams in each locality, involving clinical and nursing staff with Social Work Addiction Staff. Single management arrangements across all addiction services are currently being considered.

In relation to Homeless People, a new Homelessness Partnership has been established involving Social Work, Health, Housing and the voluntary sector under the management of a single programme manager. Plans have been developed to close large-scale homeless hostels and to develop a range of community based support services.

In relation to Older People, Social Work Services are well advanced in the adoption and implementation of a Single Shared Assessment based on Carenap E. The planning partners, have set out within the Interim Partnership Agreement, a programme to meet the 'Bottom Line' agenda for Older People and other Community Care client groups."

There has been a large increase in the number of people in Glasgow who are receiving a community care service for physical disabilities. The number doubled between 1998 and 2000.

A Sensory Impairment Planning and Implementation Group – led by social work and including representatives from health, education, housing, the voluntary sector and users – develops and implements improvements in sensory impairment.

The Council has sought to enhance awareness training on visual impairment for social work staff. Similar work on hearing impairment is at a design stage. The Council supports a comprehensive Guide Communicator Service for Deafblind People.

The Council has moved significantly towards joint resourcing and joint management with health. Early in 2002 a Joint Community Care Committee was established with a remit to address integrated decision-making and service delivery. The joint resourcing pot is to be considered across the full range of community-based health and social care services, rather than looking solely at older people.

3. Performance: Children and Families

Balance of care – Looked after children (aged 0-17)	1999-2000 actual	1999-2000 per 1,000	Quartile	2000-2001 actual	2000-2001 per 1,000	Quartile
At home	1,113	8.5	1	1,181	9.0	1
With friends/relatives/other community	370	2.8	1	256	2.0	1
With foster carers/prospective adopters	696	5.3	1	672	5.1	1
In residential accommodation	344	2.6	1	326	2.5	1
Total	**2,523**	**19.2**	**1**	**2,435**	**18.5**	**1**

Key performance indicators	1998-1999 actual	1998-1999 per 1,000	Quartile	1999-2000 actual	1999-2000 per 1,000	Quartile
Child protection (CP) referrals (aged 0-15)	685	5.8	3	859	7.3	3
Children subject to a CP case conference (aged 0-15)	350	3.0	2	439	3.7	1
Children placed on CP register (aged 0-15)	250	2.1	3	313	2.7	1
Adoption applications in year (aged 0-17)	36	0.3	3	40	0.3	3
Stranger adopter applications (aged 0-17)	17	0.1	3	26	0.2	2

The rate of looked after children is significantly higher than in most authorities being in the top quartile in every category. High rates are living with foster carers and in residential accommodation. Over the past year there has been a significant increase in those admitted to care placements for reasons of risk, including alcohol and drug misuse, lack of parental care, physical abuse and the mental health of the carer. More recently the numbers looked after have included children of asylum seekers. This brings with it additional challenges. Work is ongoing to ensure that the specific needs of thisgroup are met.

The rate of child protection referrals increased significantly between 1998 and 2000, but the referral rate is lower than in many other authorities. However, rates of children subject to a case conference and placed on the child protection register are high. The category showing the most significant increase is neglect. The number of stranger adoption applications increased significantly between 1998 and 2000.

The Council is using the Children Services Development Fund (CSDF) - together with funds from health and the Surestart programme to develop a wide range of services including:

- enhanced community support for looked after and vulnerable children and families;
- expansion of respite care arrangements and specialist fostering for children with complex needs;
- community and school based mental health developments; and
- extra care and support to the age of 18 and beyond for looked after children.

Following publication of *Learning with Care*, the Council has established a joint protocol for education and social work services to deal with the education of looked after children. It addresses the respective roles and responsibilities of parents, education and social work staff. The Council is working towards full implementation of the recommendations throughout 2002. Notwithstanding major shortages in qualified social workers, the Council has an action plan in place for ensuring that all looked after children have a care plan. This has not yet been achieved.

Glasgow has linked its social work and education information systems (CareFirst and SEEMIS) to access information about the education of looked after children. A joint Education/Social Work team provides in-school and in-home support to looked after children. A post within Social Work Services has a dedicated remit to monitor and evaluate progress in relation to the educational achievement of looked after children.

Preparations for the new arrangements for care leavers are well advanced. In a partnership which embraces accommodation, support, education, training and health services, a specialist leaving care team assesses all young people who are looked after and accommodated at 15 years of age.

The Council sees education and employment as key determinants of the future prospects of care leavers. A Council training scheme for care leavers, with 50 places a year, provides them with vocational training, such as in horticulture or building trades and the offer of an interview for a long term job with the relevant Council department.

The Council, alongside its joint planning partners in the NHS and other external agencies has developed effective planning structures for children's services. The Joint Strategy Group, which is a multi-agency forum set up to progress strategy and planning across the spectrum of children's needs as reflected in the Children's Services Plan, is accountable to the Council's Joint Education and Social Work Children's Services Sub-Committee.

4. Performance: Criminal Justice

Key Activities	1999-2000	2000-2001	2000-2001 per 10,000	Quartile
Number of social enquiry reports submitted to the courts during the year	6,564	6,176	142.4	1
Number of community service orders made during the year	1,012	1,044	24.1	1

The proportion of social enquiry reports reported to court within target time	2000-2001	Quartile		
Proportion of social enquiry reports submitted to the courts by due date	92.0	4		
The time taken to complete community service orders				
Average length of community service (hours) for orders completed during the year	163	2		
Average hours completed per week	5.0	2		

Glasgow submitted a high rate of social enquiry reports during 2000-2001, reflecting the high crime rate in the City. A lower proportion of reports are submitted to the courts in time than in many other authorities. A high rate of community service orders were made during 2000-2001. The average length of orders was fairly long but they were completed relatively quickly, with 5 hours completed on average per week.

Drug misuse is a major problem with the rate of misuse of heroin and cocaine, the highest in Scotland. A specialist drugs court has been established together with Drug Testing and Treatment Orders (DTTOs) to address some of the difficulties. However, these developments place considerable demands on criminal justice social work resources. The increasing use of methadone as drug of choice is an added complication. In order to ensure the social care support necessary to assist addicts, addiction staff are mainstreamed in each area team.

Quality assurance for the assessment and supervision of offenders has been enhanced by the introduction of a new electronic case management system, careJust. Staff use a structured risk assessment tool, Level of Service-Revised.

The Council has established youth justice teams in two pilot areas. Operating within the same management structure as children and families, and criminal justice area teams, they have been designed to work with young offenders in the children's hearing and adult court systems. The teams will work with 14-21 year olds who are involved in serious and persistent offending.

5. Finance

Service Area (£000)	GAE 1999-2000	Final net Out turn 1999-2000	GAE 2000-2001	Final net Out turn 2000-2001
Children's Services	£50,424	£53,071	£50,493	£57,531
Community Care	£108,050	£107,752	£113,368	£110,972
Adult Offenders		-£177		£290
Other SW Services	£13,331	£38,418	£13,465	£42,520
Total	**£171,805**	**£199,064**	**£177,327**	**£211,313**
Spend per head		**1999-2000**		**2000-2001**
Spend per head		£326.67		£346.77
Quartile		1		1

Criminal justice services are funded directly by the Scottish Executive, and Glasgow received £8,562,908 in 2000-2001.

Glasgow has spent 14% more than GAE on children's services. Spend per head on social work services is high.

The Council budgeted to spend over £215m on social work services in 2001-2002, in order to provide social work services in a city where poverty and deprivation has a major impact on the lives of many people who are already vulnerable. The consequences of drug misuse have an additional serious influence on services. The costs of addressing the misuse of drugs distort a budget that might otherwise be better focused on preventative services, particularly for younger children and their families.

During the past year the Department has reduced the number of its area social work teams from 17 to 9, which enabled savings of over £1m to be redirected to frontline services.

6. Staffing

Staff	WTE 1999 actual	WTE 1999 per 1,000	Quartile 1999	WTE 2000 actual	WTE 2000 per 1,000	Quartile 2000
Managers & central staff	491	0.8	1	458	0.8	2
Frontline staff	2,164	3.5	4	2,639	4.3	3
Other	1,353	2.2	1	1,178	1.9	1
Total	**4,008**	**6.6**	**2**	**4,275**	**7.0**	**2**

Vacancies	Vacancies 2000	% Vacancies 2000	% Vacancies 2000 Scotland	Vacancies 2001	% Vacancies 2001	% Vacancies 2001 Scotland
SWs with adults	24	14.6	7.8	57	18.7	10.9
SWs with children	6	6.5	7.4	40	13.0	10.7
SWs with offenders	12	8.6	7.5	10	8.6	7.2
Generic workers	24	5.5	8.0	13	16.5	12.7
Total	**65**	**8.0**	**7.7**	**120**	**14.9**	**10.5**

The Council has a relatively high rate of managers and central staff and a high rate of other staff. The rate of frontline staff increased from 1999 to 2000 but remains lower than in most other authorities.

Vacancy levels are high and have increased between 2000 and 2001. At end 2001, the Council had 15% vacancies among qualified social work staff in children and family services, compared to a vacancy rate of 6% in community care and no vacancies in criminal justice. This situation, which should be seen within the context of a national shortage, is attributed to:

- the particular and increasing demands on social workers working with vulnerable children;
- the drift of experienced practitioners into short-term targeted initiatives where pay is higher; and
- competition with other authorities.

In response, the social work department is to develop the progression of unqualified staff to become qualified social workers - a target of ten each year. The strategy assumes that the expanding social care workforce can be populated and trained from the wider workforce in Glasgow, with its above average unemployment.

Absence rates are persistently high, particularly among social care staff in residential homes. The department provides staff with a range of tailored support to return to work following sick leave, including reduced working hours, a phased return and lighter duties. New management arrangements and an investment in the homes are having a positive impact on sickness levels.

7. Modernising services

There is a high proportion of ethnic minority residents in Glasgow, especially people of Pakistani origin. Glasgow has also received some 8,000 asylum seekers in the last two years. The provision of an appropriate and sensitive service to asylum seekers presents challenges for social work staff, including the provision of a service to unaccompanied children.

The social work services' anti-racism action plan 2001-2004 addresses all the requirements of a Race Equality Scheme. The department seeks to embed its equality activity in all its operational arms, and to widen this approach to both different faiths and sectarianism.

The Council has developed a strong citizen focus with its £2million Modernising Government Fund initiative, which includes consultation for, and access by, people with learning disabilities; placing the sign language interpreter service online; and establishing video-conferencing facilities for translation and interpreting.

An ambitious range of work under the umbrella of CareFirst has and will continue to provide electronic support to staff for work with children, adults and offenders. The fruits of this work are becoming clear to frontline staff. Increasingly management information will be drawn from electronic records.

Implementation of careFirst developments is continuing with the aim of improving data quality, enhancing existing client group information and developing reporting frameworks to improve the measurement of activity and performance within the delivery of service. Significant investment in the Care First programme over the last 2 years has begun to yield signficant results. 2,500 staff have access and a link has been developed between careFirst and Seemis,the education database to inform on attendance and attainment for looked after children. The Service has also made substantial progress in the development and implementation of Access Glasgow projects including Phase one of the Access Centre: a customer access point using modern technology to speed up response to public enquiries and improve operational efficiency.

8. The Future

To maintain the impetus that has been achieved towards joint resourcing and joint management of community care services, the Council should now agree with the Health Board the joint resourcing pot for health and social care services to be implemented from 1 April 2003.

The Council and the Health Board should, through their joint strategic planning and commissioning mechanisms develop services for young people with mental health problems.

The single management arrangements, and aligned budgets which already exist in relation to services for people with a learning disability should be extended to services to people with mental health problems.

To consolidate the progress made so far in improving the education of looked after children, the Council should as a matter of urgency complete care plans for all those children. The Council should formulate joint development and training opportunities for education and care staff.

1. Profile at 2002

Highland occupies one third of the landmass of Scotland. It has a widely scattered population of 208,600.

The area faces a larger than average decline in the number of children and younger people and an above average increase in the proportion of households with pensioners; an increase of 34% in the older population is forecast.

The unemployment level has fallen but at 4.5% (January 2002) is above the national average.

Highland has a low rate of drugs misuse (0.9% of 15-54 year olds).

The crime rate is low (578 crimes recorded per 10,000 population in 2001).

Highland Council's Corporate Plan outlines key themes of community planning with partners in the Highland Well-being Alliance. The plan emphasises the importance of local planning and delivery of services from within the 8 distinct geographical areas covered by the Council.

Housing and Social Work Services report to the same strategic committee. There are Social Work Committees for each of the 8 areas. Social work services are provided through a dedicated department, under a director who is also the chief social work officer.

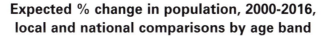

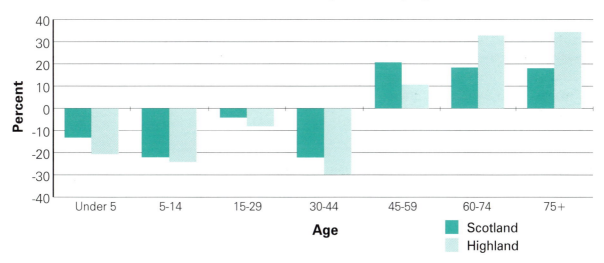

2. Performance: Community Care

Balance of care (aged 65+)	1999 actual	1999 per 1,000	Quartile	2000 actual	2000 per 1,000	Quartile
Older people in residential care homes	837	25	1	779	23	1
Older people in private nursing homes	882	27	2	839	25	2
Older people receiving home care	2,604	78	2	2,539	76	2
Older people in special needs housing	2,111	63.6	4	1,443	43	4

People receiving a community care service	1999-2000 actual	1999-2000 per 1,000	Quartile	2000-2001 actual	2000-2001 per 1,000	Quartile
Older people (aged 65+)	4,433	132.1	4	5,955	177.5	3
For mental health problems/dementia (aged 18-64)	517	4.1	2	556	4.4	2
For physical disabilities (aged 18-64)	779	6.1	4	813	6.4	4
For learning disabilities (aged 18-64)	520	4.1	2	724	5.7	1
For drug/alcohol abuse problems (aged 18-64)	65	0.5	3	71	0.6	3

The rate of older people receiving a community care service is low, in comparison to many other authorities, though it increased between 1999 and 2001. The numbers of older people in residential or nursing homes is falling but rates remain relatively high. The rate of older people in special needs housing is low and has fallen significantly between 1999 and 2000. Older people in Highland are as likely to receive home care support as elsewhere in Scotland but the intensity of support available per week is less than in other parts of Scotland.

The balance of care is relatively weighted towards residential provision. Following a strategic review of community services for older people commissioned jointly with NHS Highland, an interim report (spring 2002) recommended a shift of resources away from residential care. The Council decided to:

- implement developments in the home care service as a priority;
- appoint a development manager;
- formulate a training strategy; and
- introduce guaranteed hours.

Increased joint working with health has produced:

- a Rapid Response Team of social work, occupational therapy and physiotherapy professionals working together with support staff and carers, which provides assessment, intensive rehabilitation and home care support for up to 28 days; it takes referrals directly from GPs, hospitals and social work staff;
- a joint occupational therapy store; and
- community rehabilitation teams.

A Partnership in Practice (PiP) agreement underpins improvements in services for people with a learning disability and to date progress includes:

- development of a learning disability database;
- appointment of local area co-ordinators;
- use of direct payments; and
- appointment of review officers for people with a learning disability, to ensure individuals needs are being met.

Organised joint working between health and social care staff is focused on a pilot community learning disability team in Ross and Cromarty.

The Council and NHS Highland have developed an action plan to implement the mental health framework formulated with the help of the Mental Health and Well Being Support Group. In Ross and Cromarty a joint community mental health team has been established to support people with a severe and enduring mental illness. The team, which has a single manager, is developing joint recording and single assessment.

The implementation of single shared assessment for all community care groups is underway. A bespoke generic core assessment tool has been developed and training for health, social work and housing practitioners is being delivered from September 2002.

There are multi-agency links for services for people with a hearing impairment, but no similar arrangements are in place for people with a visual impairment. The Council has plans for a sensory impairment resource centre, based at Raigmore Hospital, to create an opportunity for a multi-agency partnership for both visually and hearing impaired people.

The Council and the Health Board have commissioned a new deaf communication service. For people who are deafblind the Council commissions supported accommodation run by Sense (Scotland) and guide/communicators provided by Deafblind Scotland.

A Joint Committee for Action in Community Care has appointed a Joint Future Implementation Manager and, on the advice of a task group, has decided to align rather than pool budgets for older people. From spring 2002 health and social work staff responsibilities at local management level were aligned, as an interim step to integration of management at area level.

3. Performance: Children and Families

Balance of care – Looked after children (aged 0-17)	1999-2000 actual	1999-2000 per 1,000	Quartile	2000-2001 actual	2000-2001 per 1,000	Quartile
At home	163	3.4	3	138	2.9	3
With friends/relatives/other community	50	1.1	2	74	1.6	1
With foster carers/prospective adopters	123	2.6	2	120	2.5	3
In residential accommodation	55	1.2	2	57	1.2	2
Total	**391**	**8.2**	**2**	**389**	**8.1**	**3**

Key performance indicators	1998-1999 actual	1998-1999 per 1,000	Quartile	1999-2000 actual	1999-2000 per 1,000	Quartile
Child protection (CP) referrals (aged 0-15)	354	8.3	2	431	10.2	1
Children subject to a CP case conference (aged 0-15)	252	6.0	1	231	5.5	1
Children placed on CP register (aged 0-15)	176	4.1	1	175	4.1	1
Adoption applications in year (aged 0-17)	21	0.4	2	15	0.3	3
Stranger adopter applications (aged 0-17)	10	0.2	2	8	0.2	3

The overall rate of looked after children is now fairly low. A relatively low rate live with foster carers and a relatively high rate are in residential accommodation. The rate living with friends or relatives is high, having increased between 1999 and 2001.

Highland has a high rate of child protection referrals and a high rate of children are subject to a case conference and have their names placed on the child protection register. This has been recognised by the Director of Social Work and the Child Protection Committee. Plans are underway to commission an independent review of trends in registration and associated practice. The rate of adoption applications is fairly low. A programme of training in permanence planning is being rolled out for all social workers, and management monitoring of permanence cases has been implemented.

The Council has published policies and procedures for the education of looked after children and has allocated resources for this aspect of service. Progress has been made in meeting the *Learning with Care* recommendations relating to:

- multi-disciplinary assessment;
- care planning;
- quality assurance;
- full-time education; and
- individual educational targets.

Following an audit of residential units, the Council has consulted each looked after and accommodated child and provided IT and other educational equipment in these units.

Highland Council has had 2 new community school pilot projects (at Inverness and Alness) designed to bring together education, social work and health services under an Integration Manager. The projects have enabled staff to train together, improved focus on individual pupils and their parents and addressed the needs of the wider communities served by the schools.

There is commitment to a major initiative in adopting the New Community School approach in all Highland Schools and this is aligned to a Family support Policy aimed at early intervention with families and young people. This programme is the key mechanism for delivery of an integrated service to children and families on a multi-agency basis and significant effort has been expended towards that aim.

The Council's action plan for the new arrangements for care leavers is implemented and co-ordinated by the social work department. A joint working group of Council departments and external agencies is:

- designing a system to operate and monitor new payment arrangements;
- organising a programme of joint staff training; and
- preparing a pooled budget in anticipation of Scottish Executive guidance on resource transfer.

A senior social worker for Throughcare and Aftercare has been appointed with the aim of developing the infrastructure for Throughcare and Aftercare services throughout Highland. The council is currently supporting four young people who were looked after through Higher Education.

A Committee on Children and Young People, representing key public and voluntary sector agencies, has the responsibility for integrating services. The Committee's 2001-2004 plan outlines objectives for improving services, including roll out of the New Community School Approach. Each of Highland's 8 areas has a Children's Services Forum, which bring together area managers from education, social work and health, provide means of integrating assessment, care planning and use of resources.

4. Performance: Criminal Justice

Key Activities	1999-2000	2000-2001	2000-2001 per 10,000	Quartile
Number of social enquiry reports submitted to the courts during the year	874	953	65.8	3
Number of community service orders made during the year	226	221	15.2	3
The proportion of social enquiry reports reported to court within target time	2000-2001	Quartile		
Proportion of social enquiry reports submitted to the courts by due date	98.2	2		
The time taken to complete community service orders				
Average length of community service (hours) for orders completed during the year	159	2		
Average hours completed per week	3.7	3		

A relatively low rate of social enquiry reports was submitted to courts in 2000-2001. A high proportion of reports was submitted by the due date. The rate of community service orders made was also relatively low. The average length of orders was longer and they took longer to complete, compared with other authorities.

Highland is part of the Northern Partnership which includes Aberdeenshire, Aberdeen City and Moray. Highland's criminal justice service has recently undergone fundamental reorganisation aimed at linking strategy and operations more closely.

The Northern Partnership is one of the three Pathfinder projects developed as part of the Getting Best Results initiative which aims to integrate quality and effectiveness across all four organisations. The partners have established a series of professional practice groups to consider how quality can be achieved and evidenced, and are currently assessing potential quality assurance structures. The use of the level of service inventory and the Scottish Executive risk assessment framework will allow all the councils to gather outcome-based information.

The Northern Partnership Provider project, established under the Scottish Executive's Getting Best Results Initiative, is designed to improve the quality of criminal justice social work delivery, with emphasis on quality assurance. A quality assurance tool has been developed which is now used across the Partnership. Practice development groups are producing common practice and protocols across the Partnership.

5. Finance

Service Area (£000)	GAE 1999-2000	Final net Out turn 1999-2000	GAE 2000-2001	Final net Out turn 2000-2001
Children's Services	£6,054	£6,405	£6,056	£5,604
Community Care	£30,769	£30,446	£32,152	£32,628
Adult Offenders		£87		£1,589
Other SW Services	£3,882	£8,489	£3,897	£9,054
Total	**£40,705**	**£45,427**	**£42,105**	**£48,875**
Spend per head		1999-2000		2000-2001
Spend per head		£217.77		£234.30
Quartile		3		2

Funding for criminal justice services is paid directly by the Scottish Executive and it amounted to £1,632,244 in 2000-2001.

Unlike most other authorities, the Council spent below GAE in 2000-2001 on children's services but over GAE on other social work services. Spend per head on social work services is relatively high.

6. Staffing

Staff	WTE 1999 actual	WTE 1999 per 1,000	Quartile 1999	WTE 2000 actual	WTE 2000 per 1,000	Quartile 2000
Managers & central staff	98	0.5	3	121	0.6	3
Frontline staff	854	4.1	3	637	3.1	4
Other	280	1.3	2	294	1.4	1
Total	**1,233**	**5.9**	**3**	**1,052**	**5.0**	**4**

Vacancies	Vacancies 2000	% Vacancies 2000	% Vacancies 2000 Scotland	Vacancies 2001	% Vacancies 2001	% Vacancies 2001 Scotland
SWs with adults	5	15.4	7.8	5	6.9	10.9
SWs with children	4	6.4	7.4	8	9.2	10.7
SWs with offenders	2	9.0	7.5	3	18.2	7.2
Generic workers	9	11.7	8.0	3	16.2	12.7
Total	**19**	**10.6**	**7.7**	**18**	**9.9**	**10.5**

The total rate of staff is low compared to other authorities, having dropped between 1999 and 2000. The rate of managers and central staff has increased, but still remains low. The rate of frontline staff has decreased significantly. The total level of staff vacancies is a little below average, but the level is higher than average in criminal justice services.

Social care facilities support the survival of local communities by providing employment as well as key services. Recruitment and retention present problems. Highland has experienced increased difficulty in recruiting qualified social workers over the last year. This has been compounded by the significant effect of experienced staff moving into fixed-term projects on secondment. On the other hand, there has been less difficulty in recruiting managers. In addition:

- Highland has no training establishment to attract new blood; and
- there are serious difficulties in attracting home care staff and occupational therapists.

Previously concentrated in the rural areas, these pressures have now spread to some of the childcare teams even in Inverness.

The Council's central strategy is to train its own staff, and it works closely with the local enterprise company to train its unqualified childcare team in different parts of Highland.

Initiatives in training are:

- a trainee/sponsorship scheme for graduates who will go on to train as social workers, with the offer of sponsored training;
- sponsorship of final year students;
- small bursaries for self-funding students; and
- (in prospect) a practice teaching post to address some of the problems of providing practice placements – which frequently lead to employment.

To attract staff into social care the Council has improved advertising and notification of vacancies (including an e-mail database) and adopted more consistent and efficient recruitment procedures.

To introduce more flexible employment, the Council has launched a pilot project for portfolio working by support staff who can work within the department's units and also provide homecare. It is hoped that the strengthening of management experience and expertise in the discrete areas of work, i.e. Criminal Justice, Community Care and Children's Services, will improve staff support and have a positive effect on retention of staff.

7. Modernising services

Highland Council has had long experience with two minority communities – Gaelic speakers in the west, and travellers, particularly during the summer months. This has provided insights for working with some black and ethnic minority families resident in the Highlands. The Council's approach to developing a Race Equality Scheme is based on a corporate equality policy, but it remains to mainstream the Scheme within social work services.

Digital Highland embraces modernising initiatives such as e-procurement, a Customer Relationship Management system and support for delivering services in Highland's 8 areas. Social work services have not been immediately involved in these developments, the priority having been to address the needs of routine high-volume customers.

The Social Work Service is upgrading its client information system. Most social work staff have either a desktop PC or a laptop (given the large amount of travel for some staff). Residential and day centre units are linked to the Council's Intranet. Internet access is provided in all establishments and offices to Team Managers and Strategic staff.

8. The Future

The Council and its health partner now need to carry through into purposeful planning and implementation within measurable time their agreement to align budgets and integrate management of community care services.

The Council should prepare an action plan to bring together a series of measures to improve and make more flexible the home care service, taking account of the diversity of needs and circumstances across Highland, and to indicate the resource priorities required to implement the changes. This would support the strategic decision to shift the emphasis of provision of care for older people from residential to community-based options.

To enhance services to people with a learning disability and mental health, the positive lessons of improved joint working between social work and health care staff derived from experience in Ross and Cromarty should be applied to the other 7 local areas of Highland.

In addition, the quality of learning disability services would benefit from closer links between social and health care and education and training interests.

Now that it has been decided to use a locally prepared tool for single shared assessment, the Council can now determine the necessary processes and provide training for its use in preparation for implementing new arrangements by a target date.

There are multi-agency links for services for people with a hearing impairment. Links for people with a visual impairment are less robust although the council, in collaboration with NHS Highland and the independent sector, are embarking on the development of a single strategy for sensory needs. This may be further advanced by the development of a sensory impairment resource centre, and the Council will take the opportunity to take forward preliminary plans for such a centre based at Raigmore Hospital, which could be the base for a partnership of service providers, including specialist voluntary organisations.

For deafblind services, the review of future needs assessment planned by the Council should be taken forward as a basis for decisions on strategic development and resource priorities.

The Council has still to bring to a conclusion action to implement a number of recommendations of *Learning with Care.* In addition attention needs to be devoted to:

- involving parents in the education of looked after children;
- improving the currently inadequate arrangements for collection, recording and analysis of data;
- reviewing the educational environment of children in foster care; and
- formulating with health a joint programme of development and training opportunities for staff who work with looked after children.

In order to secure the benefits of the partnership for criminal justice services, the Council and its partners should set a high priority on developing and implementing standardised management information systems for management and practice.

In order to address serious and continuing problems of recruitment and retention, the Council should pursue new approaches for example to:

- remuneration packages for home care workers to address the disincentives for staff who travel significant distances; and
- unqualified work as a pathway into a career in social work, especially for non-traditional groups, including men.

The Council in completing its Race Equality Scheme, should determine how it can be expressed in terms of social work, among other services.

INVERCLYDE

1. Profile at 2002

Inverclyde has a population of 84,600 in mainly urban communities. Poverty and deprivation figure prominently in urban parts of the area. An analysis of the 1991 census showed that 14.3% of households in the area could be categorised as severely or multiply deprived.

The total population is expected to fall over the next 14 years by 12.3%, wholly among those under 45. The number of older people will rise only slightly.

At 3.2% (January 2002), unemployment is lower than the national average and has fallen at a higher than average rate over the past year.

Inverclyde has Scotland's fourth highest drug misuse rate (2.8% of 15-54 year olds).

Inverclyde has the sixth highest crime rate in Scotland. There were 908 recorded crimes per 10,000 population in 2001, a slight increase in comparison to 2000 figures.

Social work services are provided through a joint Social Work and Housing Service; a senior officer in that department is the designated chief social work officer.

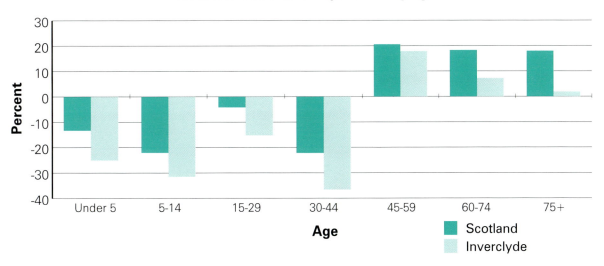

Expected % change in population, 2000-2016, local and national comparisons by age band

2. Performance: Community Care

Balance of care (aged 65+)	1999 actual	1999 per 1,000	Quartile	2000 actual	2000 per 1,000	Quartile
Older people in residential care homes	268	20	2	201	15	3
Older people in private nursing homes	284	21	3	293	21	3
Older people receiving home care	1,100	80	2	1,091	80	2
Older people in special needs housing	1,705	124.7	2	832	61.3	4

People receiving a community care service	1999-2000 actual	1999-2000 per 1,000	Quartile	2000-2001 actual	2000-2001 per 1,000	Quartile
Older people (aged 65+)	3,912	288.5	1	4,747	350	1
For mental health problems/dementia (aged 18-64)	365	7.1	1	368	7.1	1
For physical disabilities (aged 18-64)	1,001	19.4	1	1,097	21.2	1
For learning disabilities (aged 18-64)	241	4.7	1	260	5.0	1
For drug/alcohol abuse problems (aged 18-64)	660	12.8	1	646	12.5	1

The rate of older people receiving a community care service is high and increasing. The rates of older people living in nursing homes and in residential homes are low in comparison to many other authorities. A shortage of residential and nursing home places within the area is attributed to the level of financial support which can be offered to independent providers, and this contributes to delays in discharges from hospitals. The rate of people living in special needs housing is low; numbers more than halved between 1999 and 2000. A relatively high rate of older people receive home care.

A rapid response team enables people to be supported in the community rather than being admitted to hospital, thus encouraging continued independence and building confidence. The team is multi-disciplinary, developed around primary care, and is to be used as a pilot setting for single shared assessment in respect of older people.

The community learning disability team comprises solely health service staff. The Acorn Project provides community support to people with learning disabilities and is seen as a stepping stone between a traditional day centre and full community integration.

The community mental health team, comprising health, social work and housing staff, has generated its own service planning and development agenda to feed into the joint planning machinery. A co-ordinator for the mental health strategy is jointly funded. Specialist services have been developed for people with alcohol-related brain damage. The Council is working with a local housing agency to develop sheltered and supported accommodation.

The Council and its health partners have now selected the CarenapE tool as the single shared assessment tool to be used in Inverclyde, and a joint working group oversees implementation, with a sub-group working out process details.

A local strategy for sensory impairment services envisages development of a new disability resource centre in 2003 as the focus for service improvement. Changes to the purchase of services have been made following a best value review.

Reorganisation of the Council's committee structure offers the opportunity to align budgets with health partners, to match resources and to "grow" management arrangements as joint working matures. The partners are in process of scoping the pot of services. They envisage core budgets as part of joint resourcing and joint management arrangements for older people and a training and development plan for services for older people and other aspects of community care.

3. Performance: Children and Families

Balance of care – Looked after children (aged 0-17)	1999-2000 actual	1999-2000 per 1,000	Quartile	2000-2001 actual	2000-2001 per 1,000	Quartile
At home	144	7.4	1	141	7.3	1
With friends/relatives/other community	48	2.5	1	42	2.2	1
With foster carers/prospective adopters	32	1.7	4	30	1.6	4
In residential accommodation	28	1.5	2	25	1.3	2
Total	**252**	**13**	**1**	**238**	**12.3**	**1**

Key performance indicators	1998-1999 actual	1998-1999 per 1,000	Quartile	1999-2000 actual	1999-2000 per 1,000	Quartile
Child protection (CP) referrals (aged 0-15)	78	4.5	3	170	9.9	1
Children subject to a CP case conference (aged 0-15)	62	3.6	2	76	4.4	1
Children placed on CP register (aged 0-15)	43	2.5	1	8	0.5	4
Adoption applications in year (aged 0-17)	5	0.3	4	5	0.3	3
Stranger adopter applications (aged 0-17)	1	0.1	4	3	0.2	3

Inverclyde has a higher rate of looked after children than most other authorities. High rates of looked after children live at home or with friends or relatives and a fairly high rate is in residential accommodation. There is a very low rate in foster care.

The rate of child protection referrals increased substantially between 1998 and 2000 and is now higher than in most other authorities. A high rate of children were subject to a case conference in 1999-2000 but only a small rate were placed on the child protection register, following steep reductions since 1998-1999. The rate of adoption applications is relatively low.

Prompted by the Hammond Inquiry and locally-revised procedures, the Inverclyde Child Protection Committee organised multi-disciplinary seminars and workshops which provided a template for neighbouring authorities to adopt.

Joint action is in progress to implement the recommendations of *Learning with Care:*

- a formal joint assessment package is being piloted in residential units;
- social workers, health professionals and teachers are to receive joint training on assessment;
- procedures on exclusions have been revised;
- a protocol is planned to ensure continued education for looked after and accommodated children who are excluded from school; and
- a joint support project has been set up and a "lap-top library" is being established for looked after children.

The potential is being examined for monitoring progress with care plans through linked systems and shared data between social work, education and health.

A working group is in being to prepare for the new arrangements for care leavers. The structures for implementing payments have yet to be finalised, pending central guidance on resource transfers.

The Children's Services Integration Project involves education, social work, and health staff together with representatives from parents and voluntary organisations and focuses on pre-five establishments, schools, health service locations and community schools. The Project is resourced by the Changing Children's Services Fund.

4. Performance: Criminal Justice

Key Activities	1999-2000	2000-2001	2000-2001 per 10,000	Quartile
Number of social enquiry reports submitted to the courts during the year	887	929	158.4	1
Number of community service orders made during the year	144	138	23.5	1
The proportion of social enquiry reports reported to court within target time	2000-2001	Quartile		
Proportion of social enquiry reports submitted to the courts by due date	100.0	1		
The time taken to complete community service orders				
Average length of community service (hours) for orders completed during the year	109	4		
Average hours completed per week	4.4	2		

A high rate of social enquiry reports was submitted to courts in 2000-2001 in line with the high crime rate in Inverclyde. All reports were submitted by the due date. The rate of community service orders made was also high. The average length of orders was shorter than in many other authorities and they were completed relatively quickly.

The Council is part of a grouping with Renfrew and East Renfrewshire for criminal justice service provision. Following a best value review to identify and adopt the best practice of each authority, joint working arrangements are being developed. Drug Treatment and Testing Orders are to be delivered from the autumn through a joint initiative between the three councils and health partners. The "Constructs" programme for work with offenders has been adopted on a pilot basis to promote best practice in supervision.

The IT system provides monitoring information on compliance with national standards, reporting frequency and other process issues. Pending the new social work information system, a stand-alone database as been developed which supports process tracking of attendance, assessment and profiling of offenders and staff supervision.

The joint Pathways project with sex offenders which is line-managed by East Renfrewshire has attracted wide support from stakeholders. Cases provide opportunities for specialist input and for coaching in good practice to non-specialist staff. It offers assessment for both adult and youth offenders, and focuses on risk management.

5. Finance

Service Area (£000)	GAE 1999-2000	Final net Out turn 1999-2000	GAE 2000-2001	Final net Out turn 2000-2001
Children's Services	£4,663	£5,368	£4,810	£5,657
Community Care	£14,350	£11,800	£14,885	£12,557
Adult Offenders		£24		£7
Other SW Services	£1,755	£4,594	£1,749	£4,585
Total	**£20,768**	**£21,785**	**£21,443**	**£22,807**
Spend per head		**1999-2000**		**2000-2001**
Spend per head		£257.50		£269.58
Quartile		2		1

Funding for criminal justice services is paid directly by the Scottish Executive and the Council received £980,060 in 2000-2001.

The Council spent above GAE on children's services in 1999-2000 and 2000-2001 but less so than many other authorities. It spent considerably above GAE on other social work services and less on community care. Spend per head on social work services is higher than in most other authorities.

6. Staffing

Staff	WTE 1999 actual	WTE 1999 per 1,000	Quartile 1999	WTE 2000 actual	WTE 2000 per 1,000	Quartile 2000
Managers & central staff	80	0.9	1	73	0.9	1
Frontline staff	418	4.9	2	507	6.0	1
Other	143	1.7	1	104	1.2	2
Total	**641**	**7.5**	**1**	**684**	**8.1**	**1**

Vacancies	Vacancies 2000	% Vacancies 2000	% Vacancies 2000 Scotland	Vacancies 2001*	% Vacancies 2001	% Vacancies 2001 Scotland
SWs with adults	2	4.3	7.8	–	–	10.9
SWs with children	3	5.2	7.4	–	–	10.7
SWs with offenders	0	0	7.5	–	–	7.2
Generic workers	0	0	8.0	–	–	12.7
Total	**4**	**3.8**	**7.7**	**–**	**–**	**10.5**

*Inverclyde did not submit staffing vacancy figures for 2001.

Overall staffing rates are high in Inverclyde, having increased between 1999 and 2000. While the number of frontline staff increased, the number of managers and other staff reduced. Vacancy levels were below average in 2000. The situation has deteriorated since then. The Council now reports a vacancy level of 16% among qualified social workers and chronic problems with recruitment, particularly within the child protection team.

Among the most effective measures to improve recruitment and retention has been to support a disproportionately large number of practice teaching placements from which a number of appointments have been made directly and indirectly. Other actions have included shifting to specialist posts; focusing the efforts of qualified social workers on statutory tasks, while re-allocating other tasks to social work assistants; offering permanent contracts to workers on short term contracts in non-specialist posts; and seconding unqualified staff to DipSW courses.

7. Modernising services

Little specific preparation has been made for a Race Equality Scheme but a working group is looking at establishing a scheme for social work services. The social work department has been involved in the local multi-agency racial incident monitoring group, which operates a helpline for victims of racial harassment.

A history of joint working has led to a Modernising Government funded project between Inverclyde and Renfrewshire Councils and Inverclyde Primary Care NHS Trust. The project aims to support mental health services by integrating information systems and enabling partnership working and information sharing.

A new comprehensive social work information system has been procured and is to be operational by the end of 2002. All social workers and social work locations are to be linked by an Intranet by the end of 2002. Internet access will be made available to all staff.

8. The Future

Misuse of drugs and alcohol has a major impact on the range of social work services. Over 600 adults receive support, and where those adults are also parents, protection and care have to be provided for the children themselves. Criminal justice services are equally pressed, with the advent of Drug Treatment and Testing Orders. The Council should keep under review in the Drug Action Team means of enhancing its own and its partners' response to the problems presented by drug and alcohol misuse.

In order to sustain community support for older people, the Council needs as a matter of urgency to complete its best value review of home care services, to assess its recommendations, to prepare a strategic plan for improving services and to identify the resource priorities necessary to implement it.

The Council should build on the success and experience of the rapid response team to develop and introduce single shared assessment in respect of older people.

To consolidate the progress made in mental health services, the Council should:

- require departments and agencies to produce protocols to aid the transition for children with special needs entering adult services, and to assist joint working in child and adolescent mental health services;
- prepare a plan for implementing improvements needed in services for mentally disordered offenders, in light of the regional forensic unit being planned jointly with four other local authorities and the health service; and
- review with the assistance of the Scottish Development Centre the joint working required in services for older people with mental health problems.

Learning disability services would benefit from a strategic plan for development, from identification of resource priorities and greater joint working with health partners.

A searching review of procedures for assessing the future needs of people with sensory impairments is overdue, in view of the continuing time gap between registration and assessment.

The various joint actions which have been taken or are intended to prepare for improvements to the education of looked after children should be brought together into a comprehensive implementation plan dealing with the range of recommendations of *Learning with Care.*

The working group set up to prepare for the new arrangements for care leavers should identify the range of needs of young people and the different services required to meet them, pending arrangements for implementing payments.

The Council should attend to preparation of a Race Equality Scheme as a guide to future action and priorities. Meantime the working group appointed to prepare a scheme for social work services should press ahead, taking account of the experience of the local multi-agency racial incident monitoring group.

MIDLOTHIAN

1. Profile at 2002

With a population of 82,200 Midlothian is the second smallest mainland authority.

The population has risen gradually in recent years. The population of older people is set to rise by more than the national average, particularly the over 75s. Decreases in the 5 – 14 population will be smaller than the national average and there will be an increase in under 5's.

Midlothian has one of the lowest unemployment rates in Scotland (2.2% in January 2002).

The drug misuse rate is below average (1.6% of 15-54 year olds).

There is a lower than average rate of crime, 575 recorded crimes per 10,000 of population in 2001.

Midlothian Council has developed a cabinet system of government, with a Performance Panel and linked closely to developing Community Forums.

Social work services, led by a chief social work officer, are now a part of Executive Services, and linked with Corporate Policy, Business Planning and Personnel in a restructuring implemented early in 2002. Over 60% of services are purchased from external providers; there is a clear all-Lothian dimension to many of these services.

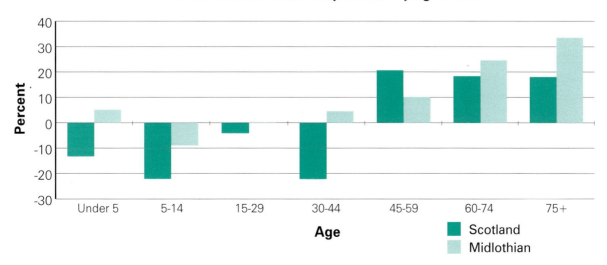

Expected % change in population, 2000-2016, local and national comparisons by age band

2. Performance: Community Care

Balance of care (aged 65+)	1999 actual	1999 per 1,000	Quartile	2000 actual	2000 per 1,000	Quartile
Older people in residential care homes	241	21	2	249	22	2
Older people in private nursing homes	209	19	4	320	28	2
Older people receiving home care	1,062	94	2	819	72	3
Older people in special needs housing	869	77	3	945	82.9	3
People receiving a community care service	1999-2000 actual	1999-2000 per 1,000	Quartile	2000-2001 actual	2000-2001 per 1,000	Quartile
Older people (aged 65+)	2,041	179	3	3,015	264.4	2
For mental health problems/dementia (aged 18-64)	268	5.1	2	224	4.3	2
For physical disabilities (aged 18-64)	1,842	35.1	1	875	16.7	2
For learning disabilities (aged 18-64)	374	7.1	1	13	0.2	4
For drug/alcohol abuse problems (aged 18-64)	36	0.7	2	21	0.4	3

Following a large increase between 1999 and 2001, the rate of older people receiving a community care service is now high. The rates of older people in residential and in nursing homes is higher than in many other authorities and the rate in nursing homes increased substantially between 1999 and 2000. The number of older people in special needs housing remains fairly low although it increased between 1998 and 2000. Older people in Midlothian are less likely to receive a home care service than their counterparts in many other Scottish authorities and the support that is available is likely to be less intensive than for older people in other areas.

Progress has been made in addressing the need to improve the flow of people from hospital through the use of early discharge teams, a joint equipment store and improved respite provision.

The number of people receiving a community care service for learning disability has drastically reduced from a high level in 1999-2000 to a very low level in 2000-2001. Midlothian Council and its partners have started taking forward an action plan from their Partnership in Practice (PiP) agreement, focusing on development of day opportunities (based on person-centred planning), expansion of advocacy, and local area co-ordination. Joint working with health at a planning level is to be strengthened with the appointment of a dedicated member of staff. At practice level there is close alignment between the community care team and health's community learning disability team.

The Council has provided group homes for the few people coming to the area following the closure of Gogarburn Hospital. One of Midlothian's two day centres, the John Chant Centre, provides the focus for enhancing day opportunities.

The Council has collaborated with the community mental health team during the reshaping of mental health services in Lothian, to achieve the shift after closure of Bangour Village to reinvestment in community-based services.

The CMHT, and the aligned community care team use close working links to provide care programmes primarily for people with more complex needs. Training, including preparation for the Adults with Incapacity Act, has been a significant feature of improving mental health services.

All-Lothian progress has been made in developing and delivering a shared assessment tool based on Carenap E. The intention is to implement the new processes for all groups, not just older people. Complementary tasks are involving health interests and developing appropriate information systems – with a target implementation date in early 2003.

The number of people receiving a community care service for physical disability more than halved between 1999 and 2001, although the rate remains higher than in many other authorities. The Council funds the Thistle Foundation to run Connect Midlothian to provide a one-to-one service, as part of the Council's services for people with a physical disability. Still at a pilot stage, the service has succeeded in building confidence and providing opportunities for people, mainly within their current living arrangements.

Midlothian leads the Lothian sensory needs joint planning group, which has prepared an action plan for service improvements. Midlothian is examining potential improvements in tracking future needs assessments for children with sensory impairment.

Under service level agreements Visual Impairment Services South East Scotland provides a service to the visually impaired and deafblind, and the Edinburgh and East of Scotland Deaf Society provides a parallel service for the deaf. Both services are being reviewed.

A joint steering group has been formed involving all local agencies and key interests, to progress the Joint Future agenda, but it has yet to offer plans for joint management or for greater service integration on the ground. The focus is on setting up joint structures and joint resourcing.

3. Performance: Children and Families

Balance of care – Looked after children (aged 0-17)	1999-2000 actual	1999-2000 per 1,000	Quartile	2000-2001 actual	2000-2001 per 1,000	Quartile
At home	102	5.6	2	89	4.9	2
With friends/relatives/other community	30	1.6	1	46	2.5	1
With foster carers/prospective adopters	57	3.1	2	41	2.2	3
In residential accommodation	33	1.8	1	37	2.0	1
Total	**222**	**12.1**	**1**	**213**	**11.6**	**1**

Key performance indicators	1998-1999 actual	1998-1999 per 1,000	Quartile	1999-2000 actual	1999-2000 per 1,000	Quartile
Child protection (CP) referrals (aged 0-15)	120	7.4	3	103	6.3	3
Children subject to a CP case conference (aged 0-15)	44	2.7	3	54	3.3	1
Children placed on CP register (aged 0-15)	37	2.3	2	46	2.8	1
Adoption applications in year (aged 0-17)	8	0.4	2	6	0.3	3
Stranger adopter applications (aged 0-17)	4	0.2	2	3	0.2	3

The rate of child protection referrals is relatively low. Though a high rate of children are subject to a case conference and the rate of children who become registered is higher than in many other authorities. There is a low rate of adoption applications.

The rate of looked after children is high. The rate of looked after children living with friends and relatives has increased, while the rate living at home has decreased. The number living with foster carers has decreased and the rate is now low, compared with many other authorities. The rate of children in residential accommodation remains high, although the number in residential schools has declined, as has the number permanently living in residential homes. Rates and numbers are affected by the impact of drug misusing parents. There has been considerable pressure on foster placements.

To develop alternative services to residential school placements, a primary and secondary school-age base has been identified and both teachers and children and family support workers are to be recruited to them. Surestart Midlothian services have been commissioned and the use of after-school care clubs has been funded for children with special needs.

Outreach services from Midfield and the Hawthorn Centres help children and young people in the community to develop self-esteem and work to prevent them becoming looked after. Outreach is supplemented by increased use of breakfast clubs, after school clubs and holiday play schemes, with social work making additional contributions to accommodate more challenging young people.

The implementation of recommendations of *Learning with Care* has still to be completed:
- all looked after children have care plans but a number of children cared for by families remain without plans;
- all but a few children have permanent full-time education;
- all schools have a designated senior member of staff to oversee looked after children;
- joint training programmes for social work and teaching staff have been undertaken and there is a programme for future training; and
- an audit of social work residential units and foster carers has led to specific funding of facilities for looked after children, including the provision of an education tool kit.

The data held by education on the educational attainment and exclusion record of looked after children is collated manually with social work records.

Throughcare and aftercare are the responsibility of the children and families team, supported where appropriate by staff in residential units. Future numbers of children leaving care have been forecast. Accommodation providers are ready to support young people leaving care, but lack of local further education provision may restrict training opportunities.

Since early 2001 Children First has run the Midlothian Young Carers Project, providing support and advice to meet the individual needs of local young people who care for a dependent relative at home. Individual and group activities are provided. About 36 young people are using the service and new referrals are still being received.

4. Performance: Criminal Justice

Key Activities	1999-2000	2000-2001	2000-2001 per 10,000	Quartile
Number of social enquiry reports submitted to the courts during the year	295	350	59.5	3
Number of community service orders made during the year	94	113	19.2	1
The proportion of social enquiry reports reported to court within target time	**2000-2001**	**Quartile**		
Proportion of social enquiry reports submitted to the courts by due date	90.0	4		
The time taken to complete community service orders				
Average length of community service (hours) for orders completed during the year	142	4		
Average hours completed per week	3.0	4		

A relatively low rate of social enquiry reports were submitted to courts in 2000-2001. A lower proportion were submitted on time than in most other authorities. The rate of community service orders made is high. The average length of orders is shorter than in most other authorities, but they take a comparatively long time to complete.

The Council is part of a criminal justice grouping with Edinburgh, East and West Lothian and Scottish Borders. It does not have effective criminal justice information systems, and has plans to remedy this. Meantime its present system has been put into an Access database to improve its usefulness for management information.

Staff use the Constructs intervention programme in work with offenders. They collaborate with SACRO on a range of joint initiatives for younger offenders plus a supported accommodation service for offenders aged 16-25. The work is overseen by a multi-agency steering group.

Despite acknowledged weakness in information management systems, feedback of information to workers to support practice is particularly well developed. In addition, all staff participate in peer review of social enquiry reports. Both these methods make a contribution to consistent practice.

5. Finance

Service Area (£000)	GAE 1999-2000	Final net Out turn 1999-2000	GAE 2000-2001	Final net Out turn 2000-2001
Children's Services	£2,899	£3,863	£3,111	£5,210
Community Care	£10,729	£12,517	£11,256	£13,382
Adult Offenders		£5		-£51
Other SW Services	£1,477	£1,244	£1,495	£1,438
Total	**£15,105**	**£17,629**	**£15,862**	**£19,979**

Spend per head		1999-2000		2000-2001
Spend per head		£214.46		£243.05
Quartile		3		2

The Council receives funding direct from the Scottish Executive for criminal justice services, and received £445,943 in 2000-2001.

The Council spent above GAE in children's services and community care in 1999-2000 and 2000-2001. Spend per head on social work services increased between the two years and is now higher than in many other authorities.

6. Staffing

Staff	WTE 1999 actual	WTE 1999 per 1,000	Quartile 1999	WTE 2000 actual	WTE 2000 per 1,000	Quartile 2000
Managers & central staff	42	0.5	3	48	0.6	3
Frontline staff	347	4.2	3	353	4.3	3
Other	89	1.1	3	74	0.9	3
Total	**478**	**5.9**	**3**	**476**	**5.8**	**3**

Vacancies	Vacancies 2000	% Vacancies 2000	% Vacancies 2000 Scotland	Vacancies 2001	% Vacancies 2001	% Vacancies 2001 Scotland
SWs with adults	6	22.2	7.8	3	11.7	10.9
SWs with children	3	9.3	7.4	5	15.1	10.7
SWs with offenders	0	0	7.5	0	0	7.2
Generic workers	0	0	8.0	0	0	12.7
Total	**9**	**13.9**	**7.7**	**8**	**12.7**	**10.5**

Staff rates are lower than many other authorities and the rate of managers and central staff is particularly low. Vacancy levels are a little above average and particularly high in children's services. The department has faced recruitment problems, primarily in children and families teams, where pressures have increased through a rise in the demands on staff from child protection referrals, or children referred as a result of neglect associated with parental drug abuse. Promotion prospects in a small authority like Midlothian are limited, making retention of able and ambitious staff more difficult.

The Council created a providers' forum, across public, private and voluntary sectors, initially for learning disability but now covering additional care groups. The forum facilitates consistency of standards and allows gaps in provision to be addressed systematically and co-operatively.

A career path has been created for social care staff, beginning with those home care staff charged with personal care tasks. Staff now make use of the competency framework. Final year students have been targeted, with a good degree of success. Workers supported through training are required to work for the Council for two years after completion.

7. Modernising services

Midlothian Council is committed to the Rooting Out Racism initiative for Lothian and Borders area and to developing an action plan to meet the implications of the Race Relations (Amendment) Act 2000. Prompted by a corporate initiative each department has carried out the Racial Equality Means Quality audit. The audit was at a high level in social work, and needs to be pursued through each individual part of the service. The process of considering the implications of the legislation includes discussion between the Commission for Racial Equality and Council members and senior officers. The Council has no local ethnic minorities' forum to allow consultation and needs to look urgently to other bodies in the Lothian region to provide expert support.

The Council's Modernising Government action plan includes developing the IT infrastructure to enable robust back-office systems to be supported. All staff are to be trained to the European Computer Driving Licence (ECDL) standard by 2004. The Council's network is being extended to remote social work sites where staff can share in improvements to data quality, information gathering, service planning and communication and have access to the client index, e-mail and the internet. The intranet site has been expanded and will allow staff to have online access to children and families procedures. Connection to the Government Secure Extranet (GSX) in the near future should allow secure transmission between various justice agencies.

Social work client information systems have corporate priority for upgrading, which will involve the purchase of new software, and allow interactivity with health, education and other information systems. This software is unlikely to be operational before 2003. A joint bid has been made with Edinburgh, East Lothian and Lothian Health for second round Modernising Government funding to develop a system for online ordering from the joint equipment stores.

8. The Future

The Council and its health partners should use the joint steering group to speed up progress on the Joint Future agenda, and to advance beyond joint structures and resourcing to prepare proposals for joint management and greater service integration.

To expand and increase the quality of home care services for older people, the Council should urgently prepare a strategic plan for improving domiciliary health and social care services and enhancing the range of personal care provided (e.g. through shopping, domestic and maintenance services) and should identify the resource priorities required to implement improvements within measurable time.

In improving home care provision for older people the Council should pay particular attention to those older people with complex problems who prefer to remain at home.

In order to consolidate the progress made in improving the education of looked after children, the Council needs to enhance the quality of information on those children and ensure links between education and social work.

To underpin the measures decided to provide effective local aftercare for young people, the Council should devise and introduce a programme of joint development and training opportunities for staff who work with looked after children.

1. Profile at 2002

With a population of 85,000 Moray is one of Scotland's smaller rural mainland authorities.

Total population is expected to fall by 6.1% over the next 14 years, but the number of older people will increase. The number of over 75s is expected to increase by more than a quarter.

At 3.1%, (January 2002), the rate of unemployment is below average. 79% of working age people in Moray are working, compared to a Scottish average of 73%.

Moray has one of the lowest mainland rates of problem drug misuse (0.9% of 15 to 54 year olds).

The crime rate is below average (622 recorded crimes per 10,000 in 2001).

Services are provided through a Department of Community Services, (social work and housing) under a director. The head of children and criminal justice services is the chief social work officer.

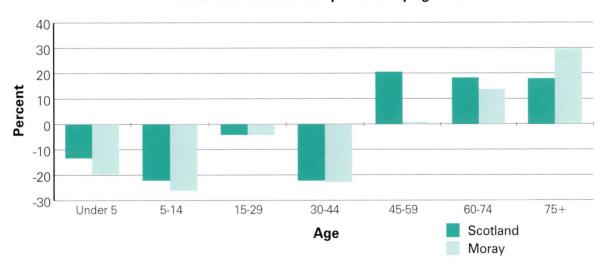

Expected % change in population, 2000-2016, local and national comparisons by age band

2. Performance: Community Care

Balance of care (aged 65+)	1999 actual	1999 per 1,000	Quartile	2000 actual	2000 per 1,000	Quartile
Older people in residential care homes	243	18	2	212	15	3
Older people in private nursing homes	287	21	3	279	21	3
Older people receiving home care	963	71	3	903	66	3
Older people in special needs housing	1,738	127.8	2	1,738	126.6	2
People receiving a community care service	**1999-2000 actual**	**1999-2000 per 1,000**	**Quartile**	**2000-2001 actual**	**2000-2001 per 1,000**	**Quartile**
Older people (aged 65+)	3,214	234.1	2	2,047	149.1	4
For mental health problems/dementia (aged 18-64)	293	5.7	1	274	5.3	1
For physical disabilities (aged 18-64)	953	18.6	1	174	3.4	4
For learning disabilities (aged 18-64)	86	1.7	4	210	4.1	2
For drug/alcohol abuse problems (aged 18-64)	102	1.9	1	142	2.8	1

The rate of older people receiving a community care service is now low in comparison with most other authorities, having fallen significantly between 1999 and 2001. Moray has a higher rate of special needs housing than many other authorities and lower rates of older people in residential and in nursing homes. Older people are less likely to receive a home care service than older people in many other authorities, but those who receive a service are more likely to receive more hours.

A current review of the development of home care services is seeking to balance the push to develop practical services with efficiencies in delivering services in rural areas. In the meantime closer working between home care, community nursing and Associated Health Professionals (AHP) has been developed in Forres as the first stage and is now rolling out across Moray.

Joint occupational therapy services have been implemented across Moray. Joint line management for all Moray's community and health OTs has led to a fresh look at some of the duties of community OTs, resulting in a better focus on the rehabilitation skills of the professional staff. A joint equipment store is being progressed. The progress has revealed the importance of compatible IT systems in the two agencies.

Learning disability services are the subject of on-going review and change. The Council has reconfigured the community infrastructure, to accord with the progress of hospital closures. A range of day services have been developed and a new centre based service is due to open in Elgin. Resource transfer is used to enhance services for all people with learning disabilities. Under the Grampian-wide Partnership in Practice agreement (PiP):

- local area co-ordinators deal with crisis, non-hospital, hospital closure, resettlement, and housing work;
- a joint multi-disciplinary community learning disability team supports resettlement and those living in the community;
- a range of day centre and community based services are provided;
- housing is made available, ranging from very sheltered housing with tenancies as well as occupancy agreements and small residential care settings; and
- A generic advocacy with specialist advocates for LD and MH advocacy is co-ordinated and provided.

Community mental health teams work in localities. A mental health framework group improves links with users and carers, with the intention of helping users become more involved in the development of services. A recently completed restructuring of rehabilitation services has led to a new facility in Elgin, managed by SAMH.

Local partners have implemented single shared assessment, building on a strong history of joint working. Key agencies and staff are involved through seminars and newsletters. Users, carers and the independent sector are being involved in locality planning. The local single shared assessment tool has been updated using Scottish Executive guidance and now consists of a generic assessment, a simple/self assessment, and a comprehensive assessment. Guidance and joint training has been delivered. The SSA has been adopted across agencies and agreed as a common document for Grampian. The lack of a shared IT client/patient record makes it difficult for staff to implement. Local priorities are being set out jointly for the use of resources, and some budgets are already aligned.

Between 1999 and 2001 there was a huge decrease in the number of people receiving a community care service for physical disability, however, this may be associated with problems experienced during 2000-2001, with maintaining client contact statistics. In 1999-2000 the rate of people receiving a service was higher than in many other authorities. By 2000-2001 it was very low.

The Moray Resource Centre provides a location for services to people with a sensory and physical impairment. In addition, Grampian Society for the Blind have their own premises in Elgin and have strong links with Moray Resource Centre. Staff from Grampian Society for the Blind, Aberdeen and North East Deaf Society and colleagues from 3 other voluntary organisations provide specialist services. A recent review of the Grampian Society has led to a shift in focus from social work towards rehabilitation.

The Moray Carers Forum has been the driving force behind a range of fresh initiatives for carers:

- organising consultation days with carers in 2000 and 2001; and
- conducting an audit of existing services, which led to an improved view of what carers themselves wanted, and what was lacking in Moray; a strategy for carers in Moray, "Carers speak out……", now articulates clearly what carers asked for, and how the various providers of services will respond.

Significant steps have been taken towards joint resourcing and joint management, building on already existing arrangements. The Moray Community Care Partnership has agreed to move to a unified management structure, with a single head of service for community care (Health and Social Care) accountable to the partnership. Staff will, for the most part, stay with their current employer, but are to be organised and managed to meet the needs of the service.

The partnership covers all council and LHCC community care resources, initially for older people and people with physical disabilities. A joint senior management group that includes the LHCC, community care, Acute Trust, health promotion and housing representatives has been set up. The scoping of the pot exercise has identified all the relevant staffing, property, equipment and budgets held by the council and LHCC. There are some jointly funded commissioning posts, an aligned OT service and aligned area teams.

3. Performance: Children and Families

Balance of care – Looked after children (aged 0-17)	1999-2000 actual	1999-2000 per 1,000	Quartile	2000-2001 actual	2000-2001 per 1,000	Quartile
At home	62	3.1	3	54	2.7	3
With friends/relatives/other community	0	0.0	4	0	0.0	4
With foster carers/prospective adopters	66	3.3	1	65	3.3	2
In residential accommodation	14	0.7	4	12	0.6	4
Total	**142**	**7.1**	**3**	**131**	**6.6**	**3**

Key performance indicators	1998-1999 actual	1998-1999 per 1,000	Quartile	1999-2000 actual	1999-2000 per 1,000	Quartile
Child protection (CP) referrals (aged 0-15)	205	11.5	1	166	9.4	1
Children subject to a CP case conference (aged 0-15)	53	3	2	34	1.9	3
Children placed on CP register (aged 0-15)	53	3	1	20	1.1	4
Adoption applications in year (aged 0-17)	15	0.7	1	15	0.8	1
Stranger adopter applications (aged 0-17)	3	0.2	3	7	0.4	1

The rate of looked after children is relatively low. The rate of children living in residential accommodation is low; a relatively high rate lives with foster carers, assisted by the development of specialised foster schemes. None of the looked after children live with friends or relatives.

Moray has a high rate of child protection referrals but only a small rate of referrals reach a case conference. The rate of children on the child protection register is lower than in most other authorities, having dropped between 1998 and 2000. The rate of stranger adoption applications is high; the number of applications more than doubled between 1998 and 2000.

Since 1998 there has been extensive development of preventive, locally based services, particularly for pre-school children, and children with a disability.

While the number of parents (and children) misusing drugs in Moray is small, the impact of drug and substance misuse on childcare has been significant. The addition of a full-time worker dedicated to working with parents and children misusing drugs has been complemented by support for a drugs and alcohol counsellor, based in the voluntary sector, to work with young people.

The Council has issued joint policy and practice guidelines on the education of looked after children, but recommendations still to be addressed are:

- joint training on the implementation of the guidelines, scheduled for later in 2002-2003; and
- collation of statistical returns on the school progress of looked after children.

Joint working between education and community services staff has included the development of procedures for joint assessment and care planning, which has a significant impact in reducing the number of pupils excluded from Moray schools, through improved support.

With the advice of a multi-agency steering group the Council has prepared an action plan for all vulnerable young care leavers over the age of 16, which in turn is linked closely to the homelessness strategy. It provides for supported accommodation, a drop-in facility, detached youth work services, improved training for young people with a disability, and a Moving On worker to enable young people to develop skills for access to employment.

The Council is currently undertaking initiatives on youth crime in an effort to address persistent offenders, including:

- more integrated working with all agencies via 'domain commitment';
- extensive joint training programmes for all staff (child care and criminal justice and voluntary agencies);
- appointment of a full time co-ordinator and staff to work exclusively with young offenders; and
- development of a 'time-out' facility for young people.

4. Performance: Criminal Justice

Key Activities	1999-2000	2000-2001	2000-2001 per 10,000	Quartile
Number of social enquiry reports submitted to the courts during the year	308	257	44.0	4
Number of community service orders made during the year	102	60	10.3	3
The proportion of social enquiry reports reported to court within target time	**2000-2001**	**Quartile**		
Proportion of social enquiry reports submitted to the courts by due date	88.0	4		
The time taken to complete community service orders				
Average length of community service (hours) for orders completed during the year	145	3		
Average hours completed per week	5.5	1		

A low rate of social enquiry reports was submitted to courts in 2000-2001; the number had fallen from the previous year. A low proportion of orders are submitted by the due date due to the offenders failing to attend interviews. The rate of community service orders is also relatively low, reflecting a drop in numbers from the previous year. The average length of orders is relatively low. Orders are completed comparatively quickly, with an average of 5.5 hours completed per week.

Moray is part of the Northern grouping of authorities for criminal justice social work, which includes Aberdeen City, Aberdeenshire and Highland. Quality assurance follows traditional models, concentrating on process rather than outcomes. The quality of social work assessments and supervision of offenders is being taken forward within the Northern Partnership project developed as part of the Getting Best Results initiative which aims to integrate quality and effectiveness across all four organisations.

5. Finance

Service Area (£000)	GAE 1999-2000	Final net Out turn 1999-2000	GAE 2000-2001	Final net Out turn 2000-2001
Children's Services	£1,639	£3,306	£1,790	£3,632
Community Care	£12,338	£13,257	£12,763	£13,659
Adult Offenders		-£26		-£23
Other SW Services	£1,554	£2,648	£1,561	£1,968
Total	**£15,531**	**£19,185**	**£16,115**	**£19,236**

Spend per head		1999-2000		2000-2001
Spend per head		£225.83		£226.43
Quartile		2		3

The Council receives funding for criminal justice services direct from the Scottish Executive, and it received £366,132 in 2000-2001.

The amounts spent on children's services were double GAEs in 1999-2000 and 2000-2001. There was a smaller overspend in community care and social work services. Spend per head on social work services is relatively high.

6. Staffing

Staff	WTE 1999 actual	WTE 1999 per 1,000	Quartile 1999	WTE 2000 actual	WTE 2000 per 1,000	Quartile 2000
Managers & central staff	44	0.5	3	57	0.7	2
Frontline staff	360	4.2	3	369	4.3	3
Other	8	0.1	4	46	0.5	4
Total	**412**	**4.8**	**4**	**472**	**5.6**	**3**

Vacancies	Vacancies 2000	% Vacancies 2000	% Vacancies 2000 Scotland	Vacancies 2001	% Vacancies 2001	% Vacancies 2001 Scotland
SWs with adults	0	0	7.8	0	0	10.9
SWs with children	0	0	7.4	0	0	10.7
SWs with offenders	0	0	7.5	0	0	7.2
Generic workers	0	0	8.0	0	0	12.7
Total	**0**	**0**	**7.7**	**0**	**0**	**10.5**

The rate of staff is lower than most other authorities, despite an overall increase between 1999 and 2000, much of it in 'other' staff. There were no vacancies for social workers in 1999 or 2000.

There are emerging recruitment problems with the field of applicants for some posts, including mental health. The workforce is stable and quite young. The local emphasis is on retention and staff development. Training is multi-disciplinary where possible and there are two new training posts in home care and childcare. There is an SVQ Centre and the Council is moving towards a structure for post-qualifying awards.

Home care could throw up future problems due to competition from the local private sector. The Council aims to make home care more attractive, by giving team leaders fixed hours and developing a joint team with community nurses based on a Finnish model.

7. Modernising services

Moray Council has a small ethnic minority population including people from the Ukraine, Turkey and China. Recently the Council subscribed to an agency able to give translation services. The Council has decided to await guidance from the Commission for Race Equality (Scotland) before taking steps to prepare a corporate Race Equality Scheme.

Moray's Open Door project, funded through Modernising Government, is designed to provide staff, patients and citizens with access to a range of health and community information and services, through contact points, access centres, and intranet and internet sites. A pilot one-stop shop is now open in Forres. Its database can be linked to CareFirst, the community services department's client information system. The Open Door project has outlets within health premises in the Moray area, but direct information exchange with health systems has still to be achieved.

The department invested heavily in client information systems following local government reorganisation, and programme modules are being upgraded on a regular basis. The Council has a mature intranet, and internet access is available to all frontline staff in the community services department.

8. The Future

Moray has a growing population of older people, and there are indications that home care support falls some way short of what the present population needs. Completion of the review of home care services is now urgent, so that the Council and its health partners can:

- prepare a strategic plan for improving the range of home care services to meet the expected growth in demand;
- assess the most cost-effective ways of meeting local needs;
- identify the resource priorities required to implement them; and
- deliver direct benefits to older people in the area within measurable time.

To complement the progress made in mental health services, the Council and its health partners should plan the linkages between acute and community services for those people who require more complex care but live at home.

Sensory impairment services in Moray are patchy and the Council should consider undertaking with health partners a strategic review of developments in the service and identify resource priorities to implement them.

As a guide to future action in dealing with questions of race the Council should commission preparatory work for the development of a full race equality scheme, for example, auditing the provision of social work services to ethnic minorities and the development of race awareness training among staff.

1. Profile at 2002

A medium sized authority, North Ayrshire has a population of 138,900.

The local population is expected to fall by 4.1% over the next 14 years. The younger age groups are likely to decrease by more than the national average and over 60s are forecast to increase at a greater rate than for Scotland as a whole.

Although it has fallen slightly, at 6.6% (January 2002), the local unemployment rate is the highest in Scotland. 65% of working age people are working compared to a Scottish average of 73%.

The rate of problem drug misuse is below average (1.8% of 15-54 year olds).

The rate of reported crime was below the Scottish average at 770 per 10,000 of population in 2001.

The Council has a streamlined Service Committee system focusing on policy, service planning and performance management.

Community care, children and families and criminal justice social work are part of a Social Services Group led by a Corporate Director who also carries the responsibilities of chief social work officer. Recent restructuring has clarified senior management responsibilities. Previously, generic Area Teams managed all local services. Management arrangements are now organised with a functional split giving clearer lines of accountability for service management and development. The introduction of Reception Services is designed to provide an improved response to initial inquiries and to free up practitioner time.

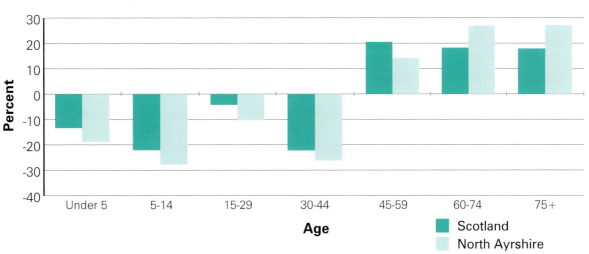

Expected % change in population, 2000-2016, local and national comparisons by age band

2. Performance: Community Care

Balance of care (aged 65+)	1999 actual	1999 per 1,000	Quartile	2000 actual	2000 per 1,000	Quartile
Older people in residential care homes	346	16	3	372	17	2
Older people in private nursing homes	727	34	1	678	32	1
Older people receiving home care	1,462	68	3	1,383	64	3
Older people in special needs housing	4,049	189.2	1	2,716	126.4	2
People receiving a community care service	1999-2000 actual	1999-2000 per 1,000	Quartile	2000-2001 actual	2000-2001 per 1,000	Quartile
Older people (aged 65+)	2,745	127.7	4	1,282	59.6	4
For mental health problems/dementia (aged 18-64)	56	0.6	4	43	0.5	4
For physical disabilities (aged 18-64)	570	6.7	4	381	4.4	4
For learning disabilities (aged 18-64)	55	0.6	4	300	3.5	2
For drug/alcohol abuse problems (aged 18-64)	3	0	4	36	0.4	3

The rate of older people receiving a community care service was lower than in most other authorities in 1999-2000 and numbers more than halved in 2000-2001. A higher proportion of older people live in nursing or residential care homes than in many other authorities; in contrast to the trend in other authorities, the number of older people in residential care increased between 1999 and 2000. Older people are less likely than counterparts in other authorities to receive a home care service, but when they do they are likely to receive more hours per week.

There are indications that the volume of community-based care is insufficient to meet demand. The existence of a persistent number of delayed discharges is attributable in part to the particular pressures on the residential sector, and in part to the need for more comprehensive services to support older people at home. The Council has set up a Best Value Strategic Review of Services for Older People.

The Ayrshire Doctors on Call scheme ensures that out-of-hours home care is available at the request of a GP or Community Nurse. The scheme was recently set up because 10% of hospital admissions were made for want of home care support. The Doctor calls Community Alarms (Alert Service) who in turn contact one of a range of home care providers. Care is provided until 12 noon the following day, by which time mainstream services can be organised. It is proposed to allocate 2 home helps to the Alert Service each evening.

The Council has developed and rationalised provision of equipment and adaptations, improved managing of community occupational therapy services and enhanced links with health service OTs. Waiting lists have now been cleared, and a joint store is in operation.

The number of people receiving a community care service for learning disability increased more than fivefold between 1999 and 2001. An all-Ayrshire Joint Partnership in Practice agreement provides a framework for development of services for learning disabilities. Partnership with housing has enabled a good number of people with learning disabilities to live independently in their own tenancies.

The Council plans to have a local Transition Planning Officer to work with young people with learning disabilities at the transition between children's and adult services. A special needs co-ordinator has been appointed to improve services for children with special educational needs.

The joint strategy for mental health services has yet to be fully implemented due to redirection of resources by health, which has prevented an action plan being completed for investment and implementation. An all-Ayrshire mental health service is in place for some children although the service offered is limited. Integrated mental health teams of social workers and community psychiatric nurses are co-located but not under single management. Recent service initiatives include the Health and Mind day service run on a clubhouse model. There is a respite flat for adults who use mental health services, which can prevent admissions to acute psychiatric services.

Joint training is being carried out on the Adults with Incapacity (Scotland) Act 2000 and a draft procedural document has been written.

Single shared assessment is being developed on an all-Ayrshire basis. A local assessment tool has been agreed and is being piloted by staff across agencies, with the aim of implementing the process for older people by spring 2003. First developments will be required to fulfil expectations to implement SSA for all core groups. Access to resources following assessment is varied: district nurses pass completed assessments to care managers to access resources and make placements, and GPs can access services directly through emergency out of hours services. Direct access by assessors in any agency will, in the long term, reduce duplication.

Between 1999 and 2000 the number of people receiving a community care service for physical disability decreased significantly.

Sensory impairment services have been merged into a single team, based in one location with a single Team Leader. Services are also provided by voluntary organisations. Following abortive efforts to develop an all-Ayrshire multi-agency resource group, a working group of the three Ayrshire councils is reviewing services issue by issue.

The development and implementation of joint planning and the Joint Future agenda is led in North Ayrshire by a Joint Planning Group. This group is developing the Local Partnership Agreement for Older People's Services. Links with the Ayrshire level Joint Development and Resource Group are maintained and focus on strategic and Ayrshire-wide issues. The Council and its health partners have reached agreement on elements of the joint resourcing pot for aligned budgets, although both the NHS Trusts have difficulty disaggregating spending on services for older people between the council areas.

3. Performance: Children and Families

Balance of care – Looked after children (aged 0-17)	1999-2000 actual	1999-2000 per 1,000	Quartile	2000-2001 actual	2000-2001 per 1,000	Quartile
At home	295	9.3	1	163	5.1	2
With friends/relatives/other community	68	2.1	1	56	1.8	1
With foster carers/prospective adopters	48	1.5	4	81	2.5	3
In residential accommodation	68	2.1	1	76	2.4	1
Total	**479**	**15**	**1**	**376**	**11.8**	**1**

Key performance indicators	1998-1999 actual	1998-1999 per 1,000	Quartile	1999-2000 actual	1999-2000 per 1,000	Quartile
Child protection (CP) referrals (aged 0-15)	144	5.1	3	97	3.4	4
Children subject to a CP case conference (aged 0-15)	69	2.5	3	65	2.3	3
Children placed on CP register (aged 0-15)	44	1.5	3	48	1.7	2
Adoption applications in year (aged 0-17)	9	0.3	3	10	0.3	3
Stranger adopter applications (aged 0-17)	3	0.1	4	6	0.2	2

Between 1999 and 2001 the number of children looked after reduced significantly (mainly in those living at home), but the rate remains higher than in most other authorities. The rate of children living with foster carers has increased, but remains relatively low. The rate living in residential accommodation has remained high and this continues to be addressed. These trends are attributed primarily to the behaviour of drug misusing parents, but the social work and education departments have together made a significant impact on the balance of care for looked after children in the last year: the numbers of children in residential schools and in residential units have reduced very significantly. A review of the youth strategy is planned.

The rate of child protection referrals is lower than in most other authorities and the rate of children subject to a case conference is also relatively low. The number of children placed on the child protection register has increased since 1998 and the rate is now relatively high. The number of stranger adoption applications doubled between 1998-1999 and 1999-2000.

The Rosemount Project aims to develop positive relationships between young people of 12-16 and their families, while maintaining the young people in the family homes and challenging inappropriate behaviour. The project group meets regularly and is intended to help identification of personal social developmental needs and the development of confidence, skills and knowledge to address those needs.

In an effort to improve the educational achievements of looked after children, joint support teams have been formed in every secondary school. The Council has addressed the recommendations of *Learning with Care:*

- all children have care plans in which learning needs are identified;
- audits of educational environments have been completed and actioned; and
- plans to link information systems are ongoing.

The exclusion policy is to be reviewed. Added support for the education of looked after children is provided through two specialist teachers and work with foster parents.

To prepare for the new arrangements for throughcare and aftercare the social work department has a dedicated team to co-ordinate services, including the Care Start project which supports young people into employment, training, or further education. Major difficulties confronting the Council are:

- uncertainties about the numbers of young people involved;
- uncertainties about the nature of the financial support; and
- the growing number of care leavers who have chaotic drug-taking behaviour, and who live in an area where unemployment is relatively high.

4. Performance: Criminal Justice

Key Activities	1999-2000	2000-2001	2000-2001 per 10,000	Quartile
Number of social enquiry reports submitted to the courts during the year	632	549	56.7	3
Number of community service orders made during the year	180	179	18.5	2
The proportion of social enquiry reports reported to court within target time	2000-2001	Quartile		
Proportion of social enquiry reports submitted to the courts by due date	100.0	1		
The time taken to complete community service orders				
Average length of community service (hours) for orders completed during the year	174	1		
Average hours completed per week	3.9	2		

The rate of social enquiry reports submitted to courts reduced in 2000-2001 and is now relatively low. All reports were submitted by the due date. A relatively high rate of community service orders were made. The average length of orders was longer than in many other authorities and they were completed comparatively quickly.

The criminal justice grouping of the three Ayrshire councils was officially launched in spring 2002. The joint working which has followed includes:

- work with women offenders developed in South Ayrshire;
- a common template for social enquiry reports; and
- joint commissioning of services from SACRO and NCH for the youth crime initiative.

North Ayrshire is to act as the lead authority of the grouping, but there is to be no single manager.

A substantial increase in community disposals is projected as a result of a change in local sentencing patterns. This has increased the need for gatekeeping of "preferred options" in social enquiry reports, which has not yet been systematically established. Monitoring of activity and of the effectiveness of interventions is based on the review of manual records through supervision.

Data collection is largely related to information required for aggregate returns. IT is not used routinely to support practice, although information such as risk assessment scores is collected. A timescale has yet to be set for the planned acquisition of the CareJust criminal justice software module.

The successful completion rate for community disposals has risen and now stands at 88% – significant since many of those on community service are young drug users. Changes in practice reflect a change in ethos: offenders are now enabled to comply with and complete community service orders whilst discipline is still maintained.

5. Finance

Service Area (£000)	GAE 1999-2000	Final net Out turn 1999-2000	GAE 2000-2001	Final net Out turn 2000-2001
Children's Services	£7,390	£7,798	£7,314	£9,096
Community Care	£21,820	£14,459	£23,178	£15,360
Adult Offenders		£24		£35
Other SW Services	£2,776	£6,882	£2,794	£7,384
Total	**£31,986**	**£29,163**	**£33,286**	**£31,875**
Spend per head		1999-2000		2000-2001
Spend per head		£210.03		£229.56
Quartile		3		2

Criminal Justice services receive funding from the Scottish Executive, and £912,315 was provided in 2000-2001.

The Council spends significantly less than GAE on community care, but spends more on children's services and much more on other social work services. Spend per head on social work services has increased and is now relatively high.

The Council anticipates continued pressure on resources for managing and developing children' services. The capital budget is under pressure to fund improvements to children's residential units to meet new standards.

6. Staffing

Staff	WTE 1999 actual	WTE 1999 per 1,000	Quartile 1999	WTE 2000 actual	WTE 2000 per 1,000	Quartile 2000
Managers & central staff	96	0.7	2	94	0.7	2
Frontline staff	614	4.4	3	714	5.1	2
Other	196	1.4	2	165	1.2	2
Total	**906**	**6.5**	**2**	**973**	**7.0**	**2**

Vacancies	Vacancies 2000	% Vacancies 2000	% Vacancies 2000 Scotland	Vacancies 2001	% Vacancies 2001	% Vacancies 2001 Scotland
SWs with adults	0	0	7.8	1	7.4	10.9
SWs with children	1	2.2	7.4	6	15.8	10.7
SWs with offenders	1	4.5	7.5	1	5.6	7.2
Generic workers	1	7.1	8.0	1	7.7	12.7
Total	**3**	**2.9**	**7.7**	**9**	**11.6**	**10.5**

There is a relatively high rate of staff, whose total number has increased between 1999 and 2000 – mainly in frontline staff. The rate of managers and central staff is relatively low. Staff vacancies are lower than average in all areas, except children's services, where they are high. Major problems have emerged in the recruitment and retention of childcare staff in fieldwork teams. A high sickness level has placed further pressure on workers.

To address these problems the Council has used social work assistants to take on tasks that do not require qualified workers. It supports assistants whose aim is to qualify as social workers. It may sponsor students through the local college with guaranteed employment on qualification. Further staff problems are foreseen as community care expands in response to the findings of the strategic review of older peoples' services.

To help retain staff, the department is creating senior practitioner posts, with appointment to the grade made on the basis of experience and qualification, as an outcome of the personal development review process. A bid has been made to the Society Of Directors Of Personnel In Scotland for consultant resources to find solutions to staff retention problems and to establish a work/life balance.

7. Modernising services

There is a small ethnic minority population, in which the largest groups are Asian and Chinese. Race equality is considered within an equal opportunities policy framework adopted by the Council in 1997. A racial incident monitoring group has been established for North Ayrshire. The Council has formed a working group to develop a race equality plan.

New technology is being used to improve the information flow between the Council and its citizens. Early successes, including the development of reception services, a telephone call centre and the Council's website, are to be followed by a second phase introducing citizen accounts and online processes. Social work has been closely involved in a detailed analysis of business processes able to be deployed on the Council's information systems.

Social work staff have access to a mature intranet, and there is a developing culture of using IT for day-to-day work based on the gradual introduction – accompanied by extensive training – of CareFirst, which commenced in summer 2001. Funds have been sought to develop links between CareFirst and health information systems. Links between CareFirst and the education information system, SEEMIS, are also planned.

8. The Future

Current shortcomings in community based provision for older people and the projected growth in the older population, which will increase demands on community care services, underline the need for the Council and its health partners to plan their strategic improvement and to identify the resource priorities for implementing improvements within measurable time. The Council should therefore pursue the current review of services for older people to a conclusion, so that it and its partners can take early decisions on an action plan to implement future changes.

The progress made by the Council and its health partners in improving services for people with a learning disability would be consolidated and enhanced by:

- establishing an integrated team of social and health care staff;
- completing a financial framework to underpin the PiP agreement;
- involving the education department closely in developments, particularly as they affect children and young people; and
- developing and expanding local area co-ordination for children and adults with learning disabilities.

The future strategy for mental health services should be completed by identification of resource priorities for implementation of the directions which the service is seen as taking in the future to meet local needs effectively. It is suggested that included in future planning should be:

- integrated mental health teams under single management; and
- close involvement of GPs and local health care co-operatives in the delivery of services

Plans for future services for people with sensory impairment should specifically include a review of future needs assessments for children with a sensory impairment and provision for transition from children's to adult services.

To capitalise on the progress made in implementing the recommendations of *Learning with Care*, the Council should complete their implementation and – with health partners – formulate a joint programme of development and training opportunities for staff who work with looked after children.

To enable the Council to play a full part in and derive benefits from the criminal justice partnership, it should regard as a priority the provision of IT support for storing, analysing and retrieving data on the performance of criminal justice services.

1. Profile at 2002

With over 327,600 people, North Lanarkshire has the fourth largest population of local authorities in Scotland. There is higher proportion of people under 35 than the national average.

The overall population is falling and is forecast to reduce slightly in the next 14 years. Overall predicted population changes are similar to the national average but the increase in the over 75 population is expected to be above average.

At 4.7% the unemployment rate is higher than the national average (January 2002).

Rates of drug misuse are below average (1.6% of 15 to 54 year olds).

The crime rate is below average (769 crimes recorded per 10,000 population in 2001) but has increased slightly since 2000.

Services are provided by a social work department under a director who is also chief social work officer. There is a supporting network of area offices. The department has recently been restructured to promote strategic planning and operational capacity.

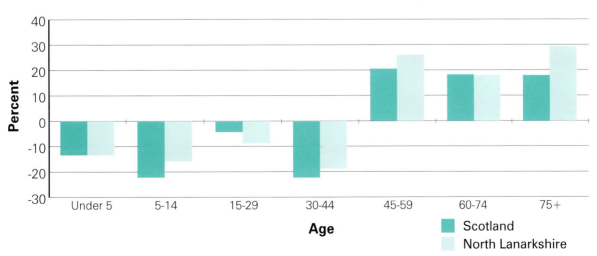

2. Performance: Community Care

Balance of care (aged 65+)	1999 actual	1999 per 1,000	Quartile	2000 actual	2000 per 1,000	Quartile
Older people in residential care homes	530	12	4	498	11	4
Older people in private nursing homes	1,093	24	2	1,175	26	2
Older people receiving home care	2,419	54	4	2,458	54	4
Older people in special needs housing	6,299	140.6	2	4,467	98.5	3
People receiving a community care service	**1999-2000 actual**	**1999-2000 per 1,000**	**Quartile**	**2000-2001 actual**	**2000-2001 per 1,000**	**Quartile**
Older people (aged 65+)	9,831	216.9	2	11,435	252.3	2
For mental health problems/dementia (aged 18-64)	690	3.3	2	838	4.1	3
For physical disabilities (aged 18-64)	4,511	21.9	1	5,080	24.6	1
For learning disabilities (aged 18-64)	497	2.4	3	578	2.8	3
For drug/alcohol abuse problems (aged 18-64)	196	0.9	2	246	1.2	2

There is a low rate of older people in residential care but a higher rate in nursing homes than in other authorities. The rate of older people receiving home care is lower than in most other authorities and there has been a decrease in the rate in special needs housing, which is now relatively low.

The Council has acted to shift the balance of care to community-based services by:

- increasing home care hours by 23% between 1999 and 2001;
- getting the independent sector to provide home care services to the value of £600,000;
- almost doubling the amount of sheltered housing for most vulnerable old people;
- providing community alarms on request to people over 75 living alone; and
- contracting 12 nursing home beds for respite care and short breaks.

The Council has carried out best value reviews on community alarms, community meals, home care, and day care for older people; changes arising from the reviews are driven forward by an implementation group which comprises elected members, senior officers and other stakeholders.

The Council is a leading local authority on services for people with learning disabilities and their carers. Change has been driven by the Council, with joint working between social work, education and housing and health:

- 70 people now have supported living;
- 45 people have been helped to get real jobs;
- 5 people have direct payments; and
- as a result of partnership with Ownership Options some now own their own homes.

People with learning disabilities are included and involved at all stages of the planning and delivery of services. The Partnership in Practice agreement is the only one in Scotland to be written in a way that is easily accessible to people with learning disabilities.

Young people with learning disabilities who are at the transition stage between children's services and adult services are no longer necessarily progressing from special school to day centre. Some young people – among them many with high support needs – now have individual support plans and they get non centre based day opportunities. There is an advocacy project specifically for young people with learning disabilities.

A costed strategy based on shared assessment of need has yet to be developed, involving health, service users and carers. There is evidence of effective partnership working at operational level between community psychiatric nurses and mental health officers and other social work staff.

A development agenda is being progressed for sensory impairment services. Action has been focused on links with Deafblind UK, and on IT developments for people with a sensory impairment. The Council has reorganised its service teams under the umbrella of independent living, with the sensory impairment teams accountable to a single manager.

The Council and its health partners have discussed but still to agree the joint resourcing pot. North Lanarkshire is one of the most advanced areas on single shared assessment, and surpassed the bottom line. A local assessment tool has been agreed and piloted and 12,000 assessments have already been done. An information sharing project, part of the eCare initiative, is highly advanced and is to go live from spring 2002.

3. Performance: Children and Families

Balance of care – Looked after children (aged 0-17)	1999-2000 actual	1999-2000 per 1,000	Quartile	2000-2001 actual	2000-2001 per 1,000	Quartile
At home	343	4.5	2	301	4.0	2
With friends/relatives/other community	50	0.7	3	54	0.7	3
With foster carers/prospective adopters	140	1.8	3	161	2.1	3
In residential accommodation	79	1.0	3	81	1.1	3
Total	**612**	**8**	**3**	**597**	**7.9**	**3**

Key performance indicators	1998-1999 actual	1998-1999 per 1,000	Quartile	1999-2000 actual	1999-2000 per 1,000	Quartile
Child protection (CP) referrals (aged 0-15)	215	3.2	4	136	2.0	4
Children subject to a CP case conference (aged 0-15)	93	1.4	4	95	1.4	4
Children placed on CP register (aged 0-15)	50	0.7	4	67	1.0	4
Adoption applications in year (aged 0-17)	30	0.4	2	18	0.2	4
Stranger adopter applications (aged 0-17)	19	0.3	1	10	0.1	3

The rate of looked after children is similar to that in many other authorities, having decreased since 1999. Lower rates of looked after children live in residential accommodation or with foster carers than in other authorities, but the number living with foster carers increased between 1999 and 2001. The Council have undertaken a series of initiatives to increase the number of foster carers, including raising the allowance, improving support for carers and recruitment campaigns.

There are low rates of child protection referrals, of children subject to a case conference and of children placed on the child protection register. The number of children on the register increased between 1998 and 2000. The number of stranger adoption applications reduced to a relatively low level in 1999-2000.

The Council has identified a dedicated senior officer, with responsibility for dealing with issues relating to the education of looked after children, and is working towards linking its social work and education information systems.

The Council has throughcare teams in place for provision of support services to young care leavers. Planning for the new arrangements for care leavers awaits clarification of the resources to be transferred.

The Council is developing an authority-wide young people's drug and alcohol service which will link closely to youth justice teams and other services. Comprising a manager and nine addiction workers, it is to offer a service to young people involved in drug and alcohol misuse. This will build on the success of the existing local Rushes Project, which provides a community based service to young people aged between 12 and 18, and their families; preventive services including education to schools; and a drop-in facility offering resources, information and training about alcohol and drugs.

A Forum of Elected Members from North Lanarkshire Council oversees the work of the Children Services Strategy Group. The Children's Services Plan outlines work to modernise and reshape services and to provide a responsive, intensive and integrated Community project, as an alternative to residential care. The plan anticipates a further roll out of the New Community School projects.

4. Performance: Criminal Justice

Key Activities	1999-2000	2000-2001	2000-2001 per 10,000	Quartile
Number of social enquiry reports submitted to the courts during the year	1,922	1,990	85.8	2
Number of community service orders made during the year	417	363	15.6	2
The proportion of social enquiry reports reported to court within target time	2000-2001	Quartile		
Proportion of social enquiry reports submitted to the courts by due date	94.5	4		
The time taken to complete community service orders				
Average length of community service (hours) for orders completed during the year	171	1		
Average hours completed per week	4.8	2		

A relatively high rate of social enquiry reports was submitted in 2000-2001. The proportion submitted to courts by the due date was lower than in most other authorities. The rate of community service orders made was also relatively high. The average length of orders made was longer than in many other authorities, but the orders were completed comparatively quickly, with 4.8 hours completed on average per week.

The Council forms with South Lanarkshire the Lanarkshire grouping for criminal justice services. A joint best value assessment of probation and court services has been carried out, using the quality assurance self-assessment process for criminal justice which was developed by COSLA in conjunction with ADSW and the Scottish Executive. Both councils have participated in the Forth and Clyde partnership of authorities to develop effective benchmarking and local performance measures for criminal justice services.

North Lanarkshire has created pilot "bridging teams" in two area teams, drawn from criminal justice and child care staff and managed by senior criminal justice staff. The aim is to improve the transition for young people between the children's hearings and adult criminal justice systems. The Council has appointed a childcare service co-ordinator with a specific remit for youth offending. Youth Justice Teams are being rolled out across the authority, a development from the "bridging teams" experience.

A protocol for managing sex offenders has been successfully taken through a joint working group of officers and elected members.

The Barnardo's CHOSI project works in partnership with the social work department and other agencies to challenge and address young people's offending behaviour. Working with young people aged between 14 and 18, the project aims to prevent 16-17 year olds progressing into the adult criminal justice system by offering alternatives through the children's hearing system, and also to prevent young people 14 plus from being placed in secure accommodation.

The Council works with other key partners such as SACRO, NCH and Includem. Each provides valuable services to the council.

5. Finance

Service Area (£000)	GAE 1999-2000	Final net Out turn 1999-2000	GAE 2000-2001	Final net Out turn 2000-2001
Children's Services	£15,544	£9,373	£15,678	£10,493
Community Care	£47,577	£46,075	£50,260	£51,567
Adult Offenders		£156		-£20
Other SW Services	£6,285	£11,966	£6,334	£10,983
Total	**£69,406**	**£67,570**	**£72,272**	**£73,023**

Spend per head		1999-2000		2000-2001
Spend per head		£206.24		£222.88
Quartile		4		3

Criminal Justice services receive funding from the Scottish Executive, and £2,052,972 was provided in 2000-2001.

North Lanarkshire spent significantly less than GAE on children's services in 1999-2000 and 2000-2001, in direct contrast to most other authorities. Expenditure on community care was slightly higher and on 'other SW services' significantly higher than GAE. Spend per head on social work services has increased, but remains relatively low.

6. Staffing

Staff	WTE 1999 actual	WTE 1999 per 1,000	Quartile 1999	WTE 2000 actual	WTE 2000 per 1,000	Quartile 2000
Managers & central staff	148	0.5	3	183	0.6	3
Frontline staff	1,366	4.2	3	1,664	5.1	2
Other	417	1.3	2	376	1.1	2
Total	**1,930**	**5.9**	**3**	**2,223**	**6.8**	**2**

Vacancies	Vacancies 2000	% Vacancies 2000	% Vacancies 2000 Scotland	Vacancies 2001	% Vacancies 2001	% Vacancies 2001 Scotland
SWs with adults	12	18.0	7.8	7	11.6	10.9
SWs with children	19	18.9	7.4	25	23.5	10.7
SWs with offenders	7	17.2	7.5	6	14.5	7.2
Generic workers	5	10.2	8.0	13	27.5	12.7
Total	**42**	**16.7**	**7.7**	**50**	**19.9**	**10.5**

An increase in total staff numbers between 1999 and 2000 means that the overall staffing rate is now relatively high. Numbers of managers, frontline staff and 'other social work services' staff all increased, but the rate of managers and central staff remains lower than in most other authorities. Vacancy levels are high in all areas and have increased from 2000 to 2001.

In early 2002 the Council had a vacancy rate of 16% for qualified social workers, in children's and criminal justice teams. In response to difficulties in recruiting social workers, occupational therapists and home care staff, the Council reviewed workforce needs and implemented measures including improvements to career structures, the introduction of social work assistants in a supportive role, and a review of the service provided by occupational therapists. There are proposals to introduce senior practitioner posts for social workers and occupational therapists. The department support unqualified workers to undertake social work qualifications through distance learning.

The Department has commissioned an external consultant to look at the reasons for the high level of sickness that prevails in the social work department.

7. Modernising services

There is a small but significant Asian population. The social work department provides funding, premises, advice and assistance to the Muslim Child and Family Alliance, which operates from the Alexander Resource Centre. Ethnic minorities are included in the carers' strategy and consideration of practice issues in children's and mental health services. The department has moved to ensure that ethnic minority staff are recruited to the home care service. The West of Scotland Race Equality Council has assisted departments to identify issues for the preparation of the Race Equality Scheme, and the social work department has established a working group to progress race equality.

There are 800 PCs in 70 different locations including all residential homes and day care centres. There is a programme of introducing case recording for all care groups, including piloting the use of voice recognition. Arrangements with Lanarkshire Health Trust for data transfer for single shared assessments are being introduced in spring 2002.

8. The Future

The Council and its health partners should build on the positive progress made on joint working in different aspects of community care.

In particular, a costed strategy, based on a shared assessment of need, is required to advance change involving all of the care agencies.

Progress on taking forward the recommendations of Sensing Progress has been slow, and further attention is needed on developing services for people with a sensory impairment.

The Council should continue its work on plans to implement the recommendations from *Learning with Care* on the education of looked after children. In particular, aligning and adjusting databases so that information can be shared, and formulating a scheme for the joint professional development of staff dealing with looked after children.

ORKNEY
ISLANDS COUNCIL

1. Profile at 2002

With 19,500 people the Orkney Council has the smallest population of all Scottish local authorities, concentrated on Mainland and spread over 17 inhabited islands.

The proportion of households with pensioners is already above the national average and the older population is projected to increase by more than the national average rate over the next 14 years. The under 45's and child population is expected to decrease at a higher than average rate.

At 2.4% (January 2002), the unemployment rate is lower than for Scotland as a whole.

Orkney has the lowest drug misuse rate in Scotland (0.3% of 15-54 year olds).

Levels of recorded crime are the lowest in Scotland (195 per 10,000 population in 2001).

The Council has a Policy and Resources Committee. Social work services are provided by the Department of Community Social Services which includes responsibility for social inclusion, housing, community safety and health. Much of their working effort has been devoted to rebuilding confidence in social work services, seriously damaged by events in the 1990s.

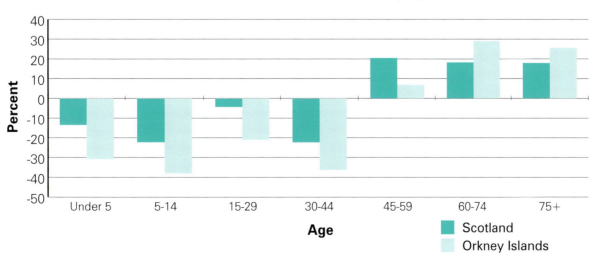

Expected % change in population, 2000-2016, local and national comparisons by age band

2. Performance: Community Care

Balance of care (aged 65+)	1999 actual	1999 per 1,000	Quartile	2000 actual	2000 per 1,000	Quartile
Older people in residential care homes	96	30	1	97	30	1
Older people in private nursing homes	0	0	4	0	0	4
Older people receiving home care	382	120	1	337	105	1
Older people in special needs housing	123	38.7	4	123	38.4	4
People receiving a community care service	1999-2000 actual	1999-2000 per 1,000	Quartile	2000-2001 actual	2000-2001 per 1,000	Quartile
Older people (aged 65+)	390	121.8	4	998	311.6	1
For mental health problems/dementia (aged 18-64)	19	1.6	4	152	12.9	1
For physical disabilities (aged 18-64)	92	7.8	4	54	4.6	4
For learning disabilities (aged 18-64)	9	0.8	4	52	4.4	2
For drug/alcohol abuse problems (aged 18-64)	3	0.2	4	58	4.9	1

Between 1999 and 2001 there was a massive increase in the number of older people receiving a community care service; the rate changed from low to high in comparison with other authorities. There are no nursing homes in Orkney. The rate of older people living in residential homes is high. The council is investing £3m in a single status residential unit. There are few special needs housing places. Orkney's Care and Repair scheme has addressed the needs of older people living in their own homes. Older people are more likely to receive a home care service than people on the mainland and are more likely to receive an intensive service (of more than 10 hours per week).

A multi-disciplinary Rapid Response service has been provided by the Council for 5 years (social care, care management and Occupational Therapy). It is currently being developed to become more formally inter-agency. A multi-disciplinary intensive home care service is already in operation. With NHS Orkney the Council is reviewing the provision of the mainstream home care service – particularly the need for contracted hours, links with community nursing, the development of career opportunities and the involvement of home carers in care planning.

The joint occupational therapy service is provided flexibly by community and hospital based occupational therapists. A joint service manager has a delegated budget. Improvements have been achieved in communications, in the management of adaptation requests and through a joint equipment store.

Community care staff work closely with partners in health, higher education and private and voluntary sector providers to provide services for the increasing number of service users who have learning disabilities. The Partnership in Practice agreement (PiP) plans for a full range of health and social services, and is clear about how the change fund is to be spent.

Following joint appointment of a local area co-ordinator, day opportunities are being expanded (including the development of SVQ modules in animal welfare and agriculture), St Colm's day centre and the voluntary sector group homes are increasingly used for people with complex needs and short breaks for carers can be arranged on Mainland or, for short periods, on individual islands.

Between 1999 and 2001 the number of people receiving a community care service for mental health problems increased significantly and the rate of provision is now high. The Council have agreed with NHS Orkney a new integrated service for mental health, and a joint mental health manager. They have provided funding to the Blide trust to assist this organisation with the purchase of their property to enable improved services for adults. It has appointed a co-ordinator to work with service users and carers, and a substance misuse worker in housing support. It is still necessary to call on psychiatric services in Aberdeen to deliver a full mental health service, a new home treatment programme in Stromness may reduce the need for some transfers.

Single shared assessment, using a locally developed tool, has been piloted with older people and is now being rolled out to all care groups, including people with a sensory impairment. Waiting times for assessments have been reduced and improvements made in access to services. Orkney has used the "resource utilisation measure" with 100 assessments and is now ready to roll out its use with single shared assessment.

Working under the joint manager for occupational therapy, a rehabilitation officer supports people with either a hearing or visual impairment. There is a visual impairment association, but no similar group for people with a hearing impairment. Resources for working with people with a sensory impairment are proportionate to the needs which the Council has identified.

There has been a large increase in the number of people receiving a community care service for drug/alcohol problems between 1999 and 2001, and the rate is now higher than in many other authorities.

A joint health and social work management team determines joint resourcing of services and manages the developing range of joint posts – notably in strategic planning, occupational therapy services, rapid response and intensive home care. Progress on a partnership agreement has been limited, because shortage of health funds has limited the capacity to deliver joint resourcing.

The Community Social Services Department and NHS Orkney are establishing an integrated training service, to cover statutory core training, joint management training, and combination of the SVQ centres to provide for care awards. Most professional post-qualifying training will continue to have to be delivered on a specialist basis. Economies are possible from integrating administrative services and combining in-house training.

3. Performance: Children and Families

Balance of care – Looked after children (aged 0-17)	1999-2000 actual	1999-2000 per 1,000	Quartile	2000-2001 actual	2000-2001 per 1,000	Quartile
At home	17	3.8	2	13	2.9	3
With friends/relatives/other community	2	0.5	3	0	0.0	4
With foster carers/prospective adopters	5	1.1	4	10	2.2	3
In residential accommodation	3	0.7	4	5	1.1	2
Total	**27**	**6**	**4**	**28**	**6.3**	**4**

Key performance indicators	1998-1999 actual	1998-1999 per 1,000	Quartile	1999-2000 actual	1999-2000 per 1,000	Quartile
Child protection (CP) referrals (aged 0-15)	39	9.7	2	40	10.1	1
Children subject to a CP case conference (aged 0-15)	3	0.8	4	11	2.8	2
Children placed on CP register (aged 0-15)	2	0.5	4	5	1.3	3
Adoption applications in year (aged 0-17)	1	0.2	4	0	0.0	4
Stranger adopter applications (aged 0-17)	1	0.2	2	0	0.0	4

The rate of children on the child protection register has been low for a number of years. The recent rise in the numbers of children being referred reflects growing confidence in the quality and operation of current child protection arrangements. Alcohol is a consistent feature of child protection. Reorganisation of the children and families team has helped staff cope with increases in child protection work.

The rate of looked after children remains low and steady. None of the looked after children live with friends or relatives. The number living with foster carers doubled between 1999 and 2001. There are difficulties in matching demand for foster carers. Three children are currently accommodated away from Orkney.

Additional funds from the Scottish Executive are being used to improve training and recruitment of carers, and to enhance support services for families with young children.

The Council has made some progress in implementing the recommendations of *Learning with Care*. It is intended to produce an integrated policy on the education of looked after children, associated with a programme of joint training for key staff. Full-time education is provided for looked after children or, for a very small number of them, education in an appropriate setting. Progress has been made in supporting the education of children and young people in residential and foster care: the Council has provided ICT equipment, homework support and quiet study areas. Comprehensive information on looked after children, is stored in accessible manual systems, and a joint education/social work database is being developed.

Services for care leavers are provided in consultation with a local throughcare and aftercare forum. Instead of a service budget the Council has specific budgets for care leavers with individual packages. The Council has still to arrange formal training, but the forum and focus groups have familiarised staff from relevant agencies with the wider needs of care leavers.

Integration of children's services is a priority reflected in the roll out of the New Community Schools project, in which social work staff work from the two main secondary schools in the islands. The need for integration is emphasised by parents of children with profound needs calling for education, social work and health to improve joint working.

4. Performance: Criminal Justice

Key Activities	1999-2000	2000-2001	2000-2001 per 10,000	Quartile
Number of social enquiry reports submitted to the courts during the year	61	50	37.2	4
Number of community service orders made during the year	19	11	8.2	4

The proportion of social enquiry reports reported to court within target time	2000-2001	Quartile
Proportion of social enquiry reports submitted to the courts by due date	100.0	1
The time taken to complete community service orders		
Average length of community service (hours) for orders completed during the year	182	1
Average hours completed per week	7.0	1

The rates of social enquiry reports submitted and of community service orders made has been lower than in most other authorities. The low numbers reflect the low crime rate in Orkney. All reports are submitted to courts by the due date. The average length of community service hours for orders completed in 2000-2001 was higher than in many other authorities and orders were completed more quickly.

The Council has observer links with the Northern Partnership for provision of criminal justice services. There is collaboration with the other two Islands on strategic planning and quality assurance. Joint training has been introduced across the whole Partnership. Staff have on-line access to the Criminal Justice Social Work Development Centre, and make use of approaches developed by other, larger authorities.

The Scottish Executive's risk assessment guidance framework (RAGF) is used to assist appropriate targeting of intervention. The low numbers involved limit formal evaluation, but performance is actively monitored through supervision.

Partnership with SACRO enables a range of services to be delivered including a four-bed supported accommodation service. A lottery funded CROP project provides people on community service and supervised attendance with work placements, producing fresh vegetables and flowers for older people, homes and day centres. A Care and Respect drink-drive programme run jointly with the police is well established and shows positive results. It also underpins the Streetwise Safe Driving Education Scheme for secondary school pupils. The mediation and reparation scheme for young offenders age up to 17 draws on SACRO's national experience and uses their local base. SACRO staff support the provision of gender-appropriate services for women offenders and provide additional capacity when departmental staff are committed elsewhere.

5. Finance

Service Area (£000)	GAE 1999-2000	Final net Out turn 1999-2000	GAE 2000-2001	Final net Out turn 2000-2001
Children's Services	£258	£1,216	£268	£1,292
Community Care	£3,081	£4,738	£3,236	£4,695
Adult Offenders		£23		£22
Other SW Services	£363	£1,035	£363	£1,048
Total	**£3,702**	**£7,012**	**£3,866**	**£7,056**

Spend per head		1999-2000		2000-2001
Spend per head		£359.95		£362.21
Quartile		1		1

Criminal Justice services receive funding direct from the Scottish Executive, which amounted to £297,147 in 2000-2001.

Expenditure on social work services in 1999-2000 and 2000-2001 was considerably above GAE levels – four and half times on children's services, but there were smaller overspends on community care services and other social work services. Spend per head on social work services is higher than in most other authorities.

6. Staffing

Staff	WTE 1999 actual	WTE 1999 per 1,000	Quartile 1999	WTE 2000 actual	WTE 2000 per 1,000	Quartile 2000
Managers & central staff	40	2.1	1	28	1.4	1
Frontline staff	222	11.3	1	194	10.0	1
Other	74	3.8	1	62	3.2	1
Total	**336**	**17.1**	**1**	**285**	**14.6**	**1**

Vacancies	Vacancies 2000	% Vacancies 2000	% Vacancies 2000 Scotland	Vacancies 2001	% Vacancies 2001	% Vacancies 2001 Scotland
SWs with adults	0	0	7.8	0	0	10.9
SWs with children	0	0	7.4	1	20.0	10.7
SWs with offenders	0	0	7.5	0	0	7.2
Generic workers	0	0	8.0	0	0	12.7
Total	**0**	**0**	**7.7**	**1**	**9.1**	**10.5**

The number of staff (both managers and frontline staff) reduced between 1999 and 2000, but staffing rates remain higher than in many other authorities. There is only one current vacancy, in children's services.

Community social services have had problems in filling management posts. The Council has taken a pro-active approach to recruitment, despite higher recruitment costs, with an average cost of £10,000 per post including advertising, interview and relocation costs.

The Council has adopted a major workforce plan to clarify recruitment and training needs, taking account of future planned service developments and the introduction of national care standards. It represents a blueprint for the social care workforce in 2005. Audit Scotland's review of home care, has prompted consideration of the need for improved conditions of service for home carers to generate a larger, more flexible workforce.

7. Modernising services

The department has lead responsibility for social inclusion and on race equality. Orkney has a small resident ethnic minority population, and the islands are visited by tourists, increasingly brought by cruise ships, from many countries. The health and social service joint management team has agreed a joint approach to preparing the Race Equality Plan. The department intends to adopt the national monitoring framework being suggested by the national data standards project, and to undertake further research on needs in Orkney.

The Council aims to introduce in 2003 a community service portal that is accessible from all rural and remote communities in Orkney. "The One Stop Shop" is to give residents access to social work, health and housing services through a variety of channels, including the internet and video conferencing. A project, supported by Modernising Government funds, is in progress to provide an improved information system, a single source for enquiries and a single route for giving personal details.

The department is purchasing a new client information system for introduction in 2003. The In4tek system can be used with mobile communications, including telephones and palmtops.

8. The Future

The Council has recently done much to earn confidence and respect of local people for social work. Greater transparency about social work, how much it spends and how it undertakes its responsibilities are conveyed in The Director's Annual Report. The major challenge is to focus on identifying developing local needs, on providing quality services at an affordable cost to the growing older population and facilitating access to services both on Mainland and in the islands, despite the difficulties and costs of local transport.

Improvements in delivery of home care services – particularly in some of the outer islands – are now due urgently. Following the joint review, the Council should formulate with its health partner priorities for progressive implementation of an up-to-date flexible service.

The implications of introducing some developments have still to be fully identified and provided for – notably professional training and information on the assessment process.

In recent years and following the Orkney Child Care Inquiry the Council has undertaken major expenditure on children and families. The time has come to reappraise resource priorities in view of other needs, particularly in different aspects of community care.

To maintain progress in improving the education of looked after children the Council faces further tasks in producing:

- care plans or placement agreements for all looked after children, based on assessments which include suitable educational targets;
- guidelines setting out the responsibilities of all agencies involved with looked after children, the procedures to be followed and arrangements for monitoring practice; and
- an out-of-school protocol for looked after children who are unable to return to mainstream schools.

The Council faces staffing problems, given the competing workforce in Orkney's buoyant employment market. It should therefore implement its staffing blue-print as a matter of urgency, to secure the service improvements which it has in train and has to plan for the future.

1. Profile at 2002

Perth and Kinross is a medium-sized mainly rural authority with a population of 133,600.

The proportions of households with pensioners and children are above the national average.

The population is expected to remain stable overall, with the largest increases in the older age group.

At 2.6% (January 2002), the unemployment rate is very low.

The rate of drug misuse is below average (1.3% of 15-54 year olds).

The crime rate is below the national average (576 crimes recorded per 10,000 population in 2001) but has increased slightly from 2000.

Perth & Kinross Council has undergone successive reorganisation. Social work services for adults has been the responsibility of a director of housing and social work (which embraces community care and criminal justice services). The director is also chief social work officer.

From early 2002 adult care services have merged with some health agencies to form Care Together, a new organisation. The director of housing and social work has been seconded to lead Care Together during its developmental phases.

Social work services for children are part of a directorate of education and children's services. The head of child care services has management responsibility for social work services to children.

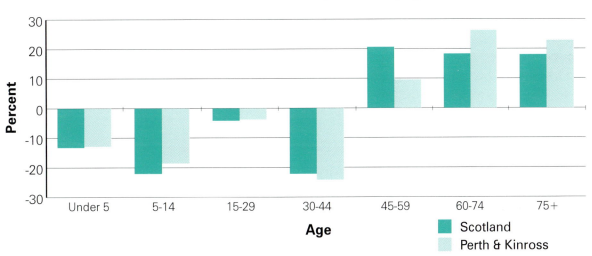

Expected % change in population, 2000-2016, local and national comparisons by age band

2. Performance: Community Care

Balance of care (aged 65+)	1999 actual	1999 per 1,000	Quartile	2000 actual	2000 per 1,000	Quartile
Older people in residential care homes	647	26	1	612	25	1
Older people in private nursing homes	733	30	1	692	28	2
Older people receiving home care	1,294	53	4	1,282	52	4
Older people in special needs housing	2,619	107.2	3	2,117	86	3

People receiving a community care service	1999-2000 actual	1999-2000 per 1,000	Quartile	2000-2001 actual	2000-2001 per 1,000	Quartile
Older people (aged 65+)	4,354	176.9	3	4,764	193.5	3
For mental health problems/dementia (aged 18-64)	237	3.0	3	237	3.0	3
For physical disabilities (aged 18-64)	1,005	12.6	3	1,121	14.0	2
For learning disabilities (aged 18-64)	256	3.2	3	266	3.3	3
For drug/alcohol abuse problems (aged 18-64)	27	0.3	3	22	0.3	4

Older people are more likely to live in residential and nursing homes in Perth & Kinross than in many other authorities, although numbers are decreasing. Provision of special needs housing is relatively low and has fallen but there are more very sheltered houses in the area than in other authorities. The Council has a lower rate of older people with home care than most other authorities and care has been provided for fewer hours per week than the Scottish average.

Changes are being made to provide more responsive care services for older people wishing to remain at home. The former home help service is gradually changing, with home carers working more flexible hours and undertaking personal care. Improvements are also being made to practical shopping, domestic and household services.

A multi-disciplinary Intensive Care at Home Service (ICAHS) has been introduced to prevent unnecessary admission and facilitate early discharge from Perth Royal Infirmary. It supports people with dementia, people with a progressive degenerative illness and carers in crisis. It also provides early supported discharges for up to 10 days. For those people leaving acute hospital but not ready to return home to rural areas, a community liaison team arranges "stepdown" care in one of five community hospitals, allowing short term rehabilitation prior to discharge.

A single learning disabilities service extends across the area, headed by a single manager and staffed by secondments from health and social work. Preparations are being made to achieve a joint budget and to develop performance indicators. Despite resources from the change fund and transitional housing benefit, many individual packages of care have proved expensive and 35-40 individuals are placed outwith the area. Firm agreement has yet to be secured on residual NHS in-patient provision, following closure of Strathmartine Hospital.

A designated officer co-ordinates future needs assessments for children with learning disabilities and engages health and education in provision of services. Vulnerable adults procedures have not yet been developed, though there are existing guidelines on abuse.

Despite joint working in the provision of mental health services, joint service developments have been restricted by NHS financial problems, and service cuts have been made to realise savings in the NHS mental health budget. There is now, however, an agreed strategy for development which includes residual in-patient provision.

Community services are provided by four community mental health teams, which do not however fit into the overall Care Together structure. Features of the present service are:

- an ongoing re-settlement programme at the Murray Royal Hospital;
- a series of day care developments; and
- an intensive care at home service.

Sensory impairment services are provided largely by Perth and Kinross Society for the Blind and Tayside Association for the Deaf. Strategic planning falls to a sub-group of the health and physical disabilities task group, comprising Care Together staff and the voluntary organisations. The lack of health or education representation inhibits its capacity to address a comprehensive sensory impairment service. A transition group – with links to the sensory impairment sub-group – manages continuity during and following future needs assessments.

Care Together, the product of a partnership agreement between the Council and NHS Tayside, became operational early in 2002. It provides social work services for adults, including learning disability and mental health, elderly acute services and old age psychiatry services. It has a general manager, with single managers for five localities. Its budget includes £26m. from the Council, equivalent to the GAE for community care services in 2001-2002.

3. Performance: Children and Families

Balance of care – Looked after children (aged 0-17)	1999-2000 actual	1999-2000 per 1,000	Quartile	2000-2001 actual	2000-2001 per 1,000	Quartile
At home	65	2.2	4	50	1.7	4
With friends/relatives/other community	38	1.3	1	35	1.2	2
With foster carers/prospective adopters	48	1.7	3	56	1.9	4
In residential accommodation	27	0.9	3	30	1.0	3
Total	**178**	**6.1**	**4**	**171**	**5.9**	**4**

Key performance indicators	1998-1999 actual	1998-1999 per 1,000	Quartile	1999-2000 actual	1999-2000 per 1,000	Quartile
Child protection (CP) referrals (aged 0-15)	296	11.5	1	236	9.3	1
Children subject to a CP case conference (aged 0-15)	93	3.7	1	62	2.4	3
Children placed on CP register (aged 0-15)	56	2.2	2	42	1.7	3
Adoption applications in year (aged 0-17)	14	0.5	2	20	0.7	1
Stranger adopter applications (aged 0-17)	5	0.2	2	8	0.3	1

The rate of looked after children is low, having remained at a similar level for 3 years. The rate of looked after children who are living in residential accommodation is relatively low. The Council has managed to cut the numbers of children in residential schools from 24 to 10, due in large part to a successful joint re-integration project. The number of children in foster care increased between 1999 and 2001 but remains low in comparison with most other authorities.

The rate of child protection referrals is higher than in many other authorities but the rate of children subject to a case conference is relatively low. The rate of children placed on the child protection register has fallen and is now relatively low. The number of adoption applications has increased between 1998 and 2000 and the rate is now higher than in most other authorities.

A recent best value audit of child protection services recommended improvements in guidance and training for education and childcare staff and also a joint assessment framework for education and social work staff.

In partnership with the voluntary sector, the Council is providing preventative services focusing on alcohol misuse and family support. A Homeless Families Co-ordination Group aims to improve inter-agency working, improve the joint assessment framework and formalise links between the Child Protection Committee, the Substance Misuse Action Team and the Domestic Violence Forum. It has prompted initiatives which address the health and welfare needs of children caught up in their parents' homelessness, substance misuse and domestic abuse. The initiatives – funded from diverse sources – range from the provision of advice and information, family support, and crisis intervention to rehabilitation.

The Council has adopted an action plan to implement recommendations of *Learning with Care*. The following action has been taken:

- designated teachers have been appointed;
- joint staff development training is in progress;
- an audit of residential homes is complete;
- targets for educational attainment are set in the Children Services Plan; and
- education and children's services are developing a management information system; a module for data on exclusions is already in use and another is being implemented for data on educational attainment from secondary schools; that data has yet to be linked to information about looked after children.

Agreement on multi-disciplinary assessments is outstanding.

Throughcare and aftercare services rely on partnership working. Wellbank has been developed as a purpose-built resource for those leaving care and for homeless young people. A Social Inclusion Partnership initiative for care leavers (the Go Project) is directed at young people age 16-26. Managed by a multi-disciplinary team, it is linked with a mentoring scheme provided in association with the Prince's Trust, and also has links with schools, careers and local colleges to extend work and training placements. The consolidation of these initiatives is the subject of a Children's Services Fund application.

The new directorate of education and children's services is a potential platform for integrating children's services. The development of area support and childcare teams, linked by Care and Learning Co-ordinators, with an integrated management structure provides opportunities for linking education, care and health services around local communities.

4. Performance: Criminal Justice

Key Activities	1999-2000	2000-2001	2000-2001 per 10,000	Quartile
Number of social enquiry reports submitted to the courts during the year	659	785	85.4	2
Number of community service orders made during the year	116	138	15.0	3
The proportion of social enquiry reports reported to court within target time	2000-2001	Quartile		
Proportion of social enquiry reports submitted to the courts by due date	100.0	1		
The time taken to complete community service orders				
Average length of community service (hours) for orders completed during the year	119	4		
Average hours completed per week	2.9	4		

A relatively high rate of social enquiry reports were submitted in 2000-2001, an increase on 1999-2000. All reports were submitted to courts by the due date. The number of community service orders made has increased, but the rate remains relatively low. The average length of community service orders completed during the year is lower than in most other authorities but the time taken to complete orders is longer, with just 2.9 average hours completed per week.

Perth and Kinross is grouped with Angus and Dundee City for the provision of criminal justice services. The intention is to build on previous collaboration by establishing a strategic group to drive the performance, quality and planning agenda, and to harmonise their different information systems as far as possible.

The Council operates a range of quality assurance mechanisms, including conversion rates and custody disposals. It is currently examining the risk/needs assessment tools to use. The inherited computer system limits the capacity for introducing a computer-based quality assurance system.

An inter-agency group oversees a number of youth crime initiatives, which feature close joint working with community learning services and voluntary agencies.

5. Finance

Service Area (£000)	GAE 1999-2000	Final net Out turn 1999-2000	GAE 2000-2001	Final net Out turn 2000-2001
Children's Services	£3,099	£6,489	£3,166	£7,680
Community Care	£21,424	£17,721	£22,537	£19,683
Adult Offenders		£23		£29
Other SW Services	£2,520	£1,962	£2,539	£2,274
Total	**£27,043**	**£26,194**	**£28,242**	**£29,666**

Spend per head		1999-2000		2000-2001
Spend per head		£196.03		£222.01
Quartile		4		3

Criminal Justice services receive funding direct from the Scottish Executive, which amounted to £864,893 in 2000-2001.

The Council has spent over twice the GAE level on children's services, but no less than £3m under GAE for community care. Spend per head on social work services has increased but is still relatively low.

6. Staffing

Staff	WTE 1999 actual	WTE 1999 per 1,000	Quartile 1999	WTE 2000 actual	WTE 2000 per 1,000	Quartile 2000
Managers & central staff	87	0.6	2	86	0.6	3
Frontline staff	508	3.8	4	461	3.5	4
Other	129	1.0	3	128	1.0	3
Total	**724**	**5.4**	**4**	**676**	**5.1**	**4**

Vacancies	Vacancies 2000	% Vacancies 2000	% Vacancies 2000 Scotland	Vacancies 2001	% Vacancies 2001	% Vacancies 2001 Scotland
SWs with adults	2	3.4	7.8	1	10.0	10.9
SWs with children	8	12.4	7.4	0	0	10.7
SWs with offenders	0	0	7.5	0	0	7.2
Generic workers	1	3.1	8.0	0	0	12.7
Total	**10**	**7.0**	**7.7**	**1**	**10.0**	**10.5**

The rates of staffing are lower than in many other authorities and total numbers have fallen between 1999 and 2000 – most of them frontline staff. In 2001 there was only one social worker vacancy in community care and none in children's service (compared with 8 in 1999).

Although the Council is not experiencing severe recruitment problems, there are some difficulties, for example in recruiting mental health officers and for posts in children's services. The recruitment process has been streamlined. The Council has led the Scottish Executive's recruitment and selection project group developing the tool-kit for the recruitment of residential child care staff. To encourage a wider range of applicants into home care, a new home carer post has been established with contracted hours and new terms and conditions.

There is a comprehensive staff support programme which includes:

- on-the-job training and work familiarisation for all staff; and
- to enable the Council to grow its own managers, secondment of service managers and senior social workers to management training at Lauder College.

The Council is considering:

- linkage of internal promotion to successful completion of professional qualification modules; and
- home working for some staff and the development of non-traditional work patterns.

It has appointed a "Health for All" worker to promote healthier lifestyles, reviewed public holidays and conducted a communications survey as part of a strategy to improve communications between services.

7. Modernising services

There is a small Chinese community and a number of travelling people. Together with the police and other agencies, the Council participates in a panel concerned with racial harassment. The lead on equality issues, including race, has been undertaken at a corporate level. Education and children's services and Care Together have few specific resources for assisting with preparation of a race equality plan.

The Council's corporate information strategy focuses on improving customer contact and developing customer care through the use of innovative technologies.

Care Together has developed strong IT links between the partners, notably the electronic single shared assessment, now available for health and social care professionals. Care Together staff have access to PCs in dispersed health offices, but not in all local authority offices: four localities are trialling the use of handheld computers.

8. The Future

The restructuring of the Council's services and the preparation required to form the entirely new Care Together has preoccupied senior managers for some time. This is now time to deploy energy and commitment to translating the opportunities provided by restructuring into planning and providing better services on the ground.

There is an urgent need to review the balance of care provided for older people in the light of population projections and in particular to plan for a higher rate of quality home care, in order to release pressures on residential resources.

To complement improvements in community mental health services, the Council should plan for residual in-patient services for mental health, when the Murray Royal Hospital retracts.

Services for children with learning disabilities require a strategy to guide their future improvement and the commitment of resources for this purpose. The strategy should embrace closer links between children's services and services for people with a learning disability. In addition the Council should reappraise its investment in assessing and planning for children with special educational needs.

To consolidate improvements in services for those with sensory impairments, the Council should give priority to training for staff working with people with a sensory impairment.

The Council should decide on its response to the recommendations made by the recent best value review for improvements in guidance and training for education and childcare staff and also a joint assessment framework for education and social work staff and decide on their priority for implementation.

To underpin the progress made and planned in the education of looked after children, the Council should press for multi-disciplinary assessments to be agreed and implemented.

The Council should join with its partners in criminal justice services in harmonising systems, procedures and practice. Establishing a strategic group could provide means for driving the performance, quality and planning agenda.

Meantime the Council should determine the requirements for developing ISCJIS (the Integrated Scottish Criminal Justice Information System) for its area.

In order to guide and inform racial equality measures, the Council should commission managers to prepare a Race Equality Plan.

1. Profile at 2002

Renfrewshire has a mainly urban population of 177,000.

The local population is expected to fall by 4.3% over the next 14 years. There is likely to be a larger than average decrease in the under 5 population and a larger than average increase in the over 75 population.

At 4.2% (January 2002), the unemployment rate is similar to the national average. It has remained static over the past year, following a faster than average fall the previous year.

Renfrewshire has the 5th highest drugs misuse rate (2.5% of 15-54 year olds).

The crime rate has risen slightly from 2000 and, at 952 crimes recorded per 10,000 population in 2001, is the fifth highest in Scotland.

Renfrewshire Council and its partners published a 10-year community plan in April 2001 following consultation through a Citizens Panel. One of the plan's 3 key themes is health and social care.

A Social Work Department provides services with a director of social work who is also chief social work officer. The Department has developed an extensive programme for consulting people using social work services.

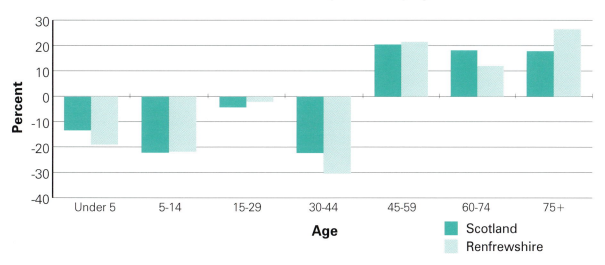

2. Performance: Community Care

Balance of care (aged 65+)	1999 actual	1999 per 1,000	Quartile	1999 actual	1999 per 1,000	Quartile
Older people in residential care homes	397	15	3	416	16	3
Older people in private nursing homes	703	27	2	528	20	3
Older people receiving home care	1,961	76	3	1,982	76	2
Older people in special needs housing	2,215	86	3	2,141	82.6	3
People receiving a community care service	1999-2000 actual	1999-2000 per 1,000	Quartile	2000-2001 actual	2000-2001 per 1,000	Quartile
Older people (aged 65+)	5,318	205.1	3	4,211	162.4	4
For mental health problems/dementia (aged 18-64)	714	6.4	1	590	5.3	1
For physical disabilities (aged 18-64)	1,678	15.2	2	1,642	14.8	2
For learning disabilities (aged 18-64)	506	4.6	1	466	4.2	2
For drug/alcohol abuse problems (aged 18-64)	545	4.9	1	768	6.9	1

In 2000 there were relatively fewer places for older people in residential and nursing homes than in many other Scottish authorities. The number of people in nursing homes decreased between 1999 and 2000 but is now growing and the number in residential homes increased. Provision of special needs housing is relatively low. The rate of older people receiving home care is relatively high and they are more likely to receive an intensive service (more than 10 hours per week) than in many other authorities.

Improvements in the home care service which are currently under way include:
- training in personal care tasks;
- extending to 6 weeks the Hospital to Home and Rapid Response Teams attached to the hospital to help prevent admission to hospital and facilitate discharge;
- expanding the community alarm service to cover greater number of clients, including those with dementia;
- implementation of the best value review of home care leading to more flexible service provision; and
- as a complementary programme, best value reviews are being undertaken on residential and day care facilities which should result in upgrading of facilities and improved staffing.

A significant number of older people have experienced delays in discharges from hospital. The Department has speeded up assessment procedures and signed off a discharge protocol. A joint commissioning plan has been agreed which will enhance community based services.

Despite past difficulties between the Council and its health partners over joint working and resource transfer and release, a Partnership in Practice Agreement (PiP) is now in place for the development of services for people with learning disabilities. The joint strategy group that developed the PiP oversees its implementation: it includes a person with learning disability, an independent advocacy worker and four family carers. A best value review of learning disability services is planned, which will include the modernisation of traditional day services.

A mental health joint strategy group has reviewed the Health Board's strategy, but its financial framework has not been agreed. An integrated community mental health team based in Paisley's Charleston Centre provides a service to people with severe and enduring mental illness.

The Council's mental health development workers link with GPs, local health care co-operatives and day centres, and undertake groupwork with people who have mental health problems.

Single shared assessment is due to be fully implemented in 2002-2003. All partners, including LHCCs and the housing department, are committed to a person-centred approach and to use of the Carenap E tool. A multi-agency reference group will ensure consistency of implementation and oversee the training programme. Three local multi-agency operational groups have been established: two have secured quicker access to services. Users are fully co-operating by signing consents to share information between agencies.

The new Mile End Resource Centre marks a major advance in services for people with a sensory impairment and for those with a multiple disability. Drawing on extensive consultation with service users, it provides assessment, equipment and skills training and access to specialist information for blind and visually impaired people and deaf or hearing impaired people. All information is provided through video in sign language and deaf people are free to use video equipment to pass and receive information in sign language or lip speaking. The Centre has a showroom and a variety of built-in loop systems facilitating the demonstration of equipment, ease of discussion and access to information. The Council's social work teams for visually and hearing impaired people and some occupational therapy services are based within the Centre. To supplement the guide/communication skills of staff, services are purchased from Deafblind Scotland.

Joint working between the Council and its health partners is progressing steadily. Under an agreed partnership arrangement (Renfrewshire Joint Care) partners are to align their relevant resources with greater transparency. Renfrewshire Joint Care is to have a joint advisory board with representatives from each of its parent bodies. A senior officer group – the membership of which may extend in future to user and carer groups, voluntary organisations and other public agencies such as Communities Scotland – will assist in implementing recommendations. A jointly appointed senior development manager post should markedly progress joint resourcing and management.

3. Performance: Children and Families

Balance of care – Looked after children (aged 0-17)	1999-2000 actual	1999-2000 per 1,000	Quartile	2000-2001 actual	2000-2001 per 1,000	Quartile
At home	224	5.5	2	219	5.4	1
With friends/relatives/other community	42	1.0	2	29	0.7	3
With foster carers/prospective adopters	70	1.7	3	80	2.0	3
In residential accommodation	88	2.2	1	100	2.5	1
Total	**424**	**10.5**	**2**	**428**	**10.6**	**2**

Key performance indicators	1998-1999 actual	1998-1999 per 1,000	Quartile	1999-2000 actual	1999-2000 per 1,000	Quartile
Child protection (CP) referrals (aged 0-15)	161	4.5	4	131	3.6	4
Children subject to a CP case conference (aged 0-15)	124	3.4	2	113	3.1	2
Children placed on CP register (aged 0-15)	88	2.4	2	79	2.2	2
Adoption applications in year (aged 0-17)	12	0.3	3	15	0.4	2
Stranger adopter applications (aged 0-17)	9	0.2	2	11	0.3	1

Between 1998 and 2000 there was a low rate of child protection referrals. A high proportion of referrals lead to a case conference and the rate of children placed on child protection registers is relatively high. There is a high rate of stranger adoption applications.

The rate of looked after children has shown a modest increase in recent years. There has been a significant increase in the number of children in residential accommodation and the rate of looked after children living in residential accommodation is higher than in most other authorities. Secure accommodation is under acute pressure. The Council is having to accommodate teenagers with significant alcohol and drug problems. Numbers in residential homes has risen. There have been some instances of residential school expulsions. There has been a significant increase in the rate of children requiring foster care, which exceeds the supply of places.

The pressures in the Council's residential units have increased due to the marked increases in the number of children needing to be accommodated coupled with insufficient placements in other care settings. Staff costs and sickness levels are rising as demand intensifies. Longcroft Children's Home was awarded a Charter Mark in 2000-2001 for the quality of its services.

A multi-disciplinary service based in Paisley (the Family Matters Project) supports vulnerable families with children under the age of 5 by:

- helping parents build on existing skills and develop new ones;
- supporting parents experiencing difficulties with stress and isolation; and
- providing training and consultancy for staff working with families with young children.

A recent external evaluation identified evidence of successful interventions and indicated ways of enhancing the work of the project.

Progress has been made in implementing most of the recommendations of *Learning with Care*. Looked after children benefit from educational support provided by three dedicated teachers whose posts are jointly funded. A particular strength is the strategic approach to family support by home/school support workers, whose priorities include looked after children. Further progress needs to be achieved in linking social work and schools information systems, producing a joint policy on promoting the education of looked after children and in training for education and social work staff.

An inter-agency working group is responsible for implementing the new arrangements for supporting care leavers. It has listed required tasks and bid for children's services funding for a dedicated post. Further progress needs to be achieved in establishing a budget and in consulting young people.

The Council's Children's Service Plan outlines the integration of planning and delivery of services for children. Education, family support and health services are to form Area Family Support Teams, as part of the roll out of New Community Schools. It is envisaged that the Changing Children's Services Fund will support developments, including the continuation and roll-out of the Family Matters Project.

4. Performance: Criminal Justice

Key Activities	1999-2000	2000-2001	2000-2001 per 10,000	Quartile
Number of social enquiry reports submitted to the courts during the year	960	1,017	81.5	2
Number of community service orders made during the year	235	232	18.6	2
The proportion of social enquiry reports reported to court within target time	2000-2001	Quartile		
Proportion of social enquiry reports submitted to the courts by due date	98.0	2		
The time taken to complete community service orders				
Average length of community service (hours) for orders completed during the year	159	2		
Average hours completed per week	4.1	2		

The relatively high rate of social enquiry reports submitted to courts reflects the high crime rate. 98% of social enquiry reports are submitted to courts by the due date. A relatively high rate of community service orders was made in 2000-2001. The average length of community service orders was relatively high, as were the average number of hours completed per week.

The Council is part of a criminal justice services grouping with East Renfrewshire and Inverclyde. An inter-authority best value review of services has been commissioned. The Council has itself speeded up the processing of social enquiry reports and has improved quality assurance by effective supervision by senior social workers, supplemented by a 10% random sampling against a standard pro forma.

Most records are manual and standardised forms are being introduced to facilitate individual case management and to monitor the achievement of national standards. It is planned to introduce Sheridan's SWIFT system to provide strategic management and quality assurance information.

The Council manages the Pathways Project which is designed to engage in partnership all agencies involved with a particular offender, in order to promote public protection through effective risk assessments. It supports the case management of offenders, both adults and young people, who have committed sex offences or displayed sexually aggressive behaviour. The Project provides a service to the three Councils involved in the Criminal Justice Grouping.

5. Finance

Service Area (£000)	GAE 1999-2000	Final net Out turn 1999-2000	GAE 2000-2001	Final net Out turn 2000-2001
Children's Services	£8,216	£8,551	£8,361	£8,019
Community Care	£25,355	£26,196	£26,602	£28,157
Adult Offenders		£23		£9
Other SW Services	£3,397	£3,770	£3,412	£5,405
Total	**£36,968**	**£38,541**	**£38,375**	**£41,590**
Spend per head		**1999-2000**		**2000-2001**
Spend per head		£217.78		£235.01
Quartile		2		2

Criminal Justice services receive funding from the Scottish Executive, and £1,344,012 was provided in 2000-2001.

Contrasting with most other authorities the Council spends slightly less than GAE levels on children's services. They spend slightly more than GAE on community care and other social work services. Spending per head on social work services is relatively high.

6. Staffing

Staff	WTE 1999 actual	WTE 1999 per 1,000	Quartile 1999	WTE 2000 actual	WTE 2000 per 1,000	Quartile 2000
Managers & central staff	127	0.7	2	156	0.9	1
Frontline staff	830	4.7	2	903	5.1	2
Other	165	0.9	4	221	1.2	2
Total	**1,123**	**6.3**	**3**	**1,280**	**7.2**	**2**

Vacancies	Vacancies 2000	% Vacancies 2000	% Vacancies 2000 Scotland	Vacancies 2001	% Vacancies 2001	% Vacancies 2001 Scotland
SWs with adults	2	7.3	7.8	4	15.2	10.9
SWs with children	4	14.2	7.4	5	14.4	10.7
SWs with offenders	3	14.0	7.5	4	17.1	7.2
Generic workers	5	19.7	8.0	12	19.5	12.7
Total	**14**	**14.2**	**7.7**	**24**	**17.1**	**10.5**

The number of staff increased between 1999 and 2000, and staffing rates are now relatively high. The rate of managers and central staff is now higher than in many other authorities. Vacancy levels are high in all areas. The Council is experiencing difficulties attracting qualified social workers and retaining home care and residential care staff – particularly good, experienced childcare workers. The situation is exacerbated by the high absentee rate in comparison with other departments. In response the Council:

- engages agency staff, with additional support;

- works to attract students and new workers; and
- uses large-scale advertising.

All new staff are provided with induction and a resource pack. Newly appointed staff have regular planned supervision and normally a protected caseload with no child protection cases in the first year. The Council is examining with Paisley University and other Councils a flexible part-time route for training unqualified workers to DipSW level.

There is a large-scale and innovative recruitment programme, with improved advertising, application packs, consistent contact with the universities and participation at recruitment fairs. Area managers give talks and offer interviews on the same day. Potential recruits are invited into team meetings and involved in training, before they actually begin working.

The demand for home care staff is expanding locally, and the Council is working with local colleges to interest students in related disciplines in undertaking work in the care sector. It is examining a career pathway through unqualified work, which will require some job enhancement.

The Council is committed to a range of staff training, from SVQ/Post Qualifying awards to a postgraduate management development course at Strathclyde University's SLAM Centre. Lunchtime professional development seminars run jointly with Paisley University.

7. Modernising services

There are small Chinese and Asian communities, and services are purchased from Glasgow organisations for some of these people. The Council ensures that documentation is translated into ethnic minority languages. The social work department has worked with Kosovar refugees. A corporate race equality working group is taking forward work on the Race Relations (Amendment) Act, within the equal opportunities framework.

The department is a partner with the Health Board, the Primary Care Trust and Inverclyde Council in one of four local e-Care projects supported from the Modernising Government Fund. It focuses on improving communications and information sharing between care professionals in mental health services. A range of information and useful links to other organisations has been created, focused on the needs of older people and carers. There is an on-going commitment to extend the Council's web content and to make more dynamic, interactive use of web-based technology to develop and improve service provision.

During 2001 the department implemented the first phase of the new SWIFT client information system, which integrates activity and financial information, and provides the foundation for further systematic development of the electronic social care record. Data interchange is being pursued between SWIFT and the education department's SEEMIS database for looked after children. Priorities for the next phase of the SWIFT implementation plan will be child protection, looked after children, interfacing with corporate financial systems, costed packages of care (community based services), Supporting People and criminal justice services (linked to the ISCJIS programme).

The department is taking the lead on behalf of the Council for developing and implementing the Supporting People initiative. Early indications show that the Supporting People Team is on target to meet all of the Executive's milestones. Another area where the department is leading for the council is in the provision of an integrated welfare benefits, debt management and money advice service.

8. The Future

The partnership agreement between the Council and the Health Board – Renfrewshire Joint Care – provides a strong platform to plan and implement improvements in the range of community care services. It is the result of gradual confidence-building in the approach adopted to the Joint Future agenda. It should achieve greater transparency about resources, which is particularly demanding for the Health Board which has to work with five local authorities.

There is, however, a formidable agenda to be tackled, notably:

- practical measures to reduce persistent delays in discharges of older people from hospital;
- agreement on funding for increased community-based support, particularly for older people;
- completion of a best value review of community-based learning disability services, which will include the modernisation of traditional day services, and decisions on the strategic development of these services and the resource priorities required to implement it;
- developing local area co-ordination for children and adults with learning disabilities;
- based on the review of the joint mental health strategy group, decisions on the future development of and resource priorities for community-based mental health services;
- plans prepared in collaboration with education and housing departments for the transition of young people with learning disabilities to adult services, and decisions on their implementation;
- completion of preparations for the introduction of single shared assessment – notably the role of health staff in financial assessment and the practical application of the assessment tool to different client groups and in different settings, such as nursing homes;
- development of a joint strategic approach to information management and technology plans, particularly technology support for information sharing and other modernised working methods;
- preparation of a strategic plan for sensory impairment services, to consolidate the benefits already achieved through joint working with audiology services, eye clinics and ophthalmology services;
- implementation of children's integrated services; and
- consolidation of the work of the new Inter-Authority Criminal Justice Grouping.

A positive improvement in children's services could be secured if the Council presses on with its intentions to expand the pool of foster carers, develop the shared care respite service and reduce the use of residential care.

To consolidate the progress made in improving the education of looked after children, the Council should:

- complete linking the information systems of social work and schools;
- formulate a joint policy on promoting the education of looked after children; and
- implement training and development opportunities for education and social work staff who work with those children.

To build on the progress already achieved by the dedicated throughcare team and its strong working links with other local agencies, the Council needs to identify in consultation the range of services needed by care leavers and establish a budget for them.

1. Profile at 2002

Scottish Borders is a medium-sized predominantly rural authority, with a population of 106,900.

Expected population changes are in the same direction as national projections, but the decrease in under 5s and 30-44 year olds is likely to be greater than the national average, as is the increase in 60-74 year olds.

At 2.7% (January 2002) the unemployment rate is below the Scottish average.

Scottish Borders has one of the lowest rates of drugs misuse (1.1% of 15-54 year olds).

The crime rate is low and has fallen since 2000 (496 recorded crimes per 10,000 of population in 2001).

In late 2001 the Council introduced a Cabinet and Scrutiny model of operation. Services are located in 5 portfolio groups one of which, Lifelong Care, includes social work, environmental health, sport & leisure, community safety and health and safety. Lifelong Learning is the portfolio that includes education. The Council continues to review its structure.

Social work services are managed by a director who carries the responsibility of Chief Social Work Officer.

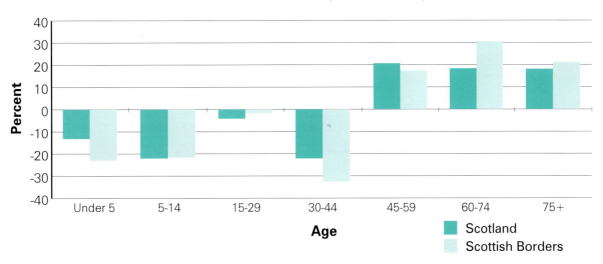

Expected % change in population, 2000-2016, local and national comparisons by age band

2. Performance: Community Care

Balance of care (aged 65+)	1999 actual	1999 per 1,000	Quartile	2000 actual	2000 per 1,000	Quartile
Older people in residential care homes	402	20	2	393	19	2
Older people in private nursing homes	546	27	2	486	24	3
Older people receiving home care	1,336	66	3	1,313	65	3
Older people in special needs housing	3,080	153.3	1	3,103	153.4	1
People receiving a community care service	1999-2000 actual	1999-2000 per 1,000	Quartile	2000-2001 actual	2000-2001 per 1,000	Quartile
Older people (aged 65+)	6,481	320.5	1	6,760	336.4	1
For mental health problems/dementia (aged 18-64)	288	4.5	2	335	5.3	1
For physical disabilities (aged 18-64)	1,152	18	2	1,232	19.4	2
For learning disabilities (aged 18-64)	374	5.8	1	369	5.8	1
For drug/alcohol abuse problems (aged 18-64)	34	0.5	3	28	0.4	3

The rates of older people who live in nursing and residential homes have reduced to levels similar to many other authorities. Since early 2000 Scottish Borders Council has purchased an additional 50 residential and nursing home places, but the waiting list for older people has risen from 50 to 80. There is a high provision of special needs housing, particularly wheelchair housing and houses with alarms. The rate of older people receiving a home care service is relatively low, with the number of hours received about the Scottish average. A recent local survey suggests a significant shift away from provision of domestic support – with fewer people receiving home care, but with higher levels of support.

The Council has recently started a best value review of home care. The current service has few staff on guaranteed hours and there has been a high turnover in staff. The Review comes at a time when there is a growing demand for services, particularly from older people.

The waiting list for Occupational Therapy (OT) assessment continues at approximately 100 people at any one time. The Council is pursuing greater efficiency and effectiveness of the service, principally through self-assessment, an integrated OT service, and a joint disability store.

A Borders Planning in Partnership agreement (PiP) has been adopted for joint implementation of the recommendations of "The Same as You?" to improve learning disability services. Day opportunities are being developed in a range of ways. It is intended to develop a locality-based learning disability service, jointly managed and resourced. Two local area co-ordinators are to be appointed.

Following review of joint commissioning arrangements, the Chief Executive of the Health Board chairs the joint commissioning group. Funding for a joint post is being created to support the group. A separate action team has been set up to tackle alcohol misuse.

The Christian Brothers run a long stay facility for people with mental health problems, which is being reorganised. There are practical difficulties in accessing in-patient beds in Lothian, despite the funding contribution made by Borders Health Board.

A new single shared assessment tool has been implemented, complete with training and monitoring and evaluation. The process will be further rolled out in 2002 along with payments for personal care and intensive care management. A joint policy for information sharing/data protection took effect from spring 2002.

Services for people with sensory impairment are dispersed. Some towns have clubs for people with a visual or hearing impairment, but initiatives are not linked with health and education services. People with a visual impairment look to hospital-based services. There is a small waiting list for those waiting for assessment following registration.

Services for people with a hearing impairment include the provision of lip-reading classes in four towns. Access to a qualified interpreter when required is afforded through external purchase. Deafblind Scotland provides awareness training for working with deafblind people, but there are no guide/communicators.

Borders Brain Injury Service was established as a Rehab Scotland service in autumn 2001. It is a unique outreach service, providing assessment, support, information, and social and skill development, including support and assistance to children. It has links with criminal justice, alcohol services and health services. Training in IT skills and numeracy is provided by partnership with Borders College, and there are links to Eyemouth Community Centre.

An overarching high level board is to be introduced, but partners have yet to agree its delegated powers. A joint executive of senior officers – with user and carer representation – is working out joint management and service arrangements. A Joint Future action plan has been developed, and a joint information group established. A new social work IT system is planned, accessible by health partners. Each care group is to have a multi-agency management/commissioning body. Joint resourcing is to apply to planning, commissioning, directly provided services and community care assessments. Also in progress is a joint development and training plan.

3. Performance: Children and Families

Balance of care – Looked after children (aged 0-17)	1999-2000 actual	1999-2000 per 1,000	Quartile	2000-2001 actual	2000-2001 per 1,000	Quartile
At home	68	3.0	3	56	2.5	4
With friends/relatives/other community	2	0.1	4	2	0.1	4
With foster carers/prospective adopters	70	3.1	2	78	3.4	1
In residential accommodation	19	0.8	3	21	0.9	3
Total	**159**	**7**	**3**	**157**	**6.9**	**3**

Key performance indicators	1998-1999 actual	1998-1999 per 1,000	Quartile	1999-2000 actual	1999-2000 per 1,000	Quartile
Child protection (CP) referrals (aged 0-15)	289	14.4	1	399	19.8	1
Children subject to a CP case conference (aged 0-15)	35	1.7	3	44	2.2	3
Children placed on CP register (aged 0-15)	24	1.2	3	34	1.7	3
Adoption applications in year (aged 0-17)	11	0.5	2	17	0.8	1
Stranger adopter applications (aged 0-17)	5	0.2	2	7	0.3	1

The number of child protection referrals increased by more than 100 between 1998 and 2000 and the rate is now the third highest of Scottish authorities. A very small proportion of referrals led to a case conference in 1999-2000, and the rate of children placed on the child protection register is fairly low. The rate of adoption applications is high, having increased between 1998 and 2000.

The rate of looked after children is relatively low. A low rate of looked after children live at home or with friends or relatives. A fairly low rate live in residential accommodation but a high rate live with foster carers, after increases between 1999 and 2001.

The Council has developed Family Support Centres as central to effective inclusive and preventative services. The family support facilities have been improved in Hawick and Eyemouth, to provide a range of structured parenting services, including courses on parenthood (for both early years and adolescents) and play.

With oversight by a multi-disciplinary group, the Council has made progress with five of the *Learning with Care* recommendations for improving educational provision for looked after children. Further progress has still to be made in:

- detailing the educational contribution to care plans and reviews;
- designating staff in schools;
- developing integrated care and education policies; and
- providing joint training and development for teachers, social workers and carers.

A lead officer has been identified for care leavers arrangements. The throughcare budget is to be re-modelled to reflect new responsibilities. Young people are being consulted by the children's rights officer and Who Cares? Scotland. It is envisaged that other key agencies will be involved through a proposed Youth Forum, which will be responsible for any necessary staff training.

The Borders Young Carers Project was established early in 2000 to provide information, advice and support to young people who are taking the kinds of responsibilities adult carers undertake. A survey early in 2002 revealed 140 young carers involved in several different geographically located groups. Evaluation has revealed the many positives which the project provides for young people and a need for increasing one-to-one support for the carers themselves.

A widely representative Borders Children's Planning Group has identified as key priority areas:

- expansion of integrated early years services for vulnerable young children; and
- support packages for children with disabilities or special physical, emotional, mental health or educational needs.

4. Performance: Criminal Justice

Key Activities	1999-2000	2000-2001	2000-2001 per 10,000	Quartile
Number of social enquiry reports submitted to the courts during the year	443	362	49.4	4
Number of community service orders made during the year	105	105	14.3	3

The proportion of social enquiry reports reported to court within target time	2000-2001	Quartile
Proportion of social enquiry reports submitted to the courts by due date	100.0	1

The time taken to complete community service orders		
Average length of community service (hours) for orders completed during the year	145	3
Average hours completed per week	3.4	3

The number of social enquiry reports submitted to courts fell between 1999 and 2001 and the rate is lower than in many other authorities. All reports are submitted to courts by the due date. The rate of community service orders made is relatively low. The average length of hours for community service orders completed in 2000-2001 was relatively low, and the time taken to complete orders was low – only 3.4 hours on average completed per week.

The Council is part of a criminal justice grouping with the three Lothian councils and Edinburgh. A consortium arrangement has been established involving elected members and chief officers from the five authorities. The five service managers are each to take a "portfolio" lead role across the grouping for areas such as performance management and practice development.

Commitment to developing information systems has supported improvements in practice. The supervision regime has recently been revised, with a move to more structured and consistent interventions delivered on a groupwork basis from a central base. Recommendations and interventions are targeted to take account of risk of harm, risk of re-conviction and risk of custody.

For offenders subject to supervision the first stage of the new supervision arrangements is an induction programme adapted from the "Think First" programme, which sets out highly specific action for the rest of their supervision. Two modules have been selected for development – general offending and anger management – and are being implemented across three of the partner authorities. They will be subject to a best value review and possibly put forward for accreditation, once this is in place in Scotland.

5. Finance

Service Area (£000)	GAE 1999-2000	Final net Out turn 1999-2000	GAE 2000-2001	Final net Out turn 2000-2001
Children's Services	£2,037	£4,688	£2,258	£4,879
Community Care	£18,552	£15,653	£19,602	£16,294
Adult Offenders		£16		£30
Other SW Services	£2,050	£2,961	£2,080	£3,087
Total	**£22,639**	**£23,317**	**£23,939**	**£24,290**
Spend per head		**1999-2000**		**2000-2001**
Spend per head		£218.11		£227.22
Quartile		2		3

Criminal Justice services receive funding from the Scottish Executive, which was £660,292 in 2000-2001.

The Council spends more than twice the GAE level on children's services. There is a historic spend below GAE on community care – currently only 78% of GAE budget. Expenditure per head on social work services is relatively low.

6. Staffing

Staff	WTE 1999 actual	WTE 1999 per 1,000	Quartile 1999	WTE 2000 actual	WTE 2000 per 1,000	Quartile 2000
Managers & central staff	75	0.7	2	93	0.9	1
Frontline staff	601	5.7	1	514	4.8	2
Other	127	1.2	3	94	0.9	3
Total	**803**	**7.5**	**1**	**702**	**6.6**	**2**

Vacancies	Vacancies 2000	% Vacancies 2000	% Vacancies 2000 Scotland	Vacancies 2001	% Vacancies 2001	% Vacancies 2001 Scotland
SWs with adults	3	5.8	7.8	12	14.5	10.9
SWs with children	0	0	7.4	5	24.6	10.7
SWs with offenders	1	11.4	7.5	0	0	7.2
Generic workers	0	0	8.0	0	0	12.7
Total	**4**	**3.5**	**7.7**	**17**	**14.7**	**10.5**

The total number of staff has decreased between 1999 and 2000 but staffing rates remain relatively high. There were reductions in the number of front-line staff and other staff, managers and central staff increased and the rate is now high compared to many other authorities. Vacancy levels are very high in community care and children's services, having increased significantly between 2000 and 2001.

Historically, the Council has not experienced significant problems of staff recruitment and retention. Exceptions have been home care staff and community-based occupational therapists. In response, the authority has created senior occupational therapist posts, and plans to retrain its home care staff to provide community support to a wider range of clients. More flexible job descriptions have been drawn up to facilitate this. However, numbers of applicants for jobs have dropped.

The Council has made use of information systems to show where service users with specific needs are concentrated and where skilled staff can be most effectively deployed.

7. Modernising services

The Council has worked closely with asylum seekers and travellers. The Council is a founding member of the Race Equality Partnership (with Edinburgh and the Lothian councils) which intends to establish an ethnic minority advice and resource centre as one of its first priorities. Social work has an action plan designed to meet the requirements of a Race Equality Scheme, including work to monitor, evaluate and report on access and take-up of social work services by people from differing racial and ethnic origins.

The Council runs a major Modernising Government project aimed at the electronic delivery of services. A strategy for public contact through the phone, internet and one-stop shops was developed following a front-line services review which included a survey to establish public preferences for accessing services.

A new social work information system is being introduced, consistent with e-government. It will be web-compliant and capable of linking to other corporate systems, including education, and to client and service information in other agencies, including health. Scottish Borders and its health and voluntary sector partners are part of the eCare club and have used Modernising Government funds for the joint disability store. The partnership hopes for second round funding for an eCare store – defined as a secure data repository accessible by all community care partner agencies – to support single shared assessment and other joint working.

As part of the Integrated Scottish Criminal Justice Information System (ISCJIS) programme the Council is establishing common data standards and inter-connectivity between criminal justice and related functions.

8. The Future

Numbers of older people who need community care are relatively high and will continue to increase. Against a background of severe local budgetary problems, the Council has not spent up to GAE level on community care. The Council now needs to invest more heavily in community-based support for older people, particularly in home care. It should progress urgently its best value review of home care, as the basis for decisions on its future development to meet local needs for quality services and on the resource priorities required to implement the necessary improvements.

Mental health provision calls for urgent joint attention. Community services need to be strengthened by involvement of social workers to complement the skills of health professionals in local teams. A joint team in the hospital-based mental health unit would seem more effective than the present arrangements, which are limited to attachment of social workers. In addition there is a need to assess how best to meet the current shortage of psychological services for depressive illness, adjustment disorders and life stresses. Any review of services should take serious account of the contribution which can be made by specialist voluntary organisations.

As advocated by the Mental Health and Well Being Support Group, there is a need for the local partners to review the range of in-patient services necessary to meet the needs of people with a learning disability and to determine the resource priorities for making improvements.

Sensing Progress recommended developing a strategic framework to guide the planning and implementation of services for people with a sensory impairment. This approach seems completely suited to the circumstances of Scottish Borders, and the Council and its health partner could commission a joint expert group for the purpose.

SHETLAND ISLANDS COUNCIL

1. Profile at 2002

With 22,400 people spread over comparatively remote island communities, Shetland has the second smallest population of Scottish authorities.

The population is expected to fall by 3.7% over the next 14 years. The 60-74 year old population is expected to increase by 41.5%. The increase in the 45-59 age group is likely to be much smaller than the national average.

Unemployment has fallen since 2000 and is now very low (1.5% at January 2002). 81% of working age people in Shetland are working compared to a Scotland average of 73%.

The drug misuse rate is below average (0.9% of 15-54 year olds), but three times higher than Orkney.

The crime rate has risen from 2000 but remains the third lowest among Scottish authorities (289 crimes were recorded per 10,000 population in 2001).

Shetland Islands Council has 3 Service Committees, including one for Community Services.

Social Care Services are part of the Department of Community Services which also includes housing, education and community development. The Head of Social Care is the chief social work officer. Restructuring, which started in autumn 2000, is not yet fully implemented.

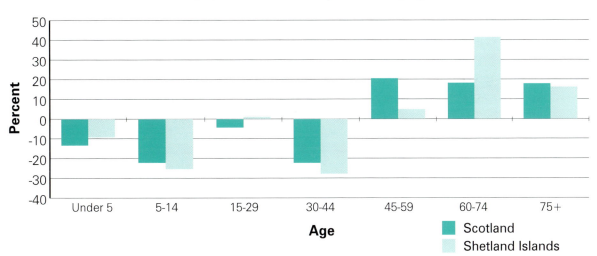

Expected % change in population, 2000-2016, local and national comparisons by age band

225

2. Performance: Community Care

Balance of care (aged 65+)	1999 actual	1999 per 1,000	Quartile	2000 actual	2000 per 1,000	Quartile
Older people in residential care homes	113	38	1	126	42	1
Older people in private nursing homes	0	0	4	0	0	4
Older people receiving home care	444	149	1	567	188	1
Older people in special needs housing	658	221.2	1	388	128.7	2

People receiving a community care service	1999-2000 actual	1999-2000 per 1,000	Quartile	2000-2001 actual	2000-2001 per 1,000	Quartile
Older people (aged 65+)	606	201.1	3	858	284.7	1
For mental health problems/dementia (aged 18-64)	26	1.9	3	30	2.2	4
For physical disabilities (aged 18-64)	240	17.4	2	268	19.5	1
For learning disabilities (aged 18-64)	15	1.1	4	26	1.9	4
For drug/alcohol abuse problems (aged 18-64)	2	0.1	4	14	1.0	2

There has been a 40% increase in the rate of older people who receive a community care service between 1999 and 2001. There are no nursing homes in Shetland but the rate of older people living in residential homes is high. The rate of older people in special needs housing has dropped significantly, but it remains relatively high. A high rate of older people receive home care, after a major increase between 1999 and 2000.

A comprehensive review of home-delivered services has resulted in a development project in the island of Unst to promote a local integrated social and health care service and to explore ways of providing more flexible care together with locally supervised home carers. Subject to evaluation and available resources, this type of devolved provision is to be rolled out to other rural areas.

Learning disability services have been well developed in Shetland over the years. There is an established independent living project, a range of supported accommodation and respite care, and a resource centre. The Partnership in Practice agreement reflects the joint approach to service improvement. The number of adults with learning disabilities – some with severe learning difficulties – is projected to increase over the next ten years, and the rebuilding of the Kantersted residential home is planned to provide additional permanent and respite accommodation. The budget for people with learning disabilities is projected to rise over 10 years from £2.2m to £3.5m – a significant proportion of the community care budget.

The Eric Gray Resource Centre for people with learning disabilities supports 32 adults: it has developed education, training and employment programmes, and brings together social and health care, and voluntary organisations, under one roof. Staff supervise various activities and training for independent living. A key worker devises a programme of activities to help people to learn new skills and develop existing ones.

Led by NHS Shetland and including a psychiatric social worker, the community mental health team (CMHT) is part of a redesign of services in Shetland. Psychiatric services for adults are provided by a resident consultant who gives leadership to the CMHT, and is supported by visiting consultants (who provide support for other care groups). Most in-patient treatment for people with a mental illness, including children, adolescents and older people with dementia, is provided in Aberdeen. Where practical and justified by needs, treatment is provided in Shetland, if suitable beds or GP support are available.

A pre-existing joint assessment process – developed in consultation with staff, users, carers and the voluntary sector – is being refined to meet the requirements of single shared assessment, and of Supporting People. A community care assessment form is the core tool, with additions for further assessment to be used as necessary. The procedure already routinely seeks the consent of users to information sharing.

A joint working group is developing detailed proposals for a redesign of sensory impairment services, including speech and language therapy. Progress is monitored by an advisory team, including the community care forum and stakeholders from both the statutory and voluntary sector. There are no sensory impairment associations within Shetland.

Proposed service developments include:

- extension of the specialist services offered to school-age children and young adults; and
- resource centre facilities to host specialist services for adults.

The needs for the service were assessed in consultation with service users and carers. Individual assessments of need are followed by access to specialist resources as required. There is a social worker specialising in sensory impairment.

The Council and NHS Shetland have established a joint implementation group which plans and oversees the management of community care services. Existing Joint Future partners are involved – health, housing and social work. It is intended to align budgets in the first instance and assess the scope and value of the joint resourcing pot, particularly around the inclusion of more hospital based services. The partners have developed a statement of intent for staff, a joint staff forum, and are in the early stages of drawing up a joint training and development plan.

3. Performance: Children and Families

Balance of care – Looked after children (aged 0-17)	1999-2000 actual	1999-2000 per 1,000	Quartile	2000-2001 actual	2000-2001 per 1,000	Quartile
At home	20	3.5	3	13	2.3	4
With friends/relatives/other community	0	0.0	4	1	0.2	4
With foster carers/prospective adopters	11	2.0	3	15	2.7	2
In residential accommodation	6	1.1	2	4	0.7	4
Total	**37**	**6.6**	**4**	**33**	**5.8**	**4**

Key performance indicators	1998-1999 actual	1998-1999 per 1,000	Quartile	1999-2000 actual	1999-2000 per 1,000	Quartile
Child protection (CP) referrals (aged 0-15)	106	20.7	1	39	7.7	2
Children subject to a CP case conference (aged 0-15)	35	6.9	1	4	0.8	4
Children placed on CP register (aged 0-15)	26	5.1	1	2	0.4	4
Adoption applications in year (aged 0-17)	1	0.2	4	6	1.1	1
Stranger adopter applications (aged 0-17)	0	0	4	2	0.4	1

The rate of child protection referrals is relatively high, but has reduced considerably from an exceptionally high rate in 1998-1999. Rates of children subject to a case conference and on the child protection register have also dropped sharply and are now lower than in most other authorities. Adoption application rates are high, having increased from a low level in 1998-1999.

Family Support Worker posts have been created to complement the social worker establishment for child protection. The development of the New Community Schools project in the North Mainland will make a significant contribution to the early intervention, prevention and protective services available in the area.

The overall rate of looked after children is low. The rate of looked after children living with foster carers increased between 1999 and 2001 and is now relatively high.

The Council has established a professional foster care service in the past year, and recruitment campaigns have resulted in the approval of 10 new foster carers.

The Social Care Service and the Shetland Child care Partnership have created a Family Centre Services team, based in Lerwick, which offers family support services throughout Shetland on an outreach basis. Parent support groups, a crèche, play opportunities, the use of the mobile Play Van are among services on offer.

The Council has so far made limited progress in implementing the recommendations of *Learning with Care*:

- all looked after children have care plans but not educational targets;
- guidelines are to be produced to clarify the responsibilities of staff in all agencies involved;
- a new post of independent childcare co-ordinator is to keep under review the educational needs of looked after children and carry out the six-monthly reviews;
- all looked after children are in full-time education or are educated in an appropriate setting; and
- some joint training has involved teachers, social workers, school auxiliaries and nurses.

Parents are invited and helped to attend reviews of their children and are sent copies of all reports. The educational environment of children and young people in residential or foster care has been enhanced by providing ICT equipment, additional homework support and study areas.

A multi-disciplinary working party is preparing for the new arrangements for care leavers and is drawing up an action programme, in consultation with other islands councils and national and regional groups preparing for the transfer. A local service budget and the future payment arrangements required by care leavers living throughout the islands have yet to be worked out. It is intended to develop specific budgets for individual care leavers. The Council is to use its inclusiveness project to provide training for staff from relevant agencies who need to broaden their knowledge of the needs of care leavers.

4. Performance: Criminal Justice

Key Activities	1999-2000	2000-2001	2000-2001 per 10,000	Quartile
Number of social enquiry reports submitted to the courts during the year	110	96	62.4	3
Number of community service orders made during the year	13	15	9.7	4
The proportion of social enquiry reports reported to court within target time	2000-2001	Quartile		
Proportion of social enquiry reports submitted to the courts by due date	100.0	1		
The time taken to complete community service orders				
Average length of community service (hours) for orders completed during the year	220	1		
Average hours completed per week	8.3	1		

The rate of social enquiry reports submitted to courts is low, reflecting a low crime rate. All reports are submitted to courts by the due date. The rate of community service orders made is lower than in many other authorities. The average length of orders completed is relatively higher than in most other authorities, but the orders are completed quickly, with an average of 8.3 hours completed per week.

The Council is linked to the Northern Partnership (with Aberdeen, Aberdeenshire, Moray and Highland) for provision of criminal justice services. Local staff also meet Orkney and Western Isles counterparts and conduct inter-island arm's-length reviews. The three services, having similar management and practice, audit each other's services.

Local staff are devising a template to bring together risk assessment, with a broader social work assessment. Locally devised schedules are used for monitoring effectiveness, and there are plans to upgrade the client information systems to allow for greater integration of qualitative data.

Young people's crime in Shetland is associated with alcohol and the use of recreational drugs. Alcohol awareness courses are a strong feature of local provision.

Since a number of youngsters are propelled very swiftly into court and adult disposals, youth justice provision has been developed to identify and co-ordinate resources to divert younger people from crime.

5. Finance

Service Area (£000)	GAE 1999-2000	Final net Out turn 1999-2000	GAE 2000-2001	Final net Out turn 2000-2001
Children's Services	£315	£1,099	£342	£1,695
Community Care	£3,377	£6,684	£3,454	£8,639
Adult Offenders		£159		£24
Other SW Services	£414	£1,029	£414	£238
Total	**£4,106**	**£8,970**	**£4,209**	**£10,596**
Spend per head		**1999-2000**		**2000-2001**
Spend per head		£399.73		£472.19
Quartile		1		1

Criminal Justice services receive funding direct from the Scottish Executive, which amounted to £192,157 in 2000-2001.

Shetland spent two and a half times GAE levels on social work services in 2000-2001. The spend on other social work services was below GAE but on community care it exceeded GAE by two and a half times. The spend on children's services was almost five times GAE. Expenditure per head is very high and has increased significantly since 1999-2000 – more than £100 higher than that for Orkney or Eilean Siar.

6. Staffing

Staff	WTE 1999 actual	WTE 1999 per 1,000	Quartile 1999	WTE 2000 actual	WTE 2000 per 1,000	Quartile 2000
Managers & central staff	23	1.0	1	24	1.1	1
Frontline staff	204	9.0	1	233	10.4	1
Other	53	2.3	1	51	2.3	1
Total	**280**	**12.3**	**1**	**308**	**13.7**	**1**

Vacancies	Vacancies 2000	% Vacancies 2000	% Vacancies 2000 Scotland	Vacancies 2001	% Vacancies 2001	% Vacancies 2001 Scotland
SWs with adults	0	0	7.8	5	52.9	10.9
SWs with children	0	0	7.4	1	12.0	10.7
SWs with offenders	0	0	7.5	1	14.1	7.2
Generic workers	1	8.0	8.0	0	0	12.7
Total	**1**	**5.4**	**7.7**	**6**	**25.7**	**10.5**

Total staffing rates are high, having increased between 1999 and 2000. There are high rates of both managers and frontline staff.

Vacancy levels are high. In spring 2002 the Social Care Service had 6.5 social worker vacancies among the 23 posts in the three teams, with particular gaps in childcare staffing. In the longer term the community planning board has set up a working group to consider the cross-cutting issues that affect recruitment and retention of staff, and to recommend appropriate measures.

There are growing problems in recruiting home care staff. Unemployment is low and other potential employers in both private and public sectors compete for labour.

7. Modernising services

Shetland has a multi-cultural environment which features a small resident Asian and Chinese population, seafaring people of many countries and some asylum seekers. The community planning board, which includes NHS Shetland and the Council, is now preparing an action plan.

E-government has not been a specific priority of Shetland Islands Council. This is changing and there is now a vision for a modern, fast communications network, with extensive use of e-mail internally and externally, internet and intranet sites, and a number of other active initiatives such as video-conferencing and document management.

Social work services need urgently to replace the current information system, and steps are being taken to commission new systems for social work services, housing and Supporting People, for implementation by mid-2003. The systems are also to link social work, health and education information.

8. The Future

The provision of services for older people in Shetland has consistently been at a high level, benefiting from additional funding from the Shetland Islands Council Charitable Trust. The projected steep increase in the older population will require the Council and its NHS partner to improve targeting of total resources available for community care and the cost-effectiveness of different packages of care.

The present home care services call for review, to ensure that they are sufficiently flexible to meet local needs and at the same time represent best value for the Shetland community. The Social Care Service is at present looking at re-defining the home care task, separating personal care and domestic duties, and conditions of employment. The Council will need to draw this work together into a coherent plan for future development and the resource priorities to implement it.

Other aspects of community care which require attention are:

- mental health services, whose scale of provision has been advocated by local interests, including users and carers; while development of acute services would be prohibitively expensive, the Council could assess the scope for improved rehabilitation and support and a programme of staff training, both for mental health officers and to prepare for the Adults with Incapacity (Scotland) Act 2000; and

- sensory impairment services (including speech and language therapy), which are being reviewed by a joint working group; this work should be completed as soon as practicable, so that the Council can determine a strategy for future development and resource priorities for its implementation.

To consolidate the progress which has been made in the education of looked after children, the Council should:

- complete educational targets for all such children;

- complete guidelines for professional staff who work with them;

- formulate and introduce a programme of training and development opportunities for staff; and

- complete a joint education/social work database for looked after children.

Service and budget planning for the aftercare of young people is at an early stage, and the multi-disciplinary working party should prepare its proposals for the Council as soon as practicable so that it can determine a strategy for establishing quality services and resources required for implementation.

1. Profile at 2002

South Ayrshire is a medium sized, mainly rural authority with a population of 113,900.

The local population is predicted to fall marginally (by 3.3%) to 2016. There is likely to be a smaller than average decrease in the under fives, whilst the 15-44 year old population is expected to reduce in line with the national rate. The older population is set to increase but by less than the national projection.

At 4.8% (January 2002), the unemployment rate is slightly above the national average. 16% of wards in the area have unemployment rates of more than twice the Scottish average.

South Ayrshire has one of the lower rates of drug misuse (0.8% of 15-54 year olds).

At 692 per 10,000 population the recorded crime rate is lower than the national average, but has increased slightly since 2000.

The Department of Social Work, Housing and Health, is one of 4 departments of the Council which was restructured in spring 2001. The Department is led by a Director with support from Heads of Social Work, Housing and Social Justice.

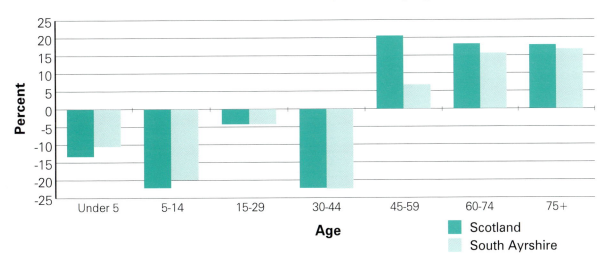

Expected % change in population, 2000-2016, local and national comparisons by age band

2. Performance: Community Care

Balance of care (aged 65+)	1999 actual	1999 per 1,000	Quartile	2000 actual	2000 per 1,000	Quartile
Older people in residential care homes	262	13	4	219	10	4
Older people in private nursing homes	616	30	1	656	31	1
Older people receiving home care	1,011	48	4	1,178	56	3
Older people in special needs housing	1,627	78	3	1,629	77.7	3
People receiving a community care service	**1999-2000 actual**	**1999-2000 per 1,000**	**Quartile**	**2000-2001 actual**	**2000-2001 per 1,000**	**Quartile**
Older people (aged 65+)	6,700	319.4	1	5,741	273.7	1
For mental health problems/dementia (aged 18-64)	446	6.5	1	450	6.5	1
For physical disabilities (aged 18-64)	1,885	27.3	1	1,621	23.5	1
For learning disabilities (aged 18-64)	275	4	2	310	4.5	1
For drug/alcohol abuse problems (aged 18-64)	99	1.4	2	75	1.1	2

The rate of older people in residential care is low, having dropped between 1999 and 2000. The rate of older people in nursing homes has increased to a higher level than in most other authorities. There is a fairly low rate of special needs housing provision. The Council has a policy of separation of housing and support services, i.e. maintenance of people in their own homes as long as possible, with support services brought to their homes.

The rate of older people receiving a home care service is relatively low, though it increased from 1999. In 2000, South Ayrshire provided a higher percentage of its clients with an intensive care service (more than 10 hours per week) than all but one other authority.

Following a best value review of services for older people, the Council has introduced a more flexible home care service, in which all carers are trained in personal care tasks, and can provide a service between 7:00 a.m. and 10:00 p.m. The Council has changed its provision of residential care, creating individual accommodation units from previous homes and retraining staff to provide care in older people's own homes.

There is a productive home care partnership with the independent sector. An independent sector forum enables independent providers to speak to each other and to consider good practice and common themes, such as staff training.

South Ayrshire has forged ahead with its own learning disability strategy, and also leads an all-Ayrshire strategy group. It has involved all the key stakeholders. The Council's priority is to continue:

- re-configuring in-patient, respite, day and residential services; and
- carrying out a programme of person-centred planning.

Day services are being changed so that people with learning difficulties get services to meet their individual needs and assist them in achieving their aspirations. Resource centres for those with challenging behaviour and complex needs will still be available. A local area co-ordinator is being appointed on a pilot basis to stimulate the modernisation of traditional services. Kirkbrae group home is to be converted into self-contained flats and the current residents' care needs are to be re-assessed.

Though joint working with health over strategy and delivery has benefited mental health services, the pace of change has been limited by resource constraints on the NHS. Mental health teams for adults and older people share accommodation. The future shape of services has been agreed, but reduction of resettlement targets has resulted in blocking of acute psychiatric beds.

The area is well provided with 25 mental health officers (with an additional 5 in training). A pilot project for mentally disordered offenders, based at Ayr and Kilmarnock sheriff courts, is currently being evaluated.

The Council and its health partners are signed up to the all-Ayrshire single shared assessment tool and has identified three pilot sites for older people to commence in July, and then for all care groups, following joint training.

Further planning covers:

- guidelines for assessors to access resources; and
- protocols for sharing information and obtaining service users' consent.

The Council provides a rehabilitation and mobility service for visually impaired people, interpreting resources for profoundly deaf sign language users, communication support for all hearing impaired people, and specialist information for both visual and hearing impaired people. Its sensory impairment team has qualified guide/communicator support available. The team is involved in future needs assessments for visually impaired children but not for those with a hearing impairment.

The Council is part of the all-Ayrshire local partnership agreement which involves NHS Ayrshire and Arran and the other two Ayrshire local authorities. The Council is taking an incremental approach to the Joint Future agenda, building on established infrastructures of joint working and joint initiatives. From spring 2002 a Joint Health Committee of Council and NHS representatives is addressing joint working for both older people and children.

The Rapid Response Team and *South Ayrshire Speedy Action* are examples of aligned and pooled budgets and joint management arrangements in operation. Services are managed by one or other agency, rather than through integrated management of joint services.

3. Performance: Children and Families

Balance of care – Looked after children (aged 0-17)	1999-2000 actual	1999-2000 per 1,000	Quartile	2000-2001 actual	2000-2001 per 1,000	Quartile
At home	55	2.3	4	60	2.5	3
With friends/relatives/other community	12	0.5	3	19	0.8	3
With foster carers/prospective adopters	32	1.3	4	34	1.4	4
In residential accommodation	16	0.7	4	20	0.8	4
Total	**115**	**4.8**	**4**	**133**	**5.5**	**4**

Key performance indicators	1998-1999 actual	1998-1999 per 1,000	Quartile	1999-2000 actual	1999-2000 per 1,000	Quartile
Child protection (CP) referrals (aged 0-15)	38	1.8	4	71	3.3	4
Children subject to a CP case conference (aged 0-15)	16	0.8	4	23	1.1	4
Children placed on CP register (aged 0-15)	5	0.2	4	6	0.3	4
Adoption applications in year (aged 0-17)	7	0.3	3	7	0.3	3
Stranger adopter applications (aged 0-17)	2	0.1	4	4	0.2	3

The rate of child protection referrals almost doubled between 1998 and 2000, but remains lower than in many other authorities. The rates of children subject to a case conference and children on the child protection register are also lower than in most other authorities.

The rate of looked after children has increased between 1999 and 2001, but remains lower than in most other authorities. The rate of looked after children living in residential accommodation or with foster carers is low. Numbers of looked after children are significantly affected by drug misuse – estimated at 90% of caseloads.

The recommendations of *Learning with Care* are being progressed on a number of fronts:

- multi-disciplinary assessment and care planning processes are fully implemented;
- each school has a named co-ordinator to ensure that every looked after child has a personal education plan containing specific targets: two full-time support teachers help to achieve this aim, reviewing plans, and checking that they include provision for communication with parents;
- most looked after children have full-time educational placements, although a small number have part-time intensive support programmes;
- the Council has published an inter-agency strategy for looked after children, which outlines support requirements, procedures for inter-agency communication, and the Council's duties as corporate parent; and
- inter-agency training has taken place and more is planned.

The Council has established and equipped an IT study base in its one residential unit and provided IT and other educational equipment to all foster placements. The computerised systems of education and social work (SEEMIS and SWIS) are being integrated.

The Council is at an early stage in preparing new arrangements for care leavers. A multi-agency throughcare team plans and oversees services and works with STEP, a project that helps vulnerable young people into training or employment. A local budget is being prepared according to central guidance. Care leavers are to be consulted.

4. Performance: Criminal Justice

Key Activities	1999-2000	2000-2001	2000-2001 per 10,000	Quartile
Number of social enquiry reports submitted to the courts during the year	589	645	81.7	2
Number of community service orders made during the year	138	138	17.5	2
The proportion of social enquiry reports reported to court within target time	2000-2001	Quartile		
Proportion of social enquiry reports submitted to the courts by due date	95.8	3		
The time taken to complete community service orders				
Average length of community service (hours) for orders completed during the year	143	3		
Average hours completed per week	5.8	1		

The number of social enquiry reports submitted to courts increased between 1999 and 2001 and the rate is relatively high. The proportions of reports allocated to staff within two days and submitted to courts by the due date are relatively low. A relatively high rate of community service orders were made during 2000-2001. The average length of hours for orders completed was lower than in many other authorities but orders are completed relatively quickly, with an average of 5.8 hours completed per week.

The Council delivers criminal justice social work services in partnership with North and East Ayrshire. The priority is to have a consistent range of community based accredited services, and it has developed an all-Ayrshire reparation and mediation scheme in conjunction with SACRO. Despite the different management information systems being developed, the partnership aims to develop a quality assurance system and benchmarking across the grouping.

A structured assessment tool is employed, from which information is fed into a database, which informs management decision-making. No less than 40% of criminal justice clients have mental health problems, and drug and alcohol misuse is a feature in 80% of women offender cases and 65% of men.

The Council has developed a youth crime strategy which is integrated with the children's services and the community safety plans. It includes an initiative to tackle vandalism. The Council is considering external evaluation of the strategy.

External evaluation of services to women offenders was positive and showed an impressive reduction in the breach rate from over 50% to 4%. Resources allowing, the Council intends to have services to other client groups evaluated.

5. Finance

Service Area (£000)	GAE 1999-2000	Final net Out turn 1999-2000	GAE 2000-2001	Final net Out turn 2000-2001
Children's Services	£3,344	£3,780	£3,521	£4,193
Community Care	£19,180	£17,570	£20,099	£18,341
Adult Offenders		£728		£35
Other SW Services	£2,226	£2,189	£2,241	£1,740
Total	**£24,750**	**£24,268**	**£25,861**	**£24,309**

Spend per head		1999-2000		2000-2001
Spend per head		£213.02		£213.38
Quartile		3		4

Criminal Justice services receive direct funding from the Scottish Executive. £710,468 was provided in 2000-2001.

The Council spent above GAE on children's services, but the gap was much smaller than in other authorities. Expenditure in community care and other social work services was below GAE. Spend per head on social work services is lower than in many other authorities.

6. Staffing

Staff	WTE 1999 actual	WTE 1999 per 1,000	Quartile 1999	WTE 2000 actual	WTE 2000 per 1,000	Quartile 2000
Managers & central staff	94	0.8	1	86	0.8	2
Frontline staff	551	4.8	2	515	4.5	3
Other	126	1.1	3	111	1.0	3
Total	**771**	**6.7**	**2**	**712**	**6.3**	**3**

Vacancies	Vacancies 2000	% Vacancies 2000	% Vacancies 2000 Scotland	Vacancies 2001	% Vacancies 2001	% Vacancies 2001 Scotland
SWs with adults	0	0	7.8	1	2.8	10.9
SWs with children	2	4.7	7.4	2	4.8	10.7
SWs with offenders	0	0	7.5	1	10.0	7.2
Generic workers	3	9.2	8.0	0	0	12.7
Total	**4**	**5.6**	**7.7**	**4**	**4.6**	**10.5**

Total numbers of staff fell between 1999 and 2000 and staffing levels are now relatively low. The rate of managers and central staff remains relatively high. Vacancy levels are below average.

In spring 2002, there were no vacant social worker posts, but 70 vacancies for home care staff. The former achievement is attributable to Council efforts to meet training needs, to provide appropriate support routes to social work qualification and to protect caseloads of newly appointed staff.

A wholly qualified workforce in residential, day and home care is planned by 2005. Vacancies in the home care workforce are expected to decline as the home care review is implemented, incorporating a single status for home carers, with recognised training and guaranteed hours.

7. Modernising services

The Council is committed to delivering a practical and effective Race Equality Scheme, which is in early stages of drafting. Preparation has included close contact with the West of Scotland Community Relations Council, a detailed audit of services, and publicity about the Council's intentions. The authority is part of a racial incidents monitoring group: police statistics show a rise in race-related incidents and in addition many go unreported. There is an anti-racial harassment policy, ethnic monitoring and support for language translation.

A Modernising Government funded project is aimed at reducing the transaction time for customers accessing council services. Longer-term intentions are to create a master address database and consider call-centre technology. The Council is improving its website infrastructure.

The department, with IT staff, is developing the inherited SWIS information system, reviewing social work business processes, cleaning existing data and addressing the individual needs of different areas of service. Planned developments include a joint bid with health to implement electronic single shared assessment, and links with education and district court information systems.

8. The Future

To follow up its review of older people's services, the Council will need to continue its programme of action on:

- the role and use of sheltered housing in the range of services for older people;
- remedying the relatively low provision of extra care housing;
- increasing day care provision; and
- enhancing service standards within day care.

To complement its action to improve services for people with learning disabilities, the Council should examine closely with health partners the opportunities for expanding and improving day care. This forms part of its commitment to The Same As You.

Mental health services have benefited from recent improvements but the Council and its partners should:

- safeguard and possibly increase social work manpower to carry out the hospital resettlement; and
- formulate a joint strategy for development of services for children and adolescents to link with mental health services for adults and identify resource priorities to implement the strategy.

To underpin its preparations for a full aftercare service for young people, the Council should organise – if necessary with other councils – a programme of inter-agency training aimed at those staff who work with those young people.

1. Profile at 2002

With 307,400 people, South Lanarkshire is a partly urban, partly rural area, with the fifth largest population of Scottish authorities.

The overall population is expected to fall by 1.8% by 2016. Numbers of children and young people are currently above the national average but all age groups under 45 are set to decrease. The over 75 population is expected to increase at a greater than average rate.

Unemployment is reducing and at 3.8% (January 2002) is close to the national average.

The drug misuse rate is just below average (1.9% of 15-54 year olds).

The level of crime has fallen and is below the national average (631 crimes recorded per 10,000 population in 2001).

South Lanarkshire Council is organised into 7 Resource Groups from a previous 15 operating departments. The structure is intended to reflect the way the public wants services delivered.

An Executive Director manages Social Work Resources with support from five Heads of Service for Older People's Services, Adult Services, Child & Family Services, Strategic Services, Support Services, and a Justice Services Manager. The Director is also Chief Social Work Officer.

Access to all council services is provided through local offices which provide one-stop shops.

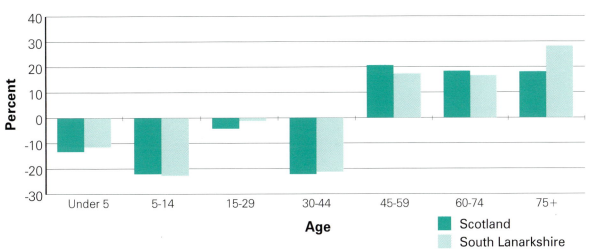

Expected % change in population, 2000-2016, local and national comparisons by age band

2. Performance: Community Care

Balance of care (aged 65+)	1999 actual	1999 per 1,000	Quartile	2000 actual	2000 per 1,000	Quartile
Older people in residential care homes	517	12	4	735	17	2
Older people in private nursing homes	1,411	33	1	1,482	34	1
Older people receiving home care	2,355	54	4	2,181	50	4
Older people in special needs housing	6,605	152.7	1	7,151	164.8	1
People receiving a community care service	**1999-2000 actual**	**1999-2000 per 1,000**	**Quartile**	**2000-2001 actual**	**2000-2001 per 1,000**	**Quartile**
Older people (aged 65+)	10,126	233.4	2	9,889	228	3
For mental health problems/dementia (aged 18-64)	133	0.7	4	1,009	5.2	2
For physical disabilities (aged 18-64)	2,788	14.4	2	2,589	13.3	2
For learning disabilities (aged 18-64)	285	1.5	4	329	1.7	4
For drug/alcohol abuse problems (aged 18-64)	550	2.8	1	478	2.5	2

A high rate of older people is in nursing home care, after a significant increase in numbers between 1999 and 2000. The number of older people living in residential homes also increased, but the rate remains relatively low. There is a high provision of special needs housing. A low rate of older people receives a home care service, but the rate of those receiving an intensive service (more than 10 hours per week) has increased from 1999. During the last year the Council has undertaken a substantial recruitment campaign in which approximately 80 new Home Carers have been recruited.

The Council has a major capital investment programme (£12m in 2002-2003 and £4m in 2003-2004) focused on providing attractive and high quality facilities. It includes:

- older people's day centres which allow flexible use and opening times;
- residential care homes embracing a broad range of needs and allowing older people to remain for their lifetime;
- an integrated adult services facility that can be used by people with dual-sensory impairment and/or multiple disabilities which affords access to personal care, privacy and IT facilities;
- a re-provisioning strategy for children's units as part of the integrated strategy to improve the support for children looked after in our care; and
- a re-provisioning strategy for adult units to support people within the community and promote social inclusion, flexibility, integration and choice.

Considerable developments in home support are in progress:

- home care workers being trained in personal and extended personal care tasks and placed on flexible rotas across the whole area;
- investment in pre-prepared meals pilot;
- development of shopping services;
- an intensive home care pilot in Rutherglen/Cambuslang;
- an integrated care project in Clydesdale – Joint Health and Social Work project;
- the formation of night care teams in each area;

- the development of the Alert System of community alarms;
- intensive training programme for all home care staff to meet new national care standards;
- development of technology;
- re-provision of two residential homes within East Kilbride; and
- continued Day Care developments as part of the Best Value Review.

The Council has established improved joint working arrangements with both NHS Lanarkshire and NHS Greater Glasgow, for the equipment and adaptations service, and expenditure from the local authority has quadrupled in the last 5 years.

The Council's learning disability strategy pre-dates Partnership in Practice Agreements (PiPs). A steering group, including service users and carers, oversees the hospital closure plan and the retraction programme for people with learning disabilities in hostel accommodation. The joint management team is planning how best to put resources into communities, using a person-centred approach and taking account of the specialist health care needs of people with learning disabilities.

Social work staffing for learning disability services has been significantly increased, for the joint rapid response team and to enhance community support teams and day centres. The Council's community support teams are tasked to respond to their own local situations.

Care management and assessment teams now work with young people and their parents on the transition to adult services, but it is not always possible to ensure that resources follow the young person. Person-centred planning may expose hidden needs for costly specialist resources, requiring the maintenance of good inter-agency working, as the emphasis shifts from hospital closures to maintaining people in their communities.

The number of people receiving a community care service for mental health problems increased more than sevenfold between 1999 and 2001. The resource network project, managed by a joint steering group, is the agreed model for the development of community mental health services, with health improvement programme investment of £2.5m. over five years. Multi-disciplinary intervention teams and outreach teams, aligned to LHCCs, are to replace the existing community mental health teams.

The Council provides social work services to the State Hospital, through a service level agreement which is due for renewal. If the West of Scotland medium secure unit is located in Lanarkshire, more services will be required for mentally disordered offenders and their relatives. Housing will need to become involved and full agreement will be needed about the type of accommodation required.

The Assessment and Care Management Module within the Social Work Information system, SWiSplus, is being re-developed. The module will incorporate Needs Assessment, Care Planning and Budgetary Commitment Accounting, and will be Carenap compliant.

Work is ongoing to agree a single shared assessment tool with health colleagues and the Council is currently working in partnership with North Lanarkshire Council and Lanarkshire NHS on the Modernising Government E-care project, which will facilitate information sharing between partner agencies. Work has been undertaken to develop the technical infrastructure and information sharing protocols to support this initiative.

A best value review of the sensory impairment service underpinned a number of achievements:

- establishment of a Multi-Agency Strategy and Resource Group with stakeholders from health, social work, the voluntary sector, education, service users and carers;
- the Multi-Agency Strategy and Resource Group has identified an impressive number of improvements and required actions; and
- sustained reduction in waiting times from 24 months to 28 days for equipment and minor adaptations and mobility/rehabilitation training.

A Multi-Agency Strategy and Resource Group has identified an impressive number of improvements and required actions.

Joint resourcing and joint management are being promoted by the South Lanarkshire Health and Care Partnership. Within this, a Health and Care Group carries out a planning function, and there are local groups with a co-ordinating role. The "bottom up" approach taken by South Lanarkshire reflects their evolutionary approach to joint management and joint resourcing. The partners' action plan focuses largely on developing joint community care services; trade unions have been fully involved. A statement of intent for staff has yet to be agreed, the joint development and training plan has yet to be initiated, and development of a joint staff forum requires preparation. Budgets are to be aligned initially.

3. Performance: Children and Families

Balance of care – Looked after children (aged 0-17)	1999-2000 actual	1999-2000 per 1,000	Quartile	2000-2001 actual	2000-2001 per 1,000	Quartile
At home	186	2.7	4	175	2.5	3
With friends/relatives/other community	70	1.0	2	84	1.2	2
With foster carers/prospective adopters	82	1.2	4	70	1.0	4
In residential accommodation	73	1.0	3	72	1.0	3
Total	**411**	**5.9**	**4**	**401**	**5.7**	**4**

Key performance indicators	1998-1999 actual	1998-1999 per 1,000	Quartile	1999-2000 actual	1999-2000 per 1,000	Quartile
Child protection (CP) referrals (aged 0-15)	342	5.5	3	279	4.5	3
Children subject to a CP case conference (aged 0-15)	99	1.6	4	105	1.7	4
Children placed on CP register (aged 0-15)	41	0.7	4	62	1.0	4
Adoption applications in year (aged 0-17)	27	0.4	2	18	0.3	4
Stranger adopter applications (aged 0-17)	17	0.2	1	10	0.1	3

There is a low child protection referral rate and a low rate of children subject to a case conference. The number of children on the child protection register increased between 1998 and 2000, but remains lower than in most other authorities. The number of adoption applications has decreased and the rate is now relatively low.

There is a low rate of looked after children.

Demands for services have mounted at a time when recruiting social work staff has been difficult, and the agenda for integrating children's services has moved ahead swiftly. The increase in demand is partly related to the impact of substance misuse on decisions about child protection and looked after children. The numbers of children with disability, and those looked after and remaining with the authority for longer periods, have also increased.

A range of innovative practice has been devised to support children in residential care:

- every children's unit has a link teacher, a named school nurse, a health visitor, a children's rights officer and a staff member of Who Cares? Scotland;
- three full-time teachers are dedicated to looked after children;
- ICT learning centres have been established in both the new and older residential units; and
- specialist links have been developed with local libraries.

The Council has made substantial progress in implementing the recommendations of Learning with Care and has:

- completed an audit of its children's residential units;
- prepared education plans for all its looked after children, though not for all its foster children;
- begun developing a shared database with education, to permit improved tracking of the attendance and educational attainment record of looked after children and also provide an alert for children who are excluded;
- provided joint training for teaching and social work staff; and
- developed an integrated Child Protection module within SWiSplus.

The Council has a dedicated throughcare/aftercare team, and an identified social worker for throughcare in each residential care home. 90 young people are currently receiving support. In 2001, 13 people moved on to independent supported accommodation. A local working group, comprising staff of the Council and key partner agencies has been preparing for the forthcoming transfer of responsibilities.

An Integrated Family Support Strategy has been developed with health and education partners. The Council is to appoint Children Services Co-ordinators for each of the 4 localities, in order to support managers from Child and Family Services, the Headteacher from the new community school cluster, the LHCC manager and other agencies involved in children's services.

4. Performance: Criminal Justice

Key Activities	1999-2000	2000-2001	2000-2001 per 10,000	Quartile
Number of social enquiry reports submitted to the courts during the year	1,640	1,707	78.1	2
Number of community service orders made during the year	400	340	15.6	2
The proportion of social enquiry reports reported to court within target time	**2000-2001**	**Quartile**		
Proportion of social enquiry reports submitted to the courts by due date	98.6	2		
The time taken to complete community service orders				
Average length of community service (hours) for orders completed during the year	160	2		
Average hours completed per week	3.9	2		

A high rate of social enquiry reports was submitted to court in 2000-2001, and a relatively high proportion of them were submitted on time. The rate of community service orders made during the year was also relatively high. The average length of community service orders is comparatively long and orders take a fairly long time to complete.

The Council is grouped with North Lanarkshire for provision of criminal justice services. The grouping has enabled the sharing of resources, consistency of approach, and joint commissioning of services, for instance from SACRO and INCLUDEM. Shared management information is currently under consideration. Following a joint best value assessment of probation and court services, the grouping has agreed on a single court team, and on a model of assessment and case management that will be jointly progressed through the training plan. Attention has been given to the particular needs of women offenders and the Grouping will pilot a programme specifically for women in the autumn. There is no dedicated funding to develop this service. It can be difficult to meet the specific needs of chaotic women including those with a mental health difficulty.

The approach to quality assurance includes the periodic sampling of cases and external chairing of reviews. They are examining the use of LSI-R as an instrument that can track change over time and provide an objective measure of the effectiveness of input, now that most staff have been trained in the use of this instrument. An electronic information system has been developed to improve workload management and improve practice.

Youth crime initiatives include:

- a reparation and mediation and restorative conferencing service for young people, commissioned from SACRO;
- a service for persistent young offenders aged 14-18, funded by criminal justice and children and families monies, and jointly commissioned from INCLUDEM by the two Lanarkshire councils; it targets those young people most at risk of residential care, secure accommodation or custody, offering individually tailored support packages, high-frequency contact and a 24-hour helpline. Includem have developed a Restorative Justice programme, aimed at persistent offenders, in conjunction with Victim Support which is funded separately; and
- training in the use of the YLS assessment tool. A small group of childcare and criminal justice staff has already received this training and the council intends to roll it out to all staff.

5. Finance

Service Area (£000)	GAE 1999-2000	Final net Out turn 1999-2000	GAE 2000-2001	Final net Out turn 2000-2001
Children's Services	£10,476	£11,981	£11,069	£12,005
Community Care	£43,135	£41,418	£45,269	£44,043
Adult Offenders		£117		£208
Other SW Services	£5,691	£4,083	£5,739	£4,640
Total	**£59,302**	**£57,600**	**£62,077**	**£60,896**

Spend per head		1999-2000		2000-2001
Spend per head		£187.37		£198.10
Quartile		4		4

South Lanarkshire Council is committed to aligning the overall Social Work budget to the GAE level over a 3-5 year period. As mentioned earlier, there has also been a significant financial investment in the Capital programme for Social Work resources.

In contrast to many other authorities, the Council spent only slightly above GAE levels on children's services in 2000-2001. Spend per head on social work services is lower than in most other authorities.

Criminal Justice services receive direct funding from the Scottish Executive, and £2,396,297 was provided in 2000-2001.

6. Staffing

Staff	WTE 1999 actual	WTE 1999 per 1,000	Quartile 1999	WTE 2000 actual	WTE 2000 per 1,000	Quartile 2000
Managers & central staff	168	0.5	3	168	0.5	4
Frontline staff	1,275	4.1	3	1,291	4.2	3
Other	280	0.9	4	276	0.9	3
Total	**1,723**	**5.6**	**3**	**1,735**	**5.6**	**3**

Vacancies	Vacancies 2000	% Vacancies 2000	% Vacancies 2000 Scotland	Vacancies 2001	% Vacancies 2001	% Vacancies 2001 Scotland
SWs with adults	6	6.0	7.8	5	5.3	10.9
SWs with children	7	6.9	7.4	4	3.9	10.7
SWs with offenders	0	0	7.5	0	0	7.2
Generic workers	0	0	8.0	0	0	12.7
Total	**13**	**5.7**	**7.7**	**9**	**4.0**	**10.5**

The Council has a low and stable rate of managers and a higher rate of front line staff. Vacancy levels are lower than the national average in all areas.

In response to the national difficulties in recruitment and retention, the Council has separate but complementary recruitment strategies for social workers and social care staff, and positive mechanisms for the retention of existing staff.

Measures to boost recruitment of social workers include:

- thematic adverts that promote both the social work service and the Council as an employer;
- named liaison officers linking directly to universities;
- informal evening sessions in different locations for students to meet the executive director and senior managers; and
- consumer feedback to ascertain the views of applicants about the recruitment process and the opportunities offered.

South Lanarkshire has developed three key employment initiatives to attract people into social care:

- a European Social Fund project, in partnership with South Lanarkshire College and private and voluntary sector providers, to bring older unemployed people back into work through the provision of HNC/SVQ 3;
- the Birkwood Project, to re-train and re-employ health board staff displaced due to hospital closure; and
- the Social Care Initiative, to establish placements for under-represented groups such as ethnic minorities, with the opportunity to complete the Progression in Care Award with a view to securing permanent posts.

To retain staff, South Lanarkshire provides formal supervision and an employee development scheme that includes a large SVQ programme.

7. Modernising services

Social work services are provided directly for the Chinese and Asian communities in South Lanarkshire, and continuing efforts are made to provide sensitive services. Social work has taken a systematic approach to developing a Race Equality Scheme within a corporate framework, and has established ways in which to recruit staff from ethnic minorities.

The Council has a substantial Modernising Government funded project to develop and implement a customer relations management system, though social work is not currently a significant partner in this initiative. Social work is, however, central to an eCare project, involving both North Lanarkshire Council and Lanarkshire NHS, to support single shared assessment by building a repository of shared information, to benefit both service users and staff. The project is being piloted in three areas, with the South Lanarkshire Council element being East Kilbride Older People's Services.

The Council is re-developing the client information system originally inherited from Strathclyde Regional Council. The system has been migrated to a modern Windows based platform, and has been re-badged as SWiSplus.

The Council has invested resources to create a SWiSplus support team who will provide training and support to staff in the use of the system. The system is effectively being re-launched, with the key objective of focusing on the system as a practitioner-based recording tool. Dedicated training facilities for SWiSplus training have also been established.

Current priorities include the re-design of Assessment and Care Management functionality to support E-care and Single Shared Assessments, and in addition, the system will provide the focus for developments in relation to Supporting People, Free Personal Care, Direct Payments and Throughcare and Aftercare.

8. The Future

The pace of progressing joint management and joint budgets for community care has been deliberate, but if they are to realise service benefits within a reasonable time, the Council with its health partners should make early progress beyond the stage of basic agreement to preparing plans and schedules for implementation of the wider Joint Futures agenda.

The Council has in train various actions to improve home care support. In view of the current balance of provision and the need to prepare for increases in the elderly population, it has the opportunity to consolidate earlier progress by planning a wider range of measures to enhance the capacity and quality of home care services and identifying resource priorities for their implementation.

To complement the progress made in learning disability services for adults, the Council should proceed to identify the requirements of younger people to achieve a smooth transition to adult services.

The Multi-Agency Strategy and Resource Group have usefully identified improvements required in sensory impairment services, which will identify the resource priorities and service developments.

Shared single assessment is recognised as an important step forward in community care services. The ground has been established for the Council to agree with health partners a common process, information-sharing and other crucial stages for implementation, and there is now an opportunity to progress without further delay.

1. Profile at 2002

One of the smaller Scottish local authorities, Stirling has a population of 85,200 people.

An overall population rise of 11.9% is expected over the next 14 years. The biggest increase is expected in the over-60 age group, which is projected to rise more quickly than the national average. In contrast to national projections, the under 5's in Stirling will increase.

The unemployment rate is below average (3.5% in January 2002).

Stirling has a below average rate of drugs misuse at 1.4% of 15-54 year olds.

The recorded crime rate is below average but has risen slightly from 2000 (607 per 10,000 population in 2001).

The Council has consolidated the restructuring undertaken in spring 2000. The Community Services Department embraces adult care and criminal justice services and the Children's Services Department embraces childcare.

The alignment and integration of services in these new configurations has required a redesign of services, and a review of the role and functions of social work. The placing of social work staff in integrated learning disability teams, and in community schools are examples of integration at the frontline.

Senior management responsibility lies with the heads of the Community and Children's Services. Professional leadership for social work rests with the Chief Social Work Officer, while scrutiny of social work functions lies with the Council's performance management and reporting framework.

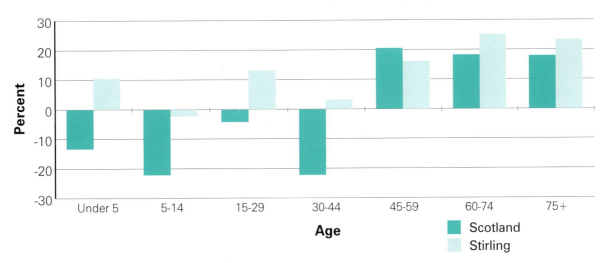

Expected % change in population, 2000-2016, local and national comparisons by age band

2. Performance: Community Care

Balance of care (aged 65+)	1999 actual	1999 per 1,000	Quartile	2000 actual	2000 per 1,000	Quartile
Older people in residential care homes	317	25	1	255	20	2
Older people in private nursing homes	497	39	1	496	39	1
Older people receiving home care	780	61	3	759	59	3
Older people in special needs housing	1,439	111.8	2	1,444	111.7	2
People receiving a community care service	1999-2000 actual	1999-2000 per 1,000	Quartile	2000-2001 actual	2000-2001 per 1,000	Quartile
Older people (aged 65+)	1,958	151.5	4	2,406	183.8	3
For mental health problems/dementia (aged 18-64)	82	1.5	4	77	1.4	4
For physical disabilities (aged 18-64)	228	4.2	4	368	6.8	4
For learning disabilities (aged 18-64)	117	2.2	4	142	2.6	3
For drug/alcohol abuse problems (aged 18-64)	10	0.2	4	12	0.2	4

The rate of older people receiving a community care service in Stirling is increasing in line with the population changes from a relatively low base. Compared to many other authorities Stirling provides a lower rate of home care support for older people – though in 2000, 21 per cent of its home care was provided in the evening or overnight (between the hours of 7 p.m. and 7 a.m.), this was the highest of all local authorities. It provides higher rates of residential and nursing home care – though the number of older people living in residential homes has fallen between 1999 and 2000. The rate of special needs housing is relatively high.

The Council is extending the range of home support services through:

- a personal care pilot project introduced in 4 areas, with active support from nursing staff;
- a bathing service established for the whole area, including provision at weekends;
- a "Tuck In" service provided Stirling-wide; and
- a "Night Link" for dementia care launched in late 2001.

Improvements to practical services and meals-on-wheels are planned.

A multi-agency strategy for older people across NHS Forth Valley and the three partner councils is nearing completion. This will inform the Local Partnership Agreement between NHS Forth Valley and Stirling Council.

Services for people with learning disabilities have focused though not exclusively on the closure of the Royal Scottish National Hospital. Joint working between agencies and the involvement of service users, have contributed to quality alternatives to institutional care. Plans for integrated social work and health services are advanced. Work is yet to move forward in relation both to direct payments, and to local area co-ordination. The Streets Ahead community-based day service is in place, and a new resource centre at Riverside is due to open.

In mental health services a joint care programme approach is in place. Voluntary organisations provide housing support. The Council's review of the assessment and care management structure, together with the introduction of single shared assessment, provides an opportunity to extend effective joint working and user involvement to all care groups.

The Council has appointed a Community Worker working within Community education Services, but only with people who have experienced or are still experiencing mental health problems. The Community Worker focuses on all areas of adult learning and essential skills, and sets up and runs a range of groups from self-help to recreational. Working across the whole of the Stirling area, the Community Worker liaises closely with health and local voluntary agencies.

A multi-agency group oversees progress on the implementation of single shared assessment. An assessment tool, part of the Council's work on e-Care, and a protocol for sharing information have been formulated. Occupational therapy assistants already do an assessment, deliver and fit single equipment in one visit, and community care staff are being trained to do single shared assessments for nursing equipment.

Progress is being made towards a more coherent service for people with sensory impairments, through a multi-agency group and a Sensing Progress implementation group of the Council. The focus is on ensuring that people have access to the services they need, and on partnership working. Services for children with sensory impairments are included, and the Council is supporting a bid by the Royal National Institute for the Deaf for an advocacy service for deaf children.

Joint working with health services is evident at the Stirling Royal Infirmary visual impairment clinic and the joint loan equipment store. Stirling is to have access to a Resource Centre being developed in Falkirk. Various avenues are being followed – in collaboration with voluntary organisations – to ensure that people have access to appropriately trained staff and to interpreting services. The numbers of referrals and assessments have risen markedly.

A Joint Community Care Forum has been formally constituted by Stirling Council and its health partners, a joint senior management group set up, and a joint action plan agreed for joint resourcing and management. It is anticipated that budgets will be aligned in the first instance. A Forth Valley-wide multi-agency human resources group is developing an action plan, building on an organisational development strategy agreed in 2000.

3. Performance: Children and Families

Balance of care – Looked after children (aged 0-17)	1999-2000 actual	1999-2000 per 1,000	Quartile	2000-2001 actual	2000-2001 per 1,000	Quartile
At home	68	3.7	3	65	3.5	2
With friends/relatives/other community	23	1.3	2	13	0.7	3
With foster carers/prospective adopters	61	3.3	1	65	3.5	1
In residential accommodation	16	0.9	3	17	0.9	3
Total	**168**	**9.1**	**2**	**160**	**8.7**	**2**

Key performance indicators	1998-1999 actual	1998-1999 per 1,000	Quartile	1999-2000 actual	1999-2000 per 1,000	Quartile
Child protection (CP) referrals (aged 0-15)	204	12.5	1	151	9.3	2
Children subject to a CP case conference (aged 0-15)	52	3.2	2	41	2.5	2
Children placed on CP register (aged 0-15)	36	2.2	2	29	1.8	2
Adoption applications in year (aged 0-17)	2	0.1	4	8	0.4	2
Stranger adopter applications (aged 0-17)	1	0.1	4	2	0.1	4

The rate of looked after children, though reduced between 1999-2000 and 2000-2001, remains relatively high compared to other authorities. A relatively low rate of looked after children is in residential accommodation, a relatively high rate in foster care.

The rate of child protection referrals is relatively high, as is the proportion of children subject to a case conference. The number of children on the child protection register has fallen recently, but the rate remains relatively high.

A comprehensive audit and evaluation of the fostering service against the national standards has been completed, which identified areas of good practice and areas in need of further development or additional resources This audit is to support the implementation of a three year plan to modernise the fostering service.

Progress has been made with aspects of education for looked after children:

- children benefit from access to learning support and the internet in all placements;
- training has been introduced for carers;
- changes have been made in the number, size and functions of children's homes (a 3-bed long-term residential unit has been opened, supported by a separate 3-bed emergency and short-term assessment unit); and
- a school doctor or community paediatrician completes a comprehensive medical assessment for each looked after child following admission.

Further developments in multi-disciplinary assessments are being developed.

The development of services for care leavers is assisted by a steering group, which includes representatives from children's services, youth support, finance, benefits advice and job centres. Two aftercare and supported accommodation workers are to be recruited and trained. Progress has been made in identifying care leavers and estimating the total costs of support but the implementation of plans is dependent on information from the Scottish Executive on resource transfer.

The Council has established an integrated model for the provision of early years, education and social work childcare services, which meet the needs of vulnerable children and families within the context of a universal service. Integrated services for children aged from birth to 5 years old have been significantly expanded.

Children's Services have structured the social work area teams around school catchment areas, to ensure integrated localised responses and to help progress the New Community Schools agenda. The Council is exploring the development of integrated, multi-professional and locality-based teams, while retaining specialist teams, such as fostering and adoption.

4. Performance: Criminal Justice

Key Activities	1999-2000	2000-2001	2000-2001 per 10,000	Quartile
Number of social enquiry reports submitted to the courts during the year	418	560	92.6	1
Number of community service orders made during the year	64	52	8.6	4
The proportion of social enquiry reports reported to court within target time	2000-2001	Quartile		
Proportion of social enquiry reports submitted to the courts by due date	99.4	2		
The time taken to complete community service orders				
Average length of community service (hours) for orders completed during the year	156	2		
Average hours completed per week	3.7	3		

The number of social enquiry reports submitted during 2000-2001 was significantly higher than in the previous year and the rate is now higher than that in many other authorities. A relatively high proportion of reports is submitted to courts by the due date. The number of community service orders made fell between 1999 and 2001 and the rate is lower than in many other authorities. The average length of orders is relatively high. Time taken to complete orders is relatively long.

Stirling is in partnership with Clackmannan and Falkirk for the provision of criminal justice services. The partnership intends to review all its assessment tools by late 2002, with a view to establishing a common framework. Meanwhile Stirling has a range of process-focused quality assurance methods including detailed six-weekly checks of all sex offender cases.

Planned improvements to data collection and management information systems include migrating from Sheridan to SWIFT. It is also planned to introduce the Level of Service Inventory as a broad assessment tool, and the Cristo Inventory on "substance misuse" for assessment in cases where offending is linked to drugs or alcohol. These would assist planning and assessing the effectiveness of interventions.

Compass for life is a dedicated support service for young people in the Stirling area who face barriers to participation. It provides a multi-agency, integrated resource for young offenders diverted from prosecution, or by way of a structured deferred sentence or referred as part of a statutory order, such as Probation. Young offenders – as well as other socially excluded groups – are offered access to learning support, employment development and vocational programmes. In addition there is specialist careers counselling, mental health and housing support, as well as a drugs service.

5. Finance

Service Area (£000)	GAE 1999-2000	Final net Out turn 1999-2000	GAE 2000-2001	Final net Out turn 2000-2001
Children's Services	£2,670	£4,156	£2,747	£4,387
Community Care	£12,636	£10,975	£13,299	£12,040
Adult Offenders		£49		£77
Other SW Services	£1,577	£2,149	£1,585	£1,503
Total	**£16,883**	**£17,329**	**£17,631**	**£18,007**

Spend per head		1999-2000		2000-2001
Spend per head		£203.34		£211.29
Quartile		4		4

Criminal Justice services receive funding direct from the Scottish Executive, and £722,740 was provided in 2000-2001.

The Council spends more than GAE on children's services, but less than GAE on community care. Spend per head on social work services is lower than in most other authorities.

6. Staffing

Staff	WTE 1999 actual	WTE 1999 per 1,000	Quartile 1999	WTE 2000 actual	WTE 2000 per 1,000	Quartile 2000
Managers & central staff	51	0.6	2	72	0.8	2
Frontline staff	338	4.0	3	350	4.1	4
Other	111	1.3	2	87	1.0	3
Total	**501**	**5.9**	**3**	**509**	**6.0**	**3**

Vacancies	Vacancies 2000	% Vacancies 2000	% Vacancies 2000 Scotland	Vacancies 2001	% Vacancies 2001	% Vacancies 2001 Scotland
SWs with adults	0	0	7.8	5	12.9	10.9
SWs with children	0	0	7.4	9	19.4	10.7
SWs with offenders	0	0	7.5	0	0	7.2
Generic workers	0	0	8.0	0	0	12.7
Total	**0**	**0**	**7.7**	**14**	**14.3**	**10.5**

Staffing rates are relatively low overall, but the rate of managers and central staff is higher than in many other authorities, after the number of managers increased significantly between 1999 and 2000. Vacancy levels are higher than average in children's services and community care.

There are problems recruiting and retaining staff in home care in rural areas and in childcare teams. Measures taken to address the problem in childcare include:

- recruiting family support workers to assist with low-level tasks;
- introducing mixed workloads to balance the pressures of statutory work;
- creating an additional tier of senior social workers/team leaders; and
- introducing a professional development programme focused on the area managers and senior social workers, to ensure quality professional leadership and practice.

The Council has increased its recruitment publicity, emphasising commitment to training and development. It provides protected time for newly qualified workers to complete their MA dissertations and guarantees the chance to undertake the Certificate in Postgraduate Social Work, paid for by the Council. A professional development co-ordinator has been appointed to implement a training programme across both children's services and community services, based on an extensive training needs analysis.

There are particular complications in providing rural services. Rural home support and residential units have to be increasingly imaginative in their use of resources, using village halls and other local buildings to provide day care, social care and PAMs services.

7. Modernising services

Stirling Council has close links with the local Race Equality Council, and has a record of tackling racial harassment and developing cultural awareness. There is a recognised need for improvement both in ethnic monitoring and in consultation with local ethnic minority groups. Support is available from an ethnic minority adviser. A Race Equality Scheme is being prepared, identifying specific functions to be addressed.

Stirling Council is committed to a citizen focus. The Access Stirling project, funded by the Modernising Government Fund, is developing a "single citizen account", based on a property index established with 14 other councils.

All social work staff are online, have internet access and use electronic records. The Council is linked to the eCare project, focusing on occupational therapy services: data sharing is advanced and a protocol is in place for the exchange of information with health.

Comprehensive information systems, based on recording, are available to managers in community care and criminal justice. Integration between social care and education information systems is well advanced. Stirling is exploring, with three other councils, ways of improving IT facilities for looked after children.

8. The Future

To maintain progress towards greater emphasis on home care for older people, the Council needs to continue attention to means of enhancing the quality and quantity of home support services, particularly in its scattered rural communities.

The progress made in services for those with learning disabilities needs to be consolidated by concluding and implementing plans for direct payments and area co-ordination.

In mental health services, the Council and its health partners should complete their review of assessment and care management as part of an action plan to enhance joint working and user involvement.

Continued progress is needed to implement progressively the recommendations of *Learning with Care*.

The Council and its criminal justice partners should complete a common framework of assessment as soon as possible, as part of its integration of management and practice which will secure the practical benefits of partnership.

1. Profile at 2002

West Dunbartonshire is a small, mainly urban authority with a population of 94,600. Poverty and deprivation heavily influence demands on all services.

Over the next 14 years the population is expected to decline by 5.5%. The over 75 population is predicted to fall only very slightly, in contrast to large increases nationally. The area faces a larger than average decrease in the number of children.

At 6.3% (January 2002) the unemployment rate is now the second highest in Scotland.

West Dunbartonshire has an above average rate of problem drug misuse (2.1% of 15-54 year olds).

The rate of crime has fallen since 2000 and, at 895 recorded crimes per 10,000 of population in 2001, is the seventh highest of Scottish authorities.

Social work services are provided through a Department of Social Work and Housing under a director, who is also the chief social work officer. Two Health Boards provide health services in West Dunbartonshire – Argyll and Clyde covering some 52% of the population and Greater Glasgow the remaining 48%.

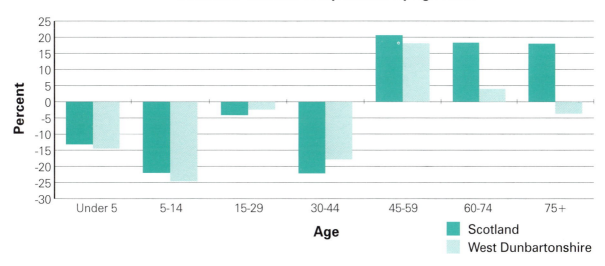

Expected % change in population, 2000-2016, local and national comparisons by age band

2. Performance: Community Care

Balance of care (aged 65+)	1999 actual	1999 per 1,000	Quartile	2000 actual	2000 per 1,000	Quartile
Older people in residential care homes	257	18	2	247	17	2
Older people in private nursing homes	330	23	3	144	10	4
Older people receiving home care	1,388	97	1	1,387	98	1
Older people in special needs housing	1,689	118.3	2	1,761	124.6	2
People receiving a community care service	1999-2000 actual	1999-2000 per 1,000	Quartile	2000-2001 actual	2000-2001 per 1,000	Quartile
Older people (aged 65+)	2,948	208.6	2	3,808	269.5	1
For mental health problems/dementia (aged 18-64)	255	4.4	2	300	5.2	2
For physical disabilities (aged 18-64)	811	14	2	1,154	20.0	1
For learning disabilities (aged 18-64)	244	4.2	2	230	4.0	2
For drug/alcohol abuse problems (aged 18-64)	128	2.2	1	275	4.8	1

The rate of older people receiving a community care service has continued to increase significantly and is now higher than in most authorities. The rates of older people living in residential and nursing home care are falling and are lower than in many other authorities. The number in nursing homes more than halved between 1999 and 2000. Although there are fewer nursing home places than in most other authorities, the Council has succeeded in reducing the numbers of delayed discharges. A higher rate of older people receives home care than in most other authorities and they are likely to receive a high number of hours per week. There is a relatively high number of special needs housing units, including houses with alarms. This housing forms a key part of community-based support.

The Council has used Transitional Housing Benefit to prepare for implementation of Supporting People, generating an additional £2m each year to fund improved provision of sheltered housing, home care, and care & repair schemes. The funds will be extended to additional housing support services for older people in residential and sheltered housing complexes.

A joint Partnership in Practice agreement is in place for people with learning disabilities. The PiP was informed by extensive consultation with people with learning disabilities and their families. Two local area co-ordinators have been appointed initially, in Clydebank and Dumbarton. A joint management board is to oversee the development of local area co-ordination. The RNIB (Royal National Institute for the Blind) provides a visual screening service for people with learning disabilities who have left long-stay hospitals. Young people with learning disabilities have access to an all-age inclusiveness project to obtain jobs and further education places. Fifty people with learning disabilities are living independently in their own tenancies.

The numbers receiving a community care service for mental health problems continue to increase. Future development in mental health services depends on agreement between the Council and Argyll and Clyde Health Board about financing and the level of resources released by the closure of psychiatric beds. An example of joint working on the ground is the Healthy Minds project, part of the Social Inclusion Partnership, through which health and social work staff support children whose parents have mental health problems.

In the absence of joint community mental health teams, there is progress in co-locating social workers, community psychiatric nurses and occupational therapists in a hospital campus in Dumbarton. A joint training programme has been introduced, partly related to the Adults with Incapacity (Scotland) Act 2000. Mental health forums in Dumbarton and Clydebank are the focus for consultation and involvement of people with mental health problems.

For single shared assessment, an agreed tool is being piloted by the Council and the Clydebank LHCC, linking with the medical requirement for an over-75s health care assessment. For an IT solution to assist in single shared assessment, the partners have prepared a bid for Modernising Government funds. A single shared assessment implementation plan is in place.

A higher rate of people is receiving a service for physical disability than in most other authorities, and the number has increased between 1999 and 2001. There is a joint physical disability strategy group, but no corresponding group for people with a sensory impairment. Joint working, including with education, operates at practice, rather than strategic, level. Progress achieved includes:

- appointment of a development worker;
- LHCC funding for a full-time worker for people with a hearing impairment;
- RNIB funding for a worker for people with a visual impairment within learning disability services; and
- (jointly with the Glasgow and West of Scotland Society for the Blind and public health staff) improved links with eye clinics.

The rate of people receiving a community care service for drug and alcohol problems is higher than in many other authorities and continues to grow at a rapid rate.

Despite the complication of two health board partners, the Council and its partners have made progress on joint resourcing and joint management and, in particular, on how decision-making will work at a strategic level. A subcommittee of the overall Health Improvement and Social Justice partnership is to act as the partnership body for joint resourcing and joint management. A joint strategy group is being set up, as will three joint posts on strategic planning, financial support and administration. Two locality planning and implementation groups have already been established.

Joint resourcing will be developed on the basis of aligned budgets. The joint resourcing "pot" is being scoped in detail, and the joint staff forum is being set up in spring 2002. The partners intend to extend joint training with further joint courses for staff, the voluntary sector and community groups.

3. Performance: Children and Families

Balance of care – Looked after children (aged 0-17)	1999-2000 actual	1999-2000 per 1,000	Quartile	2000-2001 actual	2000-2001 per 1,000	Quartile
At home	150	6.6	1	121	5.4	1
With friends/relatives/other community	8	0.4	4	18	0.8	3
With foster carers/prospective adopters	68	3.0	2	65	2.9	2
In residential accommodation	63	2.8	1	58	2.6	1
Total	**289**	**12.8**	**1**	**262**	**11.6**	**1**

Key performance indicators	1998-1999 actual	1998-1999 per 1,000	Quartile	1999-2000 actual	1999-2000 per 1,000	Quartile
Child protection (CP) referrals (aged 0-15)	221	10.9	2	102	5.1	3
Children subject to a CP case conference (aged 0-15)	87	4.4	1	54	2.7	2
Children placed on CP register (aged 0-15)	42	2.1	3	29	1.4	3
Adoption applications in year (aged 0-17)	6	0.3	4	6	0.3	3
Stranger adopter applications (aged 0-17)	3	0.1	3	4	0.2	3

The rate of looked after children, though reduced between 1999 and 2001, remains higher than in most other authorities. The rate of looked after children living in residential accommodation remains high despite a drop in numbers between 1999 and 2001. The rate of children in foster care is relatively high. The rate of children in foster care where addiction (drugs or alcohol) misuse is a contributing factor is about 70%. A relatively low rate of looked after children lives with friends or relatives but the number is increasing.

The number of child protection referrals in 1999-2000 was less than half the number in 1998-1999 and the rate is now relatively low. The number of children subject to a case conference and the number on the child protection register also decreased between 1998 and 2000. The rate of adoption applications is relatively low.

Efforts to enhance the support to children focus on:

- the development of a children with disabilities team, to achieve equity and uniformity of resources across West Dunbartonshire; it will have its first "Transitions" worker responsible for working with children through to the age of 19 and adult services; and
- following a recent study of the mental health of looked after children which found over half the children suffering from a range of distressing and disabling emotional and behavioural problems, closer links between residential staff and the children and mental health teams.

Progress in meeting the recommendations of *Learning with Care* includes:

- monitoring of the educational attainment of looked after children for the past three years, which identifies variable outcomes year on year;
- steps to provide an educationally rich environment for those children;
- engaging actively with parents through its "In from the Edge" training pack;

- offering through a pupil link worker continuity of education to looked after children who are excluded;
- weekly joint meetings between social work and education to discuss individual cases; and
- a new specialist post to provide support to looked after children affected by drug misuse (their own or that of their parents).

There is a well-established throughcare and aftercare team, which also deals with young people who are homeless. All looked after and accommodated children are automatically referred to the team at the age of 15½. The team has links with training organisations, and uses contacts with the Council's skill seekers section to secure work placements – mainly clerical and administrative – for care leavers. It also has access to 21 supported accommodation places. The Council has identified 32 young people for whom it expects to have financial responsibility.

A Special Needs in Pregnancy Service is provided for pregnant drug misusers and other vulnerable women in a neo-natal clinic. The service is provided in partnership with an obstetrician, a midwife and a specialist drugs worker. In face of a wide range of emotional, mental and financial problems, the social work role is primarily to support the mother, but the risk to the child is always a key issue.

The integration of social work and education services has developed largely around New Community Schools. The NCS has been rolled out to each secondary school (7) and their cluster primary schools in the authority. A Cluster Co-ordinator has been appointed for each cluster. There is one Integration Manager for the authority. The intention is to build integration into all levels, building up joint assessment teams that will make decisions about vulnerable children at joint meetings.

4. Performance: Criminal Justice

Key Activities	1999-2000	2000-2001	2000-2001 per 10,000	Quartile
Number of social enquiry reports submitted to the courts during the year	963	630	96.1	1
Number of community service orders made during the year	123	106	16.2	2
The proportion of social enquiry reports reported to court within target time	2000-2001	Quartile		
Proportion of social enquiry reports submitted to the courts by due date	98.0	2		
The time taken to complete community service orders				
Average length of community service (hours) for orders completed during the year	148	3		
Average hours completed per week	5.5	1		

A high rate of social enquiry reports were submitted to courts in 2000-2001 in comparison with many other authorities, but the number had decreased significantly from the previous year. The rate reflects the high crime rate in the area. A relatively high rate of community service orders were made. The average length of orders is relatively low and orders are completed quickly, with an average of 5.5 hours completed per week.

With East Dunbartonshire and Argyll and Bute, the Council forms a criminal justice service grouping with a single budget and have appointed a single manager, answering to a joint committee. It is planned to use the same assessment tools, range of interventions and evaluation regime across the grouping. The process of convergence will be supported by the adoption of one information system to support work at all levels of the service.

Youth justice benefits from a structured approach to dealing with young people. A tiered range of interventions is employed, targeted on the basis of a risk/need assessment tool designed for work with young people. The interventions are delivered either by or in partnership with childcare colleagues.

Work with women offenders, women drug users, and women who have been the subject of domestic violence are strongly linked within the authority, with opportunities for joined-up working being exploited through an inter-agency workers support group called "Praxis".

West Dunbartonshire has adopted a structured risk/needs assessment process, with a menu of programmes ("Constructs"), which are being re-written for accreditation under the Getting Best Results arrangements. The service has been restructured, with an assessment team (that also undertakes diversion work) and a programme delivery team. The programmes run on a rolling cycle, with all offenders expected to attend. Its benefits are:

- structured input of around 100 hours for someone given a year's probation;
- very rapid and predictable response to failure to attend; and
- marked improvement in the evaluation of probation by offenders: the breach rate has now dropped and completion rate without breach is 83%.

5. Finance

Service Area (£000)	GAE 1999-2000	Final net Out turn 1999-2000	GAE 2000-2001	Final net Out turn 2000-2001
Children's Services	£6,415	£6,654	£6,451	£6,630
Community Care	£14,528	£16,630	£15,170	£17,374
Adult Offenders		£57		-£62
Other SW Services	£1,936	£1,374	£1,931	£1,539
Total	**£22,879**	**£24,715**	**£23,553**	**£25,481**
Spend per head		**1999-2000**		**2000-2001**
Spend per head		£261.25		£269.35
Quartile		1		2

Criminal Justice services receive direct funding from the Scottish Executive, and £883,802 was provided in 2000-2001.

The Council is one of the higher spending authorities on Community Care. Expenditure on children's services is only slightly above GAE. Spend per head on social work services is relatively high.

6. Staffing

Staff	WTE 1999 actual	WTE 1999 per 1,000	Quartile 1999	WTE 2000 actual	WTE 2000 per 1,000	Quartile 2000
Managers & central staff	91	1.0	1	84	0.9	1
Frontline staff	611	6.4	1	636	6.7	1
Other	131	1.4	2	159	1.7	1
Total	**834**	**8.8**	**1**	**878**	**9.3**	**1**

Vacancies	Vacancies 2000	% Vacancies 2000	% Vacancies 2000 Scotland	Vacancies 2001	% Vacancies 2001	% Vacancies 2001 Scotland
SWs with adults	3	7.9	7.8	3	15.2	10.9
SWs with children	9	17.8	7.4	10	16.1	10.7
SWs with offenders	0	0	7.5	0	0	7.2
Generic workers	0	0	8.0	3	15.4	12.7
Total	**12**	**11.2**	**7.7**	**16**	**13.8**	**10.5**

The overall rate of staff is high compared to most other authorities and the total number increased between 1999 and 2000. The rate of managers and central staff decreased but remains higher than in most other authorities. Vacancy levels are high in all areas except criminal justice.

In March 2002 the department had a vacancy rate of 8%, almost entirely in childcare. An increase in specialist posts has depleted the pool of locally available workers and made it harder to maintain and recruit to core services. It is a major disadvantage for the department, with limited opportunities for offering promoted posts, to be on the boundary of a large authority.

To promote recruitment and retention the Council has:

- created a practice teaching post; and
- appointed additional seniors to provide greater supervision and support.

There have been no problems recruiting to the wider social care workforce who play a critical role in this authority, which has established itself as an SVQ accreditation centre.

7. Modernising services

The Council has a race equality policy, and a race equality officer does much to inform the Council, and the social work and housing services department. The Council has close connections with a multi-agency racial incidents monitoring group, and with a black and ethnic minorities partnership group in a local Social Inclusion Partnership area. The Race Equality Scheme is in preparation, and it is expected to have implications for social work practice.

The Council's priorities for IT development have focused on the particular needs of youth unemployment. Social work has a close interest in these developments although other departments have had a more immediate input.

Early in 2000 the department introduced the CareFirst information system, organised around the case recording needs of practitioners. Modules for Adult Services, Looked After Children, Criminal Justice and Home Care have been implemented. Child protection and financial modules are to be implemented by April 2003. Recruitment is expected to resolve the restrictions on progress created by the lack of available IT staff to support implementation. Link with education and health systems remain to be established.

The Council does not have a fully functioning intranet, although the great majority of social work staff have access to e-mail. Residential units have access to computers but not to the intranet. Access to the internet is available on a need-to-use basis.

8. The Future

The completion of a best value review of services for people with learning difficulties provides the Council with the opportunity to prepare with its health partners an action plan for future development of services and to identify resource priorities to implement it.

The pace of improvement in mental health services depends on early agreement between the Council and Argyll and Clyde Health Board about financing and the level of resources released by the closure of psychiatric beds. Securing this agreement should be a matter of priority for the partners.

While this is being pursued the partners should plan for joint mental health teams to achieve service benefits beyond those available from the current co-location of teams in parts of West Dunbartonshire, building on the joint training programme.

Sensory impairment services would benefit from a strategic lead on their future development across the whole area. The Council and its health partners should formulate a strategic plan for improvement and identify the resource priorities required for its implementation.

To build on and integrate its action to improve the education of looked after children, the Council should progress its action plan to implement the recommendations of *Learning with Care.*

The development of a fully functioning Intranet would facilitate communication among staff within the Council and would therefore play a central part in the continuing task of achieving closer integration of services.

1. Profile at 2002

West Lothian is a medium-sized authority with a population of 156,700.

The local population has grown more rapidly than in any other authority in Scotland and has doubled in the last 45 years. The proportion of households with pensioners was 25% in the 1991 Census – far lower than the Scottish average of 33%. The over 75 year old population is however projected to increase by almost forty per cent over the next 14 years. West Lothian currently has the youngest population in Scotland and the rate of under 5's is projected to increase by a further 1.8%.

At 4.3% (January 2002), unemployment is similar to the Scottish average.

At 1.2% of 15-54 year olds West Lothian has a drugs misuse rate well under average for Scotland.

The crime rate has fallen and is now slightly below the national average (734 crimes were recorded per 10,000 population in 2001).

The Council undertook an organisational review in 2001/02 to improve the effectiveness of its service delivery. The review has led to the appointment of a Head of Service, Social Policy, who reports to one of 3 Corporate Managers. Social Policy includes social work, social strategy, housing and health; the Head of Service also undertakes the duties of chief social work officer.

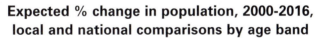

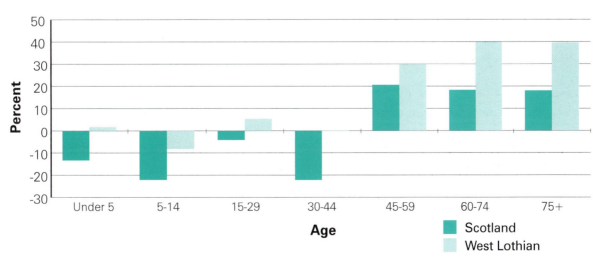

2. Performance: Community Care

Balance of care (aged 65+)	1999 actual	1999 per 1,000	Quartile	2000 actual	2000 per 1,000	Quartile
Older people in residential care homes	247	15	3	221	13	4
Older people in private nursing homes	501	30	1	581	34	1
Older people receiving home care	1,578	93	2	1,509	88	2
Older people in special needs housing	2,067	122.3	2	2,056	119.9	2
People receiving a community care service	**1999-2000 actual**	**1999-2000 per 1,000**	**Quartile**	**2000-2001 actual**	**2000-2001 per 1,000**	**Quartile**
Older people (aged 65+)	3,609	210.5	2	4,047	236.1	2
For mental health problems/dementia (aged 18-64)	204	2.0	3	206	2.0	4
For physical disabilities (aged 18-64)	996	9.7	3	1,078	10.5	3
For learning disabilities (aged 18-64)	313	3.1	3	310	3.0	3
For drug/alcohol abuse problems (aged 18-64)	28	0.3	3	34	0.3	4

The number of older people receiving a community care service in West Lothian has grown, commensurate with the increase in the number of older people and the rate is now high compared to other authorities. Rates of older people living in special needs housing and of older people receiving a home care service are high. A low rate of older people live in residential homes, the number having decreased between 1999 and 2000, but a high rate live in nursing homes.

Following a review of its home care service in autumn 2001 the Council:

- trained and introduced 240 personal care workers, working shifts from 7:00 a.m. to 10:00 p.m., 7 days a week; staff work in teams and have recently developed a personal safety system; single health and care worker posts have yet to be agreed; and

- introduced a new Home Meal Service and Shopping Service, which was extended across all areas, following a successful pilot; 100 people currently use the service; a home care assistant works alongside the delivery driver, puts the shopping away and checks that the client is eating and storing food appropriately.

Joint working between health, housing, education and social work staff have brought outcomes for people with learning disability and for people with mental health problems. For people with learning disabilities the Partnership in Practice agreement was established in summer 2001, setting out plans for an increase in the range of day opportunities and direct payments, among other developments. The closure of Bangour Village Hospital has freed resources to extend community nursing and improve services for older people with dementia in the community. This should reduce delayed discharges from hospital.

The council and its health partners have already adopted joint resourcing for projects, particularly through their considerable efforts to reduce delayed discharges. Joint resourcing will be applied initially for services for older people and then for other adults, with possible extension to children's services. The partners have drawn up the long list of services, including housing, and aim to conclude scoping the pot by spring. Single management of services – including at lower levels – is expected by summer 2002, again, firstly for older people, then for other adults. A joint staff forum is in place. The partners are therefore making good progress.

On single shared assessment, the agreed tool (Carenap E) is being rolled out from the current pilot in spring 2002. Development of the related assessment systems and information sharing is progressing but not yet concluded.

The Council has started implementing the relevant recommendations from Sensing Progress. A local multi-agency group has been established; and a sensory resource centre has been opened at St John's hospital from which the Council and voluntary organisations are delivering services and assessments for deaf and visually impaired people.

3. Performance: Children and Families

Balance of care – Looked after children (aged 0-17)	1999-2000 actual	1999-2000 per 1,000	Quartile	2000-2001 actual	2000-2001 per 1,000	Quartile
At home	212	5.7	1	171	4.6	2
With friends/relatives/other community	53	1.4	1	43	1.2	2
With foster carers/prospective adopters	108	2.9	2	146	3.9	1
In residential accommodation	42	1.1	2	44	1.2	2
Total	**415**	**11.1**	**2**	**404**	**10.8**	**1**

Key performance indicators	1998-1999 actual	1998-1999 per 1,000	Quartile	1999-2000 actual	1999-2000 per 1,000	Quartile
Child protection (CP) referrals (aged 0-15)	249	7.5	2	227	6.8	3
Children subject to a CP case conference (aged 0-15)	60	1.8	3	72	2.2	3
Children placed on CP register (aged 0-15)	54	1.6	3	69	2.1	2
Adoption applications in year (aged 0-17)	20	0.5	1	6	0.2	4
Stranger adopter applications (aged 0-17)	5	0.1	3	3	0.1	4

While the overall rate of children looked after has remained stable and relatively high. The rate of those in foster care has risen. The rate in residential accommodation is still higher than in many other authorities, most being accounted for by 25 placements in residential schools.

The rates of child protection referrals and of children who are subject to a child protection conference are relatively low. The number of children on the child protection register has increased between 1998 and 2000 and the rate is now relatively high.

Joint working with education and health staff is directed to raising attainment of looked after children:

- a local database has been established to enable the educational progress of looked after children to be tracked;
- practice and procedures are being prepared for shared assessment;
- education is fully addressed in the care plans of looked after children, all of whom have permanent full-time places in education;
- a member of staff is designated in each primary and secondary school;
- joint professional development has included curriculum awareness for social care staff; and

- the educational environment for looked after children has been developed through use of an educational psychologist to advise foster carers, the involvement of library services, and computer installations.

The Council has established a planning group for new arrangements for care leavers, and has appointed a throughcare manager. An information pack is being designed and staff anticipate the need for intensive packages for a few care leavers where a multi agency approach will be crucial.

Managed by Community Services, the new Whitdale Centre will have a community focus, encompassing Social Work, Education, Health, Surestart, and voluntary Housing staff working together on the one purpose built site. The Surestart Team provides a number of services for individuals and groups in the community addressing the needs of young families. The Intensive Support Team provides a crisis response service to reduce the number of children looked after and accommodated in foster and residential care.

Planning for children's services is led by Education, Social Work and Health Community Planning group, and there is also elected member, voluntary and user involvement in the Forum. Investment in Early years includes family centres, Bookstart, and support for voluntary sector (e.g. First Step Enable Nursery).

4. Performance: Criminal Justice

Key Activities	1999-2000	2000-2001	2000-2001 per 10,000	Quartile
Number of social enquiry reports submitted to the courts during the year	517	596	52.8	3
Number of community service orders made during the year	152	104	9.2	4
The proportion of social enquiry reports reported to court within target time	2000-2001	Quartile		
Proportion of social enquiry reports submitted to the courts by due date	99.5	2		
The time taken to complete community service orders				
Average length of community service (hours) for orders completed during the year	106	4		
Average hours completed per week	1.8	4		

The rate of social enquiry reports submitted to courts during 2000-2001 was relatively low. A relatively high proportion was submitted by the due date. The number of community service orders made was less than in the previous year and the rate is lower than in many other authorities. The average length of orders is shorter than in many other authorities but the orders take longer to complete in West Lothian, with an average of only 1.8 hours completed per week.

In providing criminal justice services, West Lothian forms part of a grouping with Edinburgh, Mid Lothian, East Lothian, and Borders. The grouping is developing a common approach to monitoring and evaluation, although the current lack of IT integration will need to be overcome to make this a reality. The Council is working on the development of a criminal justice module designed to meet operational management needs and Scottish Executive requirements. The intention is to develop common data standards based on the material developed by the Scottish Social Care Data Standards project.

The Council currently has a computerised system for maintaining annual returns and providing regular quantitative feedback to the criminal justice social work team and voluntary sector partners. In some instances evaluation has been built in.

5. Finance

Service Area (£000)	GAE 1999-2000	Final net Out turn 1999-2000	GAE 2000-2001	Final net Out turn 2000-2001
Children's Services	£6,593	£10,943	£7,108	£10,232
Community Care	£18,990	£19,372	£19,949	£20,289
Adult Offenders		£118		£33
Other SW Services	£2,782	£2,676	£2,824	£2,811
Total	**£28,365**	**£33,108**	**£29,881**	**£33,366**

Spend per head		1999-2000		2000-2001
Spend per head		£211.29		£212.94
Quartile		3		4

Criminal Justice services receive direct funding from the Scottish Executive, and £811,088 was provided in 2000-2001.

The Council spends above GAE on children's services but not so much above GAE as many other authorities. Spend per head on social work services is relatively low.

6. Staffing

Staff	WTE 1999 actual	WTE 1999 per 1,000	Quartile 1999	WTE 2000 actual	WTE 2000 per 1,000	Quartile 2000
Managers & central staff	87	0.6	2	98	0.6	3
Frontline staff	539	3.5	4	546	3.5	4
Other	104	0.7	4	120	0.8	4
Total	**729**	**4.7**	**4**	**764**	**4.9**	**4**

Vacancies	Vacancies 2000	% Vacancies 2000	% Vacancies 2000 Scotland	Vacancies 2001	% Vacancies 2001	% Vacancies 2001 Scotland
SWs with adults	4	27.9	7.8	1	6.4	10.9
SWs with children	7	10.1	7.4	9	11.4	10.7
SWs with offenders	1	10.6	7.5	0	0	7.2
Generic workers	6	18.5	8.0	6	17.1	12.7
Total	**18**	**14.0**	**7.7**	**16**	**11.4**	**10.5**

The total number of staff increased between 1999 and 2000 but levels are still lower than in many other authorities. Vacancy levels are a little higher than average.

The Council has a high level of social work vacancies, reflecting high economic activity in the local area, which offers alternative employment opportunities. The Council has developed a comprehensive and imaginative approach to recruitment and retention which includes job redesign, the organisation of resources to harness maximum benefit and significant investment in training and development.

7. Modernising services

The Council is developing a common approach to equality across race, disability and gender, mainstreaming equality in both employment and service development. The introduction of a Race Equality Scheme has implications still to be realised for social work services.

West Lothian has a long-term commitment to modernising its government processes, making full use of new technology through its Wired West Lothian initiative.

Stirling University is conducting an evaluation of the pioneering Opening Doors, a partnership with housing associations which combines support services with smart technology in houses, to enable older people with support needs to live independently in the community.

The Broxburn Partnership database will allow sharing of core personal information on mutual customers, between a range of agencies in West Lothian, including health, housing and social work services provided or purchased by the Council. Staff have an internet learning and information resource available on their PCs.

8. The Future

The Council has made significant strides in modernising its services and its business approach. It therefore has much to build on.

To meet the demands in the growth of its older population the Council needs to capitalise on its progress in developing its home care services. Priority next steps are:

- completion of the single shared assessment; and
- where appropriate, development of single health and social care worker posts.

The Council and its health partners share a common strategic direction for mental health services, but they now need to resolve the detail of joint working in order to deliver effective services. In addition, the partners will want quickly, as is planned, to finalise the outstanding issues on the Joint Future agenda, especially on single shared assessment.

To enable the development of sensory impairment services to proceed the partners should complete as soon as practicable the review of the future needs assessment process for children moving towards adulthood and facing a continuing need for support.

Appendix 1

Notes on statistics used in the local reports

Demographic, social and economic statistics (on the introductory page(s) of each report)

Population figures and projections come from the General Register Office for Scotland (GROS) 2000 based population projections. Most of the commentary relating to population are based on these figures although some comments in this section are derived from information provided by local authorities.

Figures and comments on the proportion of households with pensioners, the proportion of households with dependent children, the percentage of lone parents and those relating to minority ethnic population come from the 1991 census.

Unemployment statistics and comments are based on unemployment figures for January 2002 and come from the Scottish Executive Economic Advice and Statistics Division.

The figure for the prevalence of drug misuse is from 'Drugs Misuse Statistics Scotland 2001'.

Crime figures are from the Statistical Bulletin 'Recorded Crime in Scotland' 2001. It forms part of the Scottish Executive series of statistics bulletins on the criminal justice system.

All other figures in this section are derived from information provided by local authorities.

Facts and figures section of each report

We have used quartiles within some data tables to show where a figure for a Council (for example, older people in residential care homes per 1,000 population in 1999) lies relative to figures within the same measure for other councils.

Councils were ranked 1 to 32 (1 being the highest figure and 32 the lowest). Councils in the highest quarter, i.e. ranked 1 to 8 inclusive, were placed in quartile 1. Conversely, Councils in the lowest quarter, ranked 25 to 32, were placed in quartile 4.

Expected % changes in population, 2000-2016, local and national comparisons by age band

This graph is based on the General Register Office for Scotland (GROS) 2000 based population projections. The population figures on which the graph is based can be seen in Appendix 3.

Community Care

Figures for the number of older people in residential care homes, older people in private nursing homes, older people receiving home care and older people in special needs housing are from the Scottish Community Care Statistics 1999 and 2000 publications.

The figures for people receiving a Community Care service in 1999-2000 and 2000-2001 for older people, mental health problems, physical disabilities, learning disabilities and drug/alcohol abuse problems are from the Accounts Commission Performance Information for Scottish Councils Data Compendium for 2000/2001. This information is available from the Accounts Commission website: www.audit-scotland.gov.uk.

Children and Families

Figures are from the Scottish Executive's Information, Analysis and Communication Division (Children's Statistics).

Any other figures in the commentary section are drawn from information provided by local authorities.

Criminal Justice

All figures are derived from the Accounts Commission Performance Indicators 2000/2001 Social Work Services and the Scottish Executive's Statistical Bulletin "Criminal Justice Social Work Statistics 2000/2001".

Figures for the number of Social Enquiry Reports submitted include supplementary reports.

Any other figures in the commentary section are drawn from information provided by local authorities.

Finance

These figures are for 1999-2000 and 2000-2001 and are as reported by local authorities to the Scottish Executive.

Gross Expenditure is a total of all the costs associated with providing the service. This includes expenditure on items such as employee costs and operating costs.

Net Expenditure is the Gross Expenditure minus any income received from the service. Income received can include items such as specific grants, rents, fees and charges, sales, and income from other local authorities and Health Boards and Trusts.

Criminal Justice Services receive 100% funding from the Scottish Executive and are accounted for separately.

Please note that due to rounding totals may not add up to constituent parts.

Local authorities have questioned the extent to which these figures represent actual expenditure on services.

Appendix 1

Staffing by category of employee and whole time equivalent (WTE) as at October 1999 and October 2000

This table has been compiled from local authority staffing returns for October 1999 and 2000 to the Scottish Executive Social Work Statistics Division.

The category 'Managers/central staff' includes: Director; heads of service; service managers; other senior staff; planning, commissioning and contracting staff; registration/inspection officers; research & information officers; human resources staff, including training; finance staff.

The category 'Frontline staff' includes: social workers; occupational therapists; community service staff; supervised attendance staff; advocacy/rights staff; social work assistants; fieldwork staff; residential and day care staff; care managers; welfare rights officers; wardens.

'Other' includes administrative staff and any other staff who are not covered by the above two categories. Some local authorities have large numbers of 'other' staff while others have small numbers. Such differences appear to be largely the result of which category staff are assigned to.

As well as 'frontline staff', some senior social workers and other 'managers' may also work directly with service users and this varies across authorities.

The figures in the staffing table have been rounded independently, as a result, the totals shown may not match the sum of the categories.

There was a change in how posts were allocated to categories between 1999 and 2000 so direct comparisons between the two years may not be accurate.

Vacancy figures for 2001 are provisional and refer to the situation as at 1 October 2001.

Appendix 2

Statistical Information

Finance

Table 1 below provides details of the actual and planned expenditure across local authorities for the past six years. The Scottish Executive, in partnership with local government, is now introducing a 3 year settlement from 2001-2002, in place of the previous annual cycle for local government finance.

Table 1 **Net Expenditure on Social Work (£000s)**[1,2]

	1995-96	1996-97	1997-98	1998-99	1999-2000	2000-2001[3]
Children's Services[4]	240,417	248,401	249,112	269,442	284,457	296,536
Community Care	706,812	727,303	721,003	747,820	785,861	803,397
Adult Offenders	4,086	5,397	3,146	5,028	3,892	3,713
Non Specific Expenditure	228,867	204,215	195,592	166,227	152,744	157,500
Total	**1,180,183**	**1,185,315**	**1,168,853**	**1,188,517**	**1,226,955**	**1,261,146**

[1] Loan Charges have been excluded for all years.

[2] Figures have been adjusted to reflect current prices using GDP deflators.

[3] 2000-01 figures are provisional and may change.

[4] Includes Children's Panels. Source: SEDD Local Government Finance Statistics – LFR3 Return.

The categories under which expenditure is recorded were changed between 1994 and 1995, and again between 1997 and 1998. It is therefore difficult to make comparisons, for some categories over the full period.

Specific Grant Expenditure

Each year, in addition to the funds allocated to the general provision of social work services, the government makes specific grants to local authorities for expenditure on areas of priority need. The table below shows the expenditure on these grants for the year 1999-2000 and the specific grants which will be available to the local authorities until the year 2000-2003.

Table 2 **Specific grant to local authorities**

	1999-00 £m	2000-01 £m	2001-02 £m	2002-03 £m
Social Work Training, Specific Grant	3.7	2.7	2.2	2.2
Mental Health Specific Grant	18	19	19	19

Children's Services

- Just over 7,200 children were referred to local authorities for child protection inquiries in the year ended 31 March 2000. 36% of those referred were the subject of an inter-agency case conference.

- In 88% of instances where children were subject to a case conference the children in question were living at home prior to being referred.

- In 78% of all case conferences, the primary source of abuse/risk to the child was known or suspected to be the child's birth parent(s).

- 73% of case conferences occurring as a result of children referred in the year ending 31 March 2000 resulted in the child being placed on the local child protection register.

- There were just over 2,100 children removed from child protection registers in the year to 31 March 2000. Two thirds of these children had been on the register for less than a year with nearly 11% having spent at least 2 years on the register. Of these 2,100 de-registrations 40% were for children whose main category of abuse had been identified as physical injury.

- As at 31 March 2000, 2,050 children were on local child protection registers, a decrease of just over 300 on the number one year previously.

- At 31 March 2001, just under 10,900 children were 'looked after' by the local authorities

- In the year ended 31 December 2001, 418 applications were made for adoption compared to 405 the year before.

- At 31 March 2000, the number of children in residential accommodation was 1,960.

Figure 1

Children registered as a result of a case Conference: Breakdown by Category of abuse/risk identified by case conference.

Percentage breakdown by category of abuse 2000

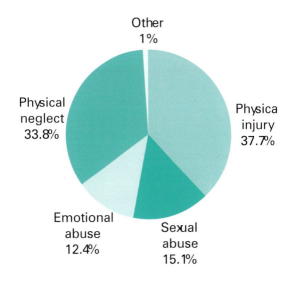

Community Care Services

Table 3 below outlines the number of people receiving different types of community care services in the year to 31 March 2000.

Table 3

Service	Number of service users
Home Care services for older people	59,232
Home Care services for physically disabled adults	53,540
Home Care services for adults with a mental health problem	2,256
Home Care services for adults with learning disabilities	1,469
Home Care services for other client groups[1]	9,918
Residential care homes for older people	13,762
Residential care homes for physically disabled adults	773
Residential care homes for adults with mental health problems	1,146
Residential care homes for adults with learning disabilities	4,394
Residential care homes for other client groups[1]	994
Day care attendance for older people	12,362
Day care attendance for adults with learning disabilities	8,587
Day care attendance for physically disabled adults	2,482
Day care attendance for adults with mental health problems	815
Day care attendance for other client groups[1]	265

Source: SEHD, Social Work Statistics Division

Note:

In 1998 a new methodology was introduced for dealing with non-response for the home care, day care and residential care data collections. Therefore, care must be taken when comparing data over time if the time period covers data before and after 1998.

Specific Notes:

[1] Other client groups include people with drug and alcohol problems, HIV and AIDS, ex-offenders, homeless people and other vulnerable groups.

Criminal Justice Services

Table 4 below sets out the numbers of offenders on whom social enquiry reports were prepared or who were supervised by social work services in 2000-2001.

Table 4 **Number of Social Enquiry Reports, Probation Orders and Community Service Orders**

	Number of Reports/Orders
Social enquiry report	31,398
Probation orders[1]	6,100
Community service orders[2]	4,506
Probation Orders with a condition of unpaid work	1,717

Source: SEHD, Social Work Statistics Division

[1] Includes Probation Orders with a condition of unpaid work

[2] Excludes Probation Orders with a condition of unpaid work

Social Work Services Staffing

As at 2 October 2000, the total number of staff working in local authority social work services was 44,909 and employed in the services outlined in Figure 2, below.

Figure 2

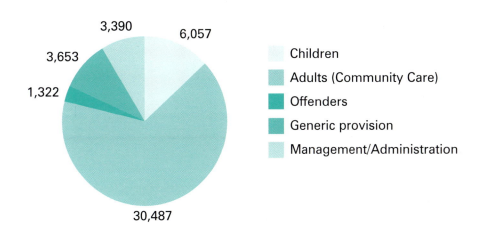

Number of Staff by Client Group

The majority (85%) of all staff in 2000 were female. This proportion was highest for staff providing services for adults, where 90% were female, and lowest for staff providing services for offenders (56%).

There were 34,161 whole time equivalent (WTE) staff employed by Scottish Local Authority Social Work Services in October 2000. Table 5 details the primary occupations in social work services.

Table 5 **Primary occupations in social work services**

Staff Role	WTE
Home Care Managers/Staff	9,482
Residential Services for Older People	4,765
Fieldwork, Services for Children	2,700
Day services for people with learning disabilities	2,221
Fieldwork, Services for Adults	2,481
Residential Services for Children & Young People	2,009
Fieldwork, Services for Offenders	1,146

Social Work staff also work in prisons, hospitals, primary health care teams, schools and other locations.

Appendix 3

Aberdeen City	2000	2016
Under 5	11.2	8.2
5-14	24.9	17.1
15-29	42.7	40.0
30-44	52.9	27.8
45-59	37.9	47.7
60-74	27.4	31.1
75+	14.2	16.2
	211.3	188.0

Aberdeenshire	2000	2016
Under 5	13.2	11.8
5-14	31.1	23.7
15-29	40.6	38.3
30-44	53.2	41.9
45-59	47.1	50.8
60-74	28.0	42.3
75+	14.0	19.2
	227.2	228.0

Angus	2000	2016
Under 5	6.0	4.5
5-14	14.1	10.2
15-29	19.6	17.8
30-44	23.1	17.6
45-59	22.1	22.5
60-74	15.8	19.6
75+	8.4	9.8
	109.2	102.0

Argyll and Bute	2000	2016
Under 5	4.3	3.4
5-14	10.3	6.9
15-29	15.3	12.3
30-44	18.7	13.2
45-59	18.3	18.5
60-74	14.0	17.2
75+	7.9	9.0
	88.8	80.5

Clackmannanshire	2000	2016
Under 5	2.9	2.3
5-14	6.6	4.8
15-29	8.4	8.0
30-44	11.4	7.6
45-59	9.7	11.1
60-74	6.4	8.7
75+	3.2	4.1
	48.5	46.7

Dumfries & Galloway	2000	2016
Under 5	7.7	5.9
5-14	18.3	12.8
15-29	22.2	20.2
30-44	31.1	19.4
45-59	30.0	31.6
60-74	24.4	29.4
75+	12.2	16.0
	145.8	135.2

Dundee City	2000	2016
Under 5	8.0	5.5
5-14	17.5	11.1
15-29	27.3	23.4
30-44	31.8	15.3
45-59	24.9	27.8
60-74	22.1	20.6
75+	11.2	11.8
	142.7	115.6

East Ayrshire	2000	2016
Under 5	6.8	5.3
5-14	16.0	11.0
15-29	21.6	19.4
30-44	26.9	18.5
45-59	23.4	25.7
60-74	17.7	20.5
75+	8.2	10.0
	120.6	110.3

East Dunbartonshire	2000	2016
Under 5	5.7	5.4
5-14	13.4	10.7
15-29	21.9	17.8
30-44	24.5	24.0
45-59	22.4	23.2
60-74	16.4	19.2
75+	6.5	10.9
	110.8	111.2

East Lothian	2000	2016
Under 5	5.4	5.6
5-14	11.6	10.5
15-29	16.3	18.3
30-44	20.9	20.3
45-59	17.5	21.8
60-74	12.7	16.3
75+	6.9	8.4
	91.3	101.2

East Renfrewshire	2000	2016
Under 5	5.2	5.6
5-14	11.7	10.6
15-29	16.2	17.0
30-44	20.6	19.8
45-59	18.1	20.8
60-74	12.0	16.2
75+	6.0	8.4
	89.8	98.4

Edinburgh	2000	2016
Under 5	23.9	22.5
5-14	49.6	42.2
15-29	102.6	104.5
30-44	113.8	99.2
45-59	75.6	106.8
60-74	55.8	62.3
75+	32.1	33.3
	453.4	470.8

Eilean Siar	2000	2016
Under 5	1.4	0.8
5-14	3.6	2.2
15-29	4.2	2.7
30-44	5.7	3.3
45-59	5.6	5.6
60-74	4.3	5.1
75+	2.4	2.7
	27.2	22.4

Falkirk	2000	2016
Under 5	8.3	7.0
5-14	18.3	15.1
15-29	26.2	25.8
30-44	34.8	26.4
45-59	27.5	34.6
60-74	20.2	23.9
75+	9.1	11.5
	144.3	144.3

Fife	2000	2016
Under 5	19.4	17.0
5-14	45.5	35.3
15-29	64.9	63.2
30-44	79.9	61.3
45-59	67.3	79.3
60-74	48.2	62.0
75+	25.3	30.3
	350.4	348.4

Glasgow	2000	2016
Under 5	34.7	31.1
5-14	75.4	56.7
15-29	137.1	131.4
30-44	153.7	123.7
45-59	92.0	139.4
60-74	76.6	71.4
75+	39.9	33.4
	609.4	587.1

Highland	2000	2016
Under 5	12.0	9.5
5-14	27.6	20.9
15-29	33.9	31.2
30-44	46.5	32.6
45-59	43.5	48.1
60-74	30.7	40.8
75+	14.4	19.4
	208.6	**202.5**

Inverclyde	2000	2016
Under 5	4.9	3.6
5-14	11.2	7.7
15-29	15.1	12.8
30-44	19.5	12.4
45-59	16.0	18.8
60-74	11.9	12.8
75+	6.0	6.1
	84.6	**74.2**

Midlothian	2000	2016
Under 5	4.8	5.1
5-14	10.5	9.6
15-29	16.7	16.7
30-44	18.3	19.2
45-59	16.3	17.9
60-74	10.9	13.6
75+	4.7	6.2
	82.2	**88.3**

Moray	2000	2016
Under 5	5.1	4.1
5-14	11.4	8.4
15-29	16.7	16.0
30-44	17.9	13.8
45-59	15.7	15.8
60-74	12.2	13.9
75+	5.9	7.7
	85.0	**79.7**

North Ayrshire	2000	2016
Under 5	7.7	6.2
5-14	18.5	13.4
15-29	25.6	23.0
30-44	31.1	23.0
45-59	27.0	30.8
60-74	19.6	24.8
75+	9.5	12.0
	138.9	**133.2**

North Lanarkshire	2000	2016
Under 5	20.1	17.4
5-14	42.9	36.1
15-29	65.5	59.8
30-44	78.0	63.5
45-59	59.4	74.9
60-74	42.8	50.5
75+	19.0	24.6
	327.6	**326.8**

Orkney	2000	2016
Under 5	1.0	0.7
5-14	2.7	1.7
15-29	3.0	2.3
30-44	4.3	2.8
45-59	4.1	4.4
60-74	2.9	3.7
75+	1.5	1.9
	19.5	**17.5**

Perth and Kinross	2000	2016
Under 5	7.1	6.2
5-14	16.5	13.4
15-29	22.3	21.4
30-44	28.3	21.5
45-59	27.3	29.9
60-74	20.7	26.1
75+	11.4	14.0
	133.6	**132.5**

Renfrewshire	2000	2016
Under 5	10.5	8.6
5-14	23.3	18.2
15-29	31.8	31.2
30-44	42.6	29.7
45-59	33.4	40.7
60-74	24.8	27.8
75+	10.6	13.4
	177.0	**169.4**

Scottish Borders	2000	2016
Under 5	5.8	4.5
5-14	13.1	10.3
15-29	15.9	15.6
30-44	23.4	15.8
45-59	22.1	26.0
60-74	17.0	22.2
75+	9.5	11.5
	106.9	**105.8**

Shetland	2000	2016
Under 5	1.4	1.3
5-14	3.4	2.5
15-29	4.0	4.0
30-44	5.2	3.8
45-59	4.5	4.7
60-74	2.6	3.7
75+	1.4	1.7
	22.4	**21.6**

South Ayrshire	2000	2016
Under 5	5.8	5.2
5-14	14.0	11.2
15-29	19.6	18.8
30-44	24.4	19.0
45-59	22.7	24.3
60-74	17.7	20.5
75+	9.7	11.3
	113.9	**110.2**

South Lanarkshire	2000	2016
Under 5	17.5	15.5
5-14	40.4	31.3
15-29	58.4	57.6
30-44	73.1	57.5
45-59	58.7	68.9
60-74	41.9	48.8
75+	17.4	22.3
	307.4	**302.0**

Stirling	2000	2016
Under 5	4.8	5.3
5-14	10.4	10.2
15-29	18.0	20.4
30-44	18.4	19.0
45-59	16.3	19.0
60-74	11.3	14.1
75+	6.0	7.4
	85.2	**95.3**

West Dunbartonshire	2000	2016
Under 5	5.6	4.8
5-14	13.1	9.8
15-29	19.3	18.8
30-44	21.6	17.7
45-59	16.4	19.3
60-74	12.6	13.1
75+	6.0	5.8
	94.6	**89.4**

West Lothian	2000	2016
Under 5	10.1	10.3
5-14	21.3	19.5
15-29	32.2	34.0
30-44	39.4	39.4
45-59	29.3	38.0
60-74	17.4	24.4
75+	6.9	9.7
	156.7	**175.2**

Glossary

ADSW	Association of Directors of Social Work
Bottom Line	Steps that agencies should have in place by 1 April 2002 to implement fully both joint working/joint management of services and single shared assessment in 2003
CareFirst	Community services client information system
Carenap	An assessment tool for use with elderly clients for needs identification with application for specialist assessment including dementia
Charter Mark	An award scheme for recognising and encouraging excellence in public service
CSDF	Children Services Development Fund
CHOSI	Barnardo's project to address young people's offending behaviour
Citizen Focus	Modernising Government funded project
CMHT	Community Mental Health Trust
Constructs	Programme for work with offenders
COSLA	Convention of Scottish Local Authorities
Cristo Inventory	Assessment tool for substance misuse
CROP	Project to provide work placements for those under court orders
DipSW	Diploma in Social Work
eCare	Programme of work funded by the Executive's 21st Government Unit to promote modernisation of service delivery through information sharing to place the citizen first and improve service delivery
eMPOWER	Project which focuses on educational, recreational & therapeutic uses of IT
ECDL	European Computer Driving Licence
ESF	European Social Fund
GAE	Grant Aided Expenditure
GSX	Government Secure Extranet, secure transmission between Justice agencies
GP	General Practitioner
ICT	Information & Communications Technology
Includem	Youth Crime project to support young people
Intranet	Internal communications network

ISCJIS	Integrated Scottish Criminal Justice Information System
ISO 9002	International quality assurance standard
IT	Information Technology
Joint Future Agenda	A strategy of measures to provide improved results for people through better joint working between health and local authorities
Joint resourcing	Health, housing and social work together plan, resource, manage and deliver the full range of services that communities need and can sustain locally
KPIs	Key Performance Indicators
LHCC	Local health care co-operative
LSI-R	Risk assessment tool
MGF	Modernising Government Fund
NCH	National Childrens Homes
NCS	New Community Schools
NHS	National Health Service
OASys	Risk assessment tool
OLM CareJust	Information system
OT	Occupational Therapist
PAMs	Professions allied to Medicine
PiP	Partnership in Practice
Pathfinder Initiative	Getting Best Results initiative for criminal justice
Pathways Project	Partnership of agencies working with offenders
PCs	Personal computers
PQ	Post-qualifying awards
Praxis	Inter-agency workers support group for work with women
Quartile	The measure we have used to show where a value lies relative to other values in the same data set
Quaser	Tool to assess the quality of social enquiry reports
RAGF	Risk Assessment Guidance Framework (Scottish Executive)
RNIB	Royal National Institute for the Blind
RSNH	Royal Scottish National Hospital
SACRO	Scottish Association for the Care and Resettlement of Offenders
Single Shared Assessment	Joint community care needs assessment with Health

Glossary

SIP	Social Inclusion Partnership
Supporting People Agenda	Accommodation strategy
Surestart	Programme to support vulnerable children
SVQ	Scottish Vocational Qualifications
SWIS	Social work information system
SWs	Social Workers
WTE	Whole Time Equivalents